Value-Driven IT Management

Value-Driven IT Management

Iain Aitken

OXFORD AMSTERDAM BOSTON LONDON NEW YORK PARIS
SAN DIEGO SAN FRANCISCO SINGAPORE SYDNEY TOKYO

Butterworth-Heinemann
An imprint of Elsevier
Linacre House, Jordan Hill, Oxford OX2 8DP
200 Wheeler Road, Burlington, MA 01803

First published 2003

British Library Cataloguing in Publication Data
A catalogue record for this book is available from the British Library

ISBN 0 7506 59254

For information on all Butterworth-Heinemann publications visit
our website at www.bh.com

Composition by Genesis Typesetting, Rochester, Kent
Printed and bound in Great Britain by MPG Books Ltd, Bodmin

Contents

Contents

Contents

Computer Weekly Professional Series

There are few professions which require as much continuous updating as that of the IT executive. Not only does the hardware and software scene change relentlessly, but also ideas about the actual management of the IT function are being continuously modified, updated and changed. Thus keeping abreast of what is going on is really a major task.

The Butterworth-Heinemann – *Computer Weekly* Professional Series has been created to assist IT executives keep up to date with the management ideas and issues of which they need to be aware.

One of the key objectives of the series is to reduce the time it takes for leading edge management ideas to move from the academic and consulting environments into the hands of the IT practitioner. Thus this series employs appropriate technology to speed up the publishing process. Where appropriate some books are supported by CD-ROM or by additional information or templates located on the Web.

This series provides IT professionals with an opportunity to build up a bookcase of easily accessible, but detailed information on the important issues that they need to be aware of to successfully perform their jobs.

Aspiring or already established authors are invited to get in touch with me directly if they would like to be published in this series.

Dr Dan Remenyi
Series Editor
dan.remenyi@mcil.co.uk

Series Editor
Dan Remenyi, Visiting Professor, Trinity College Dublin

Advisory Board
Frank Bannister, Trinity College Dublin
Ross Bentley, Management Editor, *Computer Weekly*
Egon Berghout, Technical University of Delft, The Netherlands
Ann Brown, City University Business School, London
Roger Clark, The Australian National University
Reet Cronk, Harding University, Arkansas, USA
Arthur Money, Henley Management College, UK
Sue Nugus, MCIL, UK
David Taylor, CERTUS, UK
Terry White, BentleyWest, Johannesburg

Other titles in the Series
Corporate politics for IT managers: how to get streetwise
Delivering IT and e-business value
eBusiness implementation
eBusiness strategies for virtual organizations
The effective measurement and management of IT costs and benefits
ERP: the implementation cycle
A hacker's guide to project management
How to become a successful IT consultant
How to manage the IT helpdesk
Information warfare: corporate attack and defence in a digital world
IT investment – making a business case
Knowledge management – a blueprint for delivery
Make or break issues in IT management
Making IT count
Network security
Prince 2: a practical handbook
The project manager's toolkit
Reinventing the IT department
Understanding the Internet

Acknowledgements

This book has been built on the foundations of my experiences advising a wide range of major organizations in both the private and public sectors. As a business advisor I have been in a very privileged position, giving me extraordinary access to ask probing (and sometimes impertinent!) questions of people from the board to the trainee programmer. Had these people not been (generally) frank and open with me then this book could certainly not have been written. Therefore my thanks go to all those unfortunate victims over the years who have been subjected to my disarming interviewing technique!

Iain Aitken
iambic@tiscali.co.uk

My way of joking is to tell the truth.
It's the funniest joke in the world.

George Bernard Shaw (1907)

Preface: the Four Noble Truths

She took to telling the truth; she said she was forty-two and five months. It may have been pleasing to the angels, but her elder sister was not gratified.

Saki

My name is Iain Aitken and I am a management consultant. There. I've said it. Yes, I am one of those smiling suits who are brought in by senior management to see the big picture, think outside the box, stretch the envelope and go the extra mile to visualize blue sky, synergistic, holistic, proactive, client-focused, paradigm shifting, win–win, fast-track solutions to wholly insoluble problems. For years I was in denial. But when you find yourself secreting emergency jargon under the bed and in the broom closet you have to face the fact that *you* are the one who has a problem.

It is a sad (but cathartic) confession because my profession is generally perceived to be a tad unpopular. Not, perhaps, up there with used car salesmen, tort lawyers and international terrorists, but nevertheless held by many to also be an unnecessary evil. And an expensive one at that. All right, we may be perceived to be unpopular, unnecessary, evil and expensive, but are we worth it? Well, the late Douglas Adams paid us the compliment of equating our worth with that of that other great professional elite, telephone sanitizers. However, let me temper my confession by pointing out that I am now a *self-employed, semi-retired* and *independent* management consultant. This bestows upon me certain important freedoms. In particular, that freedom enshrined in the First Amendment of the American

Constitution, but denied to all of us who have products to sell, freedom of speech. I will exercise this freedom in this book and offer advice that is not necessarily the kind of advice you might expect to receive from the typical management consultant. I will attempt, in short, *to tell the truth*, even if occasionally this means my breaking the management consultants' *omertà* and apparently placing my profession under a pedestal.

Please understand that by this I do not mean to suggest that the typical management consultant is actually dishonest. Perish the thought. I spent 16 years working for 'Big 6/5/4' management consultancy firms and I can say (trust me on this) that I was never put in a position in which I was required to (explicitly) lie. I simply mean that there are times when a certain dash of disingenuousness, even a soupçon of sophistry, is required. Typically this is because consultants believe that clients don't want to be told the plain and uncomfortable truth, won't thank you for it and, most to the point, won't ask you back. Of course, the most plain and uncomfortable truth of all (which, of course, we *never* tell clients) is that often the only real hope they have of addressing their problems is to change their senior management team. That's right, the people who commissioned you and who will now *not* be paying your bill. However, that is an extreme example. More typically it is simply an issue of telling the client about his 'opportunities for improvement' (i.e. weaknesses) in the form of palatable half truths. However, as Arthur Koestler said, 'Two half truths do not make a truth.'

In my experience, most management consultants accept that on many (oh, all right, most) occasions the benefits promised from implementing the recommendations in their reports fail to materialize fully (if at all). The main reason typically given (by management consultants) is that the client failed to fully act (if at all) on the advice they were given. It is hardly the consultant's fault if the client accepts the findings and recommendations and then does little or nothing about it, is it? Plausible, very plausible, but . . .

A classic example of this occurred when I conducted a review of the IT management and delivery practices at a major food retailer. The final presentation to the CIO (chief information officer, or 'IT director') and his senior management team was quite uncompromising in its criticisms and made quite radical recommendations for change (although, as we will see in the case study in Chapter 3, perhaps not radical enough). At the end of my presentation I went round the table asking for feedback and reactions from each member of the management team. Every single one of them was unhesitating in agreeing that our findings and proposals were sound. We were congratulated on our insight into their problems and our far-reaching and uncompromising recommendations for change. It was, in short, too easy. So before leaving the venue I obtained agreement from the CIO subsequently to interview each of his managers, ostensibly just to ensure that they understood the changes they would be required to make on their own 'patch' in order to deliver on the recommendations. When I did so the response I got from every manager, without exception, demonstrated that they were wasted in an IT career and should really move into politics. Basically, everyone agreed that it was a superb piece of consultancy work, that it had accurately identified the problems and that the recommendations for change were critically required. Having gained agreement on these points I then asked them when they would be implementing the changes in *their* department. Ah, came the reply, for complex reasons, in their particular, *unique*, department, it wouldn't really be entirely appropriate, or the timing, unfortunately, was really not good or further work would, of course, be required, or the sun was, unfortunately, in Aries etc. But everyone *else* should certainly adopt our proposals immediately.

This lack of *true* buy-in to change by key stakeholders is an endemic problem in any proposed programme of change. It is fundamentally important and I will make much of it in the 'change implementation' sections of Chapters 3, 4 and 5. While human capacity for change may be huge (when needs must), human willingness to change is very limited (when there is no overwhelming mandate to change or when there are a hundred other competing pressures). In many cases of organizational change there is a fundamental lack of understanding by the sponsors of change of how people *actually* respond. The by no means atypical response of individuals who must change their behaviours or working practices to realize the benefits of change could well be characterized as follows.

- I don't really understand why they are doing this and the little I do understand I'm not sure I agree with.
- No one asked my opinion, thank you very much.
- Maybe it suits others but it sure doesn't suit the way I work.
- I don't see what's in it for me – in fact, it might make me look bad.

- I'll get no thanks for adopting this – it's just more aggravation.
- I'm stressed enough without this too.
- This just shows how little they trust me.
- OK, the way I work now may not be ideal – but it took me years to get my mind round it and it works for *me*.
- The guys at the top aren't *really* committed to this; give it a few months and it will all blow over with the next 'crisis'.
- Even the guys at the top don't really *want* to do this – they just want to be *seen* to do this so it makes them look good.
- They are going to expect me to do this in my spare time – *what* spare time?
- They are being silly about how quickly they are trying to do this.
- They made a mess of the last set of changes and they'll do the same this time.
- This is going to cost time and money that could better be spent elsewhere.
- But ... I guess I'll have to go through the motions and outwardly *pretend* to support this in order to protect my backside – what a farce!

This is sometimes (oh, all right, often) coupled with a 'corporate culture' that produces management teams that can display all the commercial acumen and entrepreneurial zeal of the average novice in a nunnery (I exaggerate only a little). We tend to think of the words 'corporate' and 'commercial' as almost being synonyms. But in my experience there is, ironically, no quality rarer in 'corporate management man' (*especially* when it is a man) than common (commercial) sense. In this culture the main way to get ahead is based far more on rhetoric than results. You talk and talk and always talk 'politically correctly' ('I'm 100 per cent behind this initiative, which will empower our greatest assets, our people, and maximize shareholder value, blah blah blah . . . ') but actually do little or nothing but keep your head below the parapet ('It will probably fail and I'm 100 per cent sure I'm not going down with this initiative'). Here you have a recipe for complacency, conservatism and stagnation, the name of the game being to 'talk the talk' but not 'walk the talk'.

Were consultants to tell the 'whole truth' they might well say at the end of their final presentation to client management, 'Those, gentlemen, were my 30 key recommendations for change . . . Mind you, quite aside from the bureaucratic and uncommercial culture that permeates your entire organization, generally low calibre of management and the total absence of anyone with the requisite leadership skills to make change actually happen, we all know you are far too frightened of change and far too busy doing things the way you have always done them to have a hope in hell of implementing a fraction of these recommendations this century. However, the good news is that I've learned a lot and billed a lot.'

My other key concern is to honestly face up to the fact that the recommendations made by consultants are typically rooted in advising clients to adopt 'industry best practices'. What could possibly be wrong with that, you may say. Well, as I hope to show in Chapter 2, 'industry best practices' may produce 'higher quality' solutions but do not necessarily produce the best *commercial outcomes*. In the first place, 'quality' has a price tag and in the second place 'quality' does not necessarily equate to value being added to the business. Were consultants to tell the whole truth they might well say, 'Those, gentlemen, were my 30 key recommendations for change. They are firmly rooted in international best practice and if you adopt them you should become a "world class IT" organization . . . Mind you, it will cost you a fortune to make and sustain all these changes and you probably won't contribute much more to the business bottom line at the end of it, but, hey, that's not my problem. Have a nice day.'

Management consultancy (like, I suspect, politics) is a job that tends to engender a degree of cynicism. You see, consultants just *can't* tell the whole truth. And if they did, then of course they wouldn't be in a position to sell on all that consultancy work to help you implement the 30 key recommendations, would they? Aside from confronting the senior management team with an honest appraisal of their leadership (in)ability, the 'whole truth' would probably include something like, 'Instead of those 30 "key" best practice recommendations for change, here are half a dozen *critical* things you should do to genuinely transform the business value of IT in your company. Given that some of these things you already do reasonably well, you should be able to make these changes, and make them stick, in the next year or so, if you really focus on them (and you have a bit of luck). At the end of it you won't get any "world class IT" awards but you will get the respect of the business you serve. Oh, and by the way, you can probably make these changes with little or no external consultancy support. In fact, we have found much the same problems in virtually all our other clients so this job was really quite simple for us. So we will only be billing you half of our original quote for the work.' This book is principally about defining those half dozen *critical* things you should do and making a success of implementing them. It is also about trying to tell the whole truth. Which leads me, of course, to Buddhism.

Buddhism has fascinated me for over 30 years (bear with me here). I am an arch rationalist (albeit a superstitious arch rationalist) and Buddhism provides a supremely elegant, logical, rational and methodical approach to the attainment of spiritual enlightenment (*nirvana*). The basic approach is set out in the Pali Canon of Buddhism, written largely in the second century BC in south India. This states that after his complete and unexcelled enlightenment, Gautama the Buddha went to the Deer Park at Benares and declaimed his doctrine in the form of his Four Noble Truths. As you will doubtless know, these are patterned on the traditional Vedic form of a physician's diagnosis and prescription, namely, the identification of the disease, the identification of its cause, an assessment of whether or not it is susceptible to cure and, if it is susceptible to cure, the prescription.

The First Noble Truth is usually translated from the Sanskrit as 'To live is to suffer' but can more usefully (if less pithily) be paraphrased as 'Fundamental dissatisfaction with life is an endemic problem.' The Second Noble Truth is that 'The cause of this dissatisfaction is attachment to ideas, based on ignorance.' The Third Noble Truth is that 'There is a cure, and that cure is to end attachment to ideas.' The Fourth Noble Truth sets out the 'prescription' for the cure in the form of the Eightfold Path to enlightenment. The Eightfold Path is essentially the 'best practice' model of Buddhism. It includes, for example, *samyag-vak* (which essentially means 'truthful speech') and *samyagajiva* (which essentially means 'noble vocation'). In my experience, not many management consultants are Buddhists. Now, it is at this point you are probably asking at least two questions, namely, (1) exactly *what* has this got to do with achieving a value-driven IT function?, and (2) exactly what drug is this guy on?

Well, I want to draw a parallel. My First Noble Truth is that 'Fundamental business dissatisfaction with its IT service is an endemic problem.' My second is that 'The cause of this dissatisfaction with IT is the typical gulf between the promise and the reality of the delivery of business value from IT.' These two 'truths' are examined in Chapter 1. My third, examined in

Chapter 2 ('Defining goals'), is that 'There is a cure, and that cure is to focus IT delivery practices on the delivery of business *value*.' Taking a reality check on the promises wouldn't hurt either. My fourth, the 'prescription', is a set of practices and initiatives precisely focused on optimizing the value added to business by IT and the cost-efficiency of the supply of IT products and services. These are examined in Chapters 3 ('Optimizing effectiveness') and 4 ('Optimizing cost-efficiency'), respectively. And my 'nirvana'? That is becoming a 'value-driven IT function'. How will you know how close you are getting to nirvana? That is examined in Chapter 5 ('Measuring success').

But first, the Introduction, and a little matter of IT conspiracy theory.

Summary

Management consultancy recommendations often take the form of palatable half truths that may compromise the best interests of the client in order to serve the best interests of the consultancy firm. The clients of these consultants may claim to accept these half truths but will often not truly buy in to the underlying changes required. As a result the potential benefits of change are often poorly realized. Furthermore, the half truths are typically rooted in industry best practices which do not necessarily produce the best commercial outcomes. The realization of potential benefits will also often be severely hindered by leadership deficiencies in the management team and a failure to adequately recognize and address the (often enormous) behavioural barriers to making real change happen. Organizations need to take a 'reality check' and identify, and *genuinely* commit to, a small and manageable set of IT practices that most critically optimize commercial outcomes.

1 Introduction

The rule is, jam tomorrow and jam yesterday – but no
jam today.

Lewis Carroll – *Through the Looking Glass*

This is a book about transforming the business value of IT. It is
about identifying what is relatively important in IT product and
service delivery (and doing it extremely well) and what is
relatively unimportant (and doing it acceptably well). It is, in
short, about jam delivery today, the jam in this case being
'value'.

A significant amount of research went into this book but I
sincerely hope that that is not readily evident because my
message is founded on practical experience, not pseudo-
academic theory. So, trust me, you won't find a single footnote
or reference clogging up the text of this book! This book isn't
science, it's personal. I generally don't have much patience with
the theories of the 'management sciences', although I confess
that I have cherry-picked a few bits of management theory that
did actually seem to correlate reality as I have experienced it.
This book is not even based on 'conventional wisdom' because,
as I intend to show, 'conventional wisdom' is often spouted by
those with an agenda (namely, to sell you something) and,
anyway, is often based on assumptions that do not bear
commercial scrutiny. Therefore my attitude to the inclusion of
advice in this book has been that if it will make a real
(commercial) difference in the real (commercial) world, it's in; if
it doesn't, it's out. My goal is to be down to earth and pragmatic
(occasional Buddhist flights of fancy aside), offering an
approach to IT value transformation that is occasionally ingen-
ious and, I hope, always ingenuous.

This book began with Chapter 5, 'Measuring success'. I was initially asked to write a proposal for a consultancy assignment to advise a client on building a 'balanced scorecard' to help measure the performance of its IT function. The potential assignment came my way because within the consultancy firm I was regarded as the IT benchmarking 'guru' (in the land of the blind, the one-eyed man is king). What this really meant was that I was well acquainted with 'conventional wisdom' in the world of IT performance measurement. The trouble was that my extensive experience of seeing that conventional wisdom put into practice had left me increasingly disillusioned with the real business value of that 'wisdom'. It had resulted in a history of 'balanced scorecards' that struck me as being highly *un*balanced, at least if you believed, as I did, that business outcomes ought to be firmly on one side of the scales. Whatever the measures told you about the performance of the IT product and service delivery 'factory' they seemed to tell you little to nothing about 'customer delight' with the quality and value of the products and services delivered. Furthermore they were typically characterized by measuring arcane things that IT people understood (or, at least, claimed to understand) and which were relatively easy to measure rather than things that actually told senior management something commercially meaningful about the value of IT to their business in a language they could understand. Pondering this caused me to back up further and ask myself questions about which practices and behaviours most critically needed to be changed or improved if we were to maximize the value of IT to the business (topics that I cover in Chapters 3 and 4). This, in turn, made me back up to the very question of 'What *is* best practice?', a topic dealt with in Chapter 2. So I have a story to tell, albeit in reverse.

What are my qualifications to write this book? Well, when I give talks and presentations I am almost invariably introduced as 'an expert in IT business management'. Fine. But what is an 'expert', other than someone who is one page ahead of you in the manual? Well, the great physicist Niels Bohr said that 'An expert is a man who has made all the mistakes, which can be made, in a very narrow field.' Thank you Niels. Got me in one. Because that is certainly my key qualification – if I haven't got it wrong personally then I have seen many a man who has. I would like to think that I have learnt something from that (although I give no guarantees). In particular, I spent 10 years 'on the inside' working in various technical and managerial roles in large IT functions (culminating in three years as an IT project manager in

Tesco Stores Ltd, Britain's biggest and most successful food retailer) and the last 18 years 'on the outside' as a management consultant specializing in the performance improvement of large IT functions. Key clients I have advised over the years have included Marks & Spencer, J. Sainsbury, Reuters, Consignia/Royal Mail, Barclays Bank, Cable & Wireless and Lloyd's of London (all of whom will be very familiar to the British reader, at least). My qualifications rest on experience, therefore – the extensive experience of trying to increase the value realized from IT investment. In business there is no more valuable commodity than experience, and my experience of value is the value of my experience! Sorry, I just couldn't resist that.

1.1 Why bother?

So do we have a problem with extracting value from our IT investments such that we need a book on the subject? Well, let's look at just one important aspect of IT delivery, namely, project management. According to the Standish Group:

- about a third of development projects are recognized to have gone seriously out of control and are cancelled (eventually);
- over half of development projects are delivered at a cost of almost double the originally estimated budget;
- around half of development projects are delivered behind schedule or with reduced functionality.

And note that this is just the projects in which someone actually recognized and reported the problem! For every one of those, how many others were there? I could go on, so I will. The recently published IBM book, *Troubled IT Projects*, states that average IT project timescale overruns are 30 per cent, with only 5 per cent coming in on time and about half of all projects overrunning by more than 30 per cent. Then there is Beam, in *Software Engineering Productivity and Quality*, who reports that 'Of all software projects incorporating over 64,000 lines of code, 25% failed to deliver anything; 60% were over budget and behind schedule, and only 1% met requirements on time and on budget.' And what about the survey of 1027 IT projects published in the 2001 *British Computer Society Review*, which showed that less than 13 per cent succeeded. Where these IT projects were software development projects, less than 1 per cent were regarded as having succeeded.

Now, admittedly, I tend to collect these sorts of statistics (yes, I know, it's sad and I should really get a life), but let's just say that there is ample evidence out there that we have a problem with the credible delivery of IT solutions, never mind delivering the *value* promised from those solutions.

In my own (pre-consultancy) experience, when I was doing a proper job working in industry, running a group of about 80 development staff, we estimated that around 20 per cent of the code we developed was never actually implemented and a further 20 per cent, although implemented (for reasons of avoided embarrassment), was never actually used by the business. This wastage arose for a variety of reasons, but principally was because either the users found that what we delivered was not what they thought they had asked for or simply because the business priorities or requirements had moved on since the initial request for the system had been made. So we knew that around 40 per cent of our effort was a *complete* waste of time and money but had no idea really about the extent to which the other 60 per cent of our effort truly added value to the business. And anyway, was that our problem?

On this basis alone it is not difficult to see that when senior business management are asked to give their views of their IT function their most typical lament can be paraphrased as 'They cost too much, they take too long and they don't deliver what they promise.' This may be a cliché but that does not make it untrue. It is basically a more prosaic way of expressing my 'First Noble Truth' about the fundamental dissatisfaction with IT delivery (although, as we will see, it actually goes deeper than that). As an IT consultant, I have been listening to this lament for over 18 years and, although increasing IT literacy in the business community generally, and e-business specifically, has somewhat increased the empathy between the business and IT communities, I do not believe the situation has improved significantly throughout those 18 years. There are obviously exceptions, but the overwhelming impression of senior managers with whom I have dealt over the years has been that while fully recognizing the importance of IT to the operation of their business, IT functions have repeatedly failed to deliver the value sought. This, quite simply, is a key driver of the 'casualty' rate of CIOs, the average CIO in the USA now surviving less than two years. They may cry out that their external benchmarking shows that (at least compared with their peers) they are *not* excessively expensive, slow or ineffective but 'perceptions are reality'. At the very least they have not effectively managed their key customers' expectations.

1.2 The nature of the problem

So why is the delivery of IT value so difficult? Like any manufacturing business 'all' we are doing is developing a product (a system), implementing it and then providing 'post-sales' support. And the internal customer has generally already decided he wants the product so we don't even have to sell it to him! All we have to do is persuade him to buy the product from us, the internal service provider rather than going directly to an external IT service provider (ESP). Since many IT functions today still are (by policy or in effect) 'protected' as monopoly suppliers of IT to the business, they might not even to have to do that bit of persuasion. Surely 'all' we have to do to be successful in our internal 'IT factory' is agree with the business which products it wants us to deliver, predictably deliver the products and then predictably run and support those products after they have been implemented, through to product obsolescence or replacement. It can be modelled very simply, as set out in Figure 1.1.

Figure 1.1

We, in the IT industry, have been doing these three things for decades but seem to be little better at delighting our customers now than in the 1960s. What are we doing wrong, and, more to the point, why do we *continue* to do it wrong?

1.3 Conspiracy theories

My experience suggests to me that the problems lie in a number of areas, but are primarily founded on a deadly combination of the 'twin towers' of collusion and illusion. By 'collusion' I mean a tacit conspiracy between the 'buyer' (the business sponsor/requester of the solution) and the supplier (the internal service supplier, the IT function). By 'illusion' I mean the typical failure of both the buyer and supplier to face certain realities that are clearly visible (but uncomfortable to confront).

First, collusion. The project sponsor *wants* the system developed. He or she sincerely believes it is important to the success of the business (or, at least, did so when the system was originally requested). And the IT function generally *wants* to develop it; it keeps them in a job, pays their mortgages and may enhance their CVs. So they immediately have a common goal, namely, to produce a project justification that will leap whatever hurdles the finance department 'bean counters' place in the way of its acceptance and, once those annoying, petty hurdles have been jumped (or sidestepped), to breathe a sigh of relief and get on with the interesting bit, the delivery of the system. In order to achieve these goals an 'unspoken conspiracy' typically arises in which, for example:

- assumptions about the importance of the proposed system to support business goals are exaggerated, the 'strategic import-ance' of the desired solution typically being based on 'decibel management' (i.e. the senior manager who shouts hardest and longest) rather than any credibly 'objective' process;
- assumptions about the business revenue that the system will generate are exaggerated (or wildly optimistic, or just wishful thinking);
- assumptions about the business savings that the system will generate are exaggerated (or wildly optimistic, or just wishful thinking);
- assumptions about the speed of full adoption of the system by the business are unrealistic (or wildly optimistic, or just wishful thinking);
- assumptions about the practical difficulties of actually realiz-ing the system benefits are unrealistic (e.g. unions resisting the laying off, or even redeployment, of staff; users not acting on information provided by the system because they do not see it as serving their best interests);
- assumptions about the stability of the market in which the business operates and the stability of the business 'strategy' while the system is in development are unrealistic;
- assumptions about the stability of functional requirements while the system is in development are unrealistic;
- assumptions about the development risks (e.g. availability of skilled staff, commitment of key users to requirements specification or testing, new technology working first time) are unrealistic (or just wildly optimistic).

The key term in all my points above is, of course, 'unrealistic assumptions', and this is where the 'illusion' bit comes in. It is not so much that such unrealistic assumptions occur occasion-ally in IT delivery; in my experience of 10 years in the IT industry delivering IT solutions and then over 18 years consulting to the IT industry, *most* of these unrealistic assumptions occur *most* of the time. Often these assumptions will not be explicitly documented. Even when they *are* documented it may simply be as a 'get out of jail free card' that the project or programme manager can use later to justify why the solution delivered is not actually delivering the benefits sought. ('Of course the project has proved to be a failure – it was inevitable, because the fairytale world in which I set it failed to materialize.') In other words, the realization of value from the solution is being predicated on 'assumptions' that pretty much anyone with any significant experience of business or the IT industry *knows* to be unrealistic, if not plain nonsense.

1.4 Case study – best practice, worst outcome?

To help illustrate the problem let me cite a case study based on my experience reviewing a project that had been performed in one of Britain's largest (and most successful) retailers. The project (to select and implement a package to improve merchandise cataloguing and buying for stores) had been justified on the basis of generating around a £200m ($300m) increase in sales (in a part of the business in which gross margins sat at around the *50 per cent* mark – yes, there is no business like apparel business). Two hundred million pounds may sound like a suspiciously nice, round, large number, but in this case the predicted sales generation figure was *not* simply plucked out of the air. Far from it. It was determined from a huge undertaking by the world's largest management consultancy firm (at that time) that drew on business estimates, variability analysis, external benchmarking evidence and widespread trials. Given the inherent difficulty of quantifying benefits in the case of this system (since so many other factors can be responsible for changes in sales figures – e.g. the saleability of the product, the availability of the product, the global economy, 11 September 2001) this huge effort (costing a six figure £ sum) was arguably expensive 'brick polishing' (to use the more polite term). However, be that as it may, the fact remained that every reasonable effort was made to quantify the benefits. Since the project costs were estimated at under £3m ($4.5m), the board of the retailer doubtless regarded the decision on the authorization of this project as a 'no-brainer'. After all, the project could come in 1000 per cent over budget and still realize massive net benefits!

The project was duly initiated amid much trumpet-blowing about how it would be key to the future success of the business. A comprehensive project charter was prepared and a strong IT development team was established, managed by a highly experienced IT project manager. A reputable package supplier was selected and an excellent relationship was established between this company and the internal IT development group. Inevitably the project suffered its share of problems but, despite these, it delivered the core functionality successfully, tolerably to budget, and exactly to the (very aggressive) deadline. During the project, 'scope creep' (an endemic problem in most IT develop-ments) was controlled well, as were key project risks and issues. Ask almost any IT project manager for a definition of a 'successful' project and I feel confident you will get an answer along the lines of 'delivered *what* you said you would deliver, *when* you said you would deliver it, for the *cost* you said'. In fact, many (IT internal) project managers would regard 'success' as delivering just the *core* functionality (by and large) on the planned delivery date (by and large), at undetermined final cost.

So our case study is a near textbook example, then, of a 'successful project'? The business strategy on which the project was founded had been clearly articulated ('develop strategy'), the project had delivered a solution of the specified quality, to budget and on schedule ('develop system'). The development team were subsequently retained and provided timely and effective support and the system ran to generally acceptable service levels ('deliver service'). How could it have been more successful than that?

It is, of course, at this point that we get to the 'crunch' question, namely, did the system realize the £200m ($300m) per annum sales uplift? The answer is that no one knew for sure (because, of course, no one was measuring it) but the best guess was that at most £10m ($15m) in sales uplift could be attributed to the new processes (albeit not necessarily to the *system* itself). The margins on this still more than 'paid' for the project but it was hardly the bonanza anticipated by the board. So why the dramatic shortfall? The answer lay predominantly in (yes, you guessed it) assumptions that were unrealistic to the point of naivety. In particular the realization of the benefits were predicated on assumptions that:

- the prevalent (dominant) business culture of 'short-termism' would, of itself, shift rapidly to one of long-term merchandise planning based on the outputs of the system;

- the existing 'power base', rooted firmly within the buying department since the dawn of the company, would, of itself, shift rapidly to one rooted in the marketing department (who were the sponsors of the project);
- the buyers would inherently trust the system-generated buying plans and predominantly buy according to plan, despite the fact that this could fundamentally undermine their role;
- the complex new product and customer categorizations that were being proposed by marketing staff (essentially increasing 40-fold the number of variables) would be rapidly understood, accepted and adopted consistently across the business (no disrespect, but these are retailers, not rocket scientists);
- identical product categorizations would be adopted by both the 'buying' and 'marketing' sides of the business (despite the fact that even before the project began there were strongly adversarial views on this, arguments that were never resolved);
- individual business departments using the new system and processes would act in the best interests of the company as a whole, even at the expense of their own department's bottom line (despite a well-recognized history of their working largely in self-interested 'silos' and the implementation of a management bonus system that very strongly incentivized the acting in silos);
- the project sponsor (who was sponsoring multiple projects) and key stakeholders across the business would commit the leadership and time to drive out the benefits sought (despite the fact that virtually no time was made available for them to do this in addition to their 'day job' responsibilities and, anyway, no sponsorship responsibilities or tasks were allocated to them, i.e. their roles were basically sinecures);
- full benefits would emerge almost immediately (despite the fact that plans produced by the system would only start to influence sales in trading seasons a year off);
- the company strategy would be stable (despite the fact that it changed radically shortly after the system was implemented).

A point that I found particularly interesting was that despite the fact that the project charter specified no less than 17 key stakeholders, not one of them was a 'buyer'. The reason given for this was that the initial actual users of the system were all on the 'marketing' side of the business. But to extract the *benefits* from the system it was key to get the buy-in of the buyers since it was essential that they act on the information provided to them by the system.

It was hardly surprising that there was widespread disappointment with the project when it was founded on such a shaky edifice of 'assumptions'. Of course not one of these 'assumptions' was written down. Yet this was most emphatically *not* just a matter of 'wisdom of hindsight'. All of these (tacit and implicit) 'assumptions' (with the arguable exception of the last one) were 'obvious' before the project ever began. You would not have to work in either IT or the retail industry for long to understand how unrealistic (not to say ridiculous) these 'assumptions' were. But it was a case of 'the Emperor's New Clothes'. It was 'truth and consequences': they didn't want to face the truth and there were serious consequences. The board *wanted* to 'flex its muscles' and be seen to initiate a flagship, business transformational project and the departmental directors greedily *wanted* their slice of the proposed benefits pie and the IT function *wanted* to be bringers of glad tidings and great joy. This is why I use the phrase 'collusion and illusion'.

What was needed, perhaps, was a 'court jester'. In medieval England the court jester was the one person in the king's court who could, without fear of reprisal, whisper into the king's ear, 'Sire, none of the snivelling toads you keep around your court is going to tell you this but today thou speaketh bosh and balderdash – pray just listen to yourself you old fool.' Our current-day court jester would, without fear for his job, whisper into the king's (CEO's) ear, 'You are (once again) about to make a monumental horse's ass of yourself – so don't listen to all the sycophantic colleagues and consultants around you telling you how brilliant the proposal on the table is and how it's going to make the company (and, by the way, you) into stars – listen to the voice of commercial reason and common sense instead. Get real and *think*.' How many doomed at birth grandiose plans would businesses (and governments) avoid if only they employed court jesters! CEOs don't need personal assistants (PAs); they need personal court jesters. Of course we couldn't actually call them court jesters. Instead I suggest we call them PMs, for personal mokitas. The word 'mokita' is from the Kiriwina language of New Guinea and it means 'the truth which no one speaks'. Of course the PM's position would be tenured and I think such a PM could, with justification, pretty much name his or her own salary.

If they had been honest with themselves, someone (but who, exactly?) should have said, 'Let's get real here and acknowledge that this project is actually founded on a lot of (unspoken) major assumptions and that these "assumptions" are actually *risks* with a near certainty of occurring and with a major impact on benefits realization.' But then no one was responsible (let alone *accountable*) for benefits realization. The project manager wasn't sure who was responsible but certainly *was* sure it was not her. The same story came from the programme manager, the project sponsor and the key stakeholders.

The key point I am trying to make is that the IT function did, generally, a truly excellent job in terms of deploying 'best practices' for *solution delivery*. But they tacitly colluded with the business in going into 'denial' about *benefits realization*.

By the way, when I presented my report 'confronting' them with the points I raise above you might well think that they would have fervently challenged my analysis of the root causes of the problems and/or roundly discredited me and/or quickly suppressed my report. But no. The response was a shrug of the shoulders, a rueful smile and the comment that the problems I was raising were endemic to pretty much all large projects in their company, IT or otherwise. But, apparently, that was just the way life was.

1.5 Twenty questions

You are perhaps thinking that the above case study is an extreme example. You are possibly also thinking that I cannot possibly be talking about *your* IT function. So let's play 'Twenty Questions' on the topic of how you justify and run 'IT projects' in your organization:

Q1: When planning and scheduling projects, do you ever assume that project staff will not be materially distracted from their project commitments by production support demands or that they will not fall ill while the project is running or that, generally, they will all spend 100 per cent of every working day productively working on the project (despite the fact that this virtually *never* happens)?

Q2: When planning projects, do you ever assume that the work and cost estimates (on which the business case, the justification for performing the project, is based) are acceptably accurate, even though most IT functions estimate their projects by no more sophisticated a method than 'gut feel', a project manager basically saying to himself, 'It looks a bit like that previous project I did but about 50 per cent bigger'?

Q3: When planning projects, do you ever assume that the work and cost estimates (on which the business case, the justification for performing the project, is based) will be stable despite the fact that at the time of the initial estimate you may not know if the system is to be bespoked (i.e. a customized solution) or realized with a tailored package, developed in-house or externally, using VB or Cobol, on a mainframe or a server etc. and that therefore the estimates almost certainly will change substantially, if not dramatically?

Q4: Do you ever submit project business cases that you *know* do not include system total life-cycle costs (i.e. the cost not just of developing it but also of subsequently maintaining, supporting and operating it) or do not include infrastructure upgrades that may be required to run the system or do not include the actual costs of the project team since the size and constitution of the team may be unknown at the time of writing the business case? (Indeed, I have seen many business cases that completely *omit* the cost of the development team and only include 'out the door' capital expenditure. I have even worked on a client project in which the tiny positive NPV on which it was justified was only arrived at by *completely omitting* the vast IT expenditure required.)

Q5: When planning projects for which you actually *know* the composition of the project team, do you ever construct cost estimates that assume a nominal cost for permanent staff, despite the fact that you know that the project will make significant use of (*far* more expensive) contract staff?

Q6: When running projects do you ever assume that when key user stakeholders sign off your detailed specification documents they actually understand what they are signing for and can mentally picture the system that will result, despite the fact that you know from experience that this has virtually *never* happened in the past?

Q7: When planning projects, do you ever assume that the project sponsor will play an active role in leading and giving direction to the project, using his influence and contacts to gain business support, despite the fact that you know from experience that this has virtually *never* happened in the past?

Q8: When planning projects, do you ever assume that key users will sign off your deliverables in a timely manner and make their time available to the team when required, when you know from experience that this has virtually *never* happened in the past?

Q9: While running projects, do you ever fail to accrue to the budget the overtime costs that you run up (especially as the deadline looms) or do you ever fail to accrue to the budget the full indirect costs that the project runs up (such as database designers, capacity planners etc.)?

Q10: Do you ever assume that as the project develops and the users understand better what they *actually* want, the requirements will not expand and the scope will not creep, despite the fact that this virtually *always* happens?

Q11: Do you ever assume that as the project develops, the technical complexity of developing what the users want will not increase, despite the fact that this virtually *always* happens?

Q12: Do you ever assume that 90 per cent complete project tasks have 10 per cent of the work left to run when this has virtually *never* happened in the past? (Remember: the first 90 per cent of the task takes 90 per cent of the budgeted time and the remaining 10 per cent takes the other 90 per cent.)

Q13: Do you ever assume that when project staff are inexperienced in a new technology, their learning curve will not materially increase the project costs and time, despite the fact that this virtually *always* happens?

Q14: Do you ever assume that the business staff reductions upon which the business case is predicated will actually happen, despite the fact that this virtually *never* happens (as a result of union resistance, staff actually just being 'moved sideways', or plain 'cold feet')?

Q15: Do you ever assume that capex or working capital reductions (for example, as a result of inventory reduction) upon which the project business case is predicated will actually happen, despite the fact that you know that it will be *much* more difficult in practice to actually deliver those reductions?

Q16: Do you ever artificially 'engineer' anticipated benefits values to ensure that the business case beats the return on investment or return on capital employed or net present value 'hurdle' set for project acceptance?

Q17: Do you ever set project benefit values 'arbitrarily' (e.g. branch turnover will increase by 0.2 per cent), when you know that it might be a fraction of that figure (but are secure in the thought that it will be unprovable post-implementation anyway)?

Q18: Do you ever assume that during the many months of systems development, the business strategy will be static and the market conditions will be unchanged, despite the fact that this virtually *never* happens?

Q19: Do you ever assume that, on systems implementation, users will immediately change their established ways of working and embrace the new system rapidly, quickly realizing the full benefits, despite the fact that this virtually *never* happens?

Q20: Do you ever assume that the post-implementation support and running costs will not rise with time, despite the fact that this virtually *always* happens as a result of the difficulty of maintaining increasingly amended code, key staff leaving the company, lack of maintained systems documentation etc.?

If you have answered 'no' to all 20 questions, then either:

(a) you don't run projects in your IT function (at least, not any more), or
(b) you are being somewhat abstemious in the matter of veracity, or
(c) you are the long-standing CIO of a major IT function and in your deluded (though doubtless happy) way have long since lost all touch with the reality of what is *actually* going on out there, or
(d) the sky is pink in your world.

By the way, project managers who feel that they have learned things to their advantage in the above list are referred to Figure 1.2.

In short, we *know* that many (if not most) project business cases would not fly (or even make it to the end of the runway) if we were realistic in stating the *true* costs, benefits and risks. We *know* that once approved, the business case almost invariably becomes *less* credible during the development as the actual development costs prove greater than we originally estimated (and that they will inexorably rise) and the ability to actually deliver the originally promised benefits fades. We *know* that once we implement the system the support and running costs

Make believe: 20 ways to ensure that you get your project business case accepted	
1	Pretend that all project staff will spend 100% of every working day productively working on the project
2	Pretend that your initial work and cost estimates are not actually just guesstimates
3	Pretend that initial work and cost estimates will not rise
4	Pretend that the total lifetime costs of the system will end the day it goes live
5	Pretend that the project will be staffed by nominally costed permanent staff, even if expensive contractors are to be used
6	Pretend that the users understand exactly what they are signing up for
7	Pretend that the project sponsor will play a leading role
8	Pretend that the users won't introduce any delays
9	Pretend that there will be no overtime costs and no indirect costs
10	Pretend that the business requirements will not change
11	Pretend that the technical complexity will not grow
12	Pretend that the project team will complete all tasks on budget
13	Pretend that there is going to be no learning curve
14	Pretend that business staff who will have to be sacked to make your business case work will actually be sacked
15	Pretend that the business capex reductions needed to make your business case work will actually happen
16	Pretend that you haven't 'massaged' the benefits to ensure you beat the ROI hurdle rate
17	Pretend that you haven't dreamed up the benefits figure (and then doubled it)
18	Pretend that the business strategy and market conditions will be static
19	Pretend that when the system goes live all the benefits will materialize from day 1
20	Pretend that support costs won't rise with time (or see no. 4)

Figure 1.2

will be higher than predicted and will rise. And we *know* that the benefits predicted are extremely unlikely to be fully (or even partially) realized. And so on.

All this we know and yet through a combination of the unspoken conspiracy with the business and 'forgetting' our repeated experience we plough on regardless and profess surprise when projects fail and fail again (or at least fail to deliver what they promised). Is this the result of a battle between conscience ('No way is this project viable ... ') and career (' ... but it will be interesting to do, will keep me in a job and look good on my CV') in which conscience rarely prevails? Is it some sort of 'collective dementia'? Or is it that corporate man is 'just doing a job' and so doesn't really care too much about the commercial whys and wherefores? I don't know. But

I do know that instead of managing the 'IT factory' based on commercial reality we repeatedly manage based on illusions, even though we *know* that they are illusions.

If we built comprehensive, commercially thorough, honest business cases that complemented the cost/benefit equation with a truly honest and realistic examination of the risks, not only of project delivery, but also of benefits realization, then I suspect that many (perhaps most) projects would not even be approved – and this is as it *should* be. If we *maintained* approved, comprehensive, commercially realistic business cases and risks throughout the development process, ensuring that the cost/ benefit/risk case reflected the project as it existed at that time, then I suspect that many (perhaps most) would be terminated (or at least descoped) long before they were implemented – and this is *also* as it should be.

However, no one wants to be the one to say, 'Look, I'm sorry, but this pet project of yours is just not viable (i.e. going to deliver the promised value) in the real world so let's not even start it.' No one wants to be the one to say, 'Look, I'm sorry, I know we have spent a small fortune on this project already but it just isn't going to realize its business case, at least not in its current state today, so let's kill it now.' No one (least of all the project sponsor) wants to be the one to say, 'Look, I'm sorry, but this system we just spent a small fortune on developing is costing more to run and support than the benefits it is actually delivering so let's kill it.' As we saw in the case study above, no one even wants to say, 'Look, I'm sorry, although this project is commercially viable, the level of benefits you are pinning your hopes on are simply

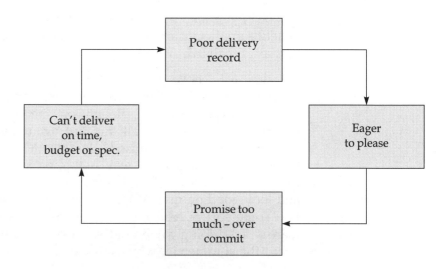

Figure 1.3

not remotely achievable in the real world and, anyway, we can probably get a bigger bang for our buck investing elsewhere.'

This 'management by illusion' practice is arguably self-perpetuating, as Terry White sets out in his book, *Reinventing the IT Department* (Butterworth-Heinemann 2001), as the 'vicious circle of IT esteem', which I repeat in Figure 1.3. As he puts it, 'something unhealthy is happening here, which is not good for either party in this sad cycle: business people are learning not to trust IT people, and IT people are setting themselves up to fail'.

1.6 Real world management

Until those in the 'IT industry' cease to quietly collude with their customers and cease to 'manage by illusion', the project failure statistics will continue (and remember, those are only the ones we have had the courage to *admit* as failures) and internal IT functions will continue to be regarded with suspicion and distrust (because they did not have the courage to face the commercial reality of the difficulty of what they were doing). You could call it shifting from 'managing projects for solution delivery' to 'managing projects for value delivery'. But I could just call it 'real world management'. Once again, it is about truth.

Now, I know that the term 'real world' has very negative connotations. T.S. Eliot said that 'Human kind cannot bear very much reality.' And when someone says to you, 'Welcome to the real world', they are never referring to a world that is sunny, carefree and innocent but rather one that is menacing, melancholy and Machiavellian. But none of these adjectives apply to 'real world management', which I hope to demonstrate as being an honest approach to management that is more immediate, exciting and fulfilling (if, occasionally, a little scary).

The pressure is on IT managers to just 'play the game'. They don't really want to tell unpalatable truths to users (who really don't want to know that their pet project is actually a benefits no-hoper). Quite aside from any other consideration, admitting to this, if not completely challenging the reason for their existence, at least diminishes their 'forward order book'. Yet it is precisely here that IT functions should be demonstrating their key value over ESPs, namely, they should not have the commercial agenda of the supplier at heart; they should instead have the commercial agenda of the *business* in which they work.

The idea that the preferred model for running an IT function is to 'emulate' an ESP is fine up to a point, that key point being that the ESP wants to make money out of you. You contract with them to deliver (and perhaps also to support and operate) a solution for a price. They are hardly going to say to you, 'Please don't buy our service to supply this system, because if we are honest we both actually know that even if we can deliver it to budget and deadline it won't realize the benefits you seek.' The IT function does not have to make a profit or reward shareholders and so should not only be able to undertake work without commercial bias, it should also generally be able to do it *cheaper* than an ESP (a point that I will expand upon in Chapter 4)!

IT functions that refuse to continue the charade risk, at first, being labelled 'politically naive' for not just continuing to play the corporate game. But until they have the courage to do this they will not win the full trust and support of senior business management. If they simply continue to 'play the game' they perhaps run a bigger risk of being outsourced to an ESP who, ironically, can be assured of playing the game like a grand master!

1.7 Managing for value delivery

My contention in this book is that IT functions (and, crucially, businesses as a whole) need to ensure that there is a fundamental sharpening of focus on managing IT for *value delivery*. This is certainly not to say that managing the inputs (e.g. people, organization, technology) and processes to deliver products and services is unimportant. It is simply that the only reason for the IT function's existence (the only reason, indeed, for *IT's* existence) is to deliver products and services of the 'right' commercial quality that *add value* to the business (whether that be by revenue enhancement, cost reduction or risk reduction).

A system delivered to budget and to schedule and which provides the functionality requested may well be very satisfactory for the IT function but is not in itself a success. It is only successful if the deliverables are of commercially appropriate quality and they (to a tolerable margin) add the promised value to the business. Therefore my contention is that the key focus of IT management generally (and IT performance improvement initiatives specifically) must be on the *outcomes* of IT product and service delivery and that successes and failures in those outcomes will help us understand where (commercially) best to

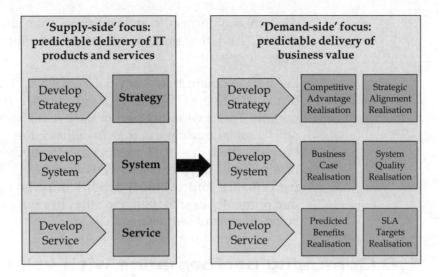

Figure 1.4

focus our energies (and money) to improve the inputs and processes of IT delivery. It is a question of a shift in focus from the supply side of delivery to the demand side of delivery, as illustrated in Figure 1.4.

Being effective at strategy development by adopting strategy development 'best practices' is only ultimately 'good' if it actually results in an IT function that is well aligned with the business goals, IT solutions that are well aligned with business priorities and business unit performance goals and, ideally, the realization of competitive advantage from IT. Being effective at systems development by adopting system development 'best practices' is only ultimately 'good' if it actually results in a system that will realize the business case that was used to justify the development and produces a solution of commercially appropriate quality. Being effective at service delivery by adopting service delivery 'best practices' is only ultimately 'good' if it actually results in the delivery of a service that meets commercial service level needs for an acceptable price and supports systems that realize the benefits set out in the business case that was used to justify the development of the system. As Terry White puts it in *Reinventing the IT Department*, 'The traditional information system development process requires accurate specification of business requirements, sign-off on specification documents, and (some time later, perhaps six months, one year, two years or worse), user acceptance testing. Research suggests that businesses frequently do not know exactly what they want, change their minds, and are more concerned with results and outcomes than the production of a system. And this systems development method has been far from successful.'

Let me say again that I am not suggesting for a moment that being effective at IT product and service delivery is unimportant. This is certainly part of the overall 'value equation'. But what I am suggesting is that to *optimize* the value of IT to the business the focus of IT management activity (and I don't just mean IT management activity within the IT function) and IT performance improvement activity must be on those practices that optimally *improve business value*. In short, the focus needs to be on successful *outcomes*.

1.8 Confusing performance with value

I would make a comparison here with the world of high-fidelity (as it was 30 years ago). Hi-fi was then truly a do-it-yourself hobby in which 'solutions' were custom built rather than bought. Since you ask, I designed and built my first amplifier from basic components, designed and built my turntable (utilizing a Garrard 401 deck and 12" SME arm set in a massive base of concrete) and designed and built my speakers (12" units set in a corner base reflex mounting of several buckets of sand sandwiched between $\frac{3}{4}$" chipboard sheets – and then bolted to the wall). You had to have muscles to be a hi-fi buff in those days. Everything revolved around the measured performance of the equipment. Components were assessed and selected on the basis of their wow and flutter, harmonic distortion, intermodulation distortion, their frequency response or whatever. These *were* the measures of 'best practice'. Equipment like the Quad 303, with its fantastic tolerances, was the (financially unattainable for non-Lottery winners) nirvana we sought. And then, in the early 1970s, someone said, 'Hang on a minute. I know this isn't possible but some of the equipment with the poorer specifications actually *sounds* better.' And he was right. It was a shock, I can tell you. For years we had been confusing performance and value (the value of a hi-fi system should surely be indicated by how good it sounds, not how well it is engineered).

In this book I will set out (in Chapter 2) a framework for creating a value-driven IT function. In Chapter 3 I will set out the practices that I believe are most valuable in an IT product and service delivery practice (i.e. the 'best value practices') and explain how to make a success of implementing these practices.

These are my 'half dozen things' you must critically get right if you are to optimize value-added to the business. Next, in Chapter 4, I will set out the equivalent practices for optimizing the cost-efficiency of IT product and service delivery. My objective in Chapters 3 and 4 is to help you create an IT improvement programme to create the value-driven IT function. Finally, in Chapter 5, I will set out an approach to measuring how close to your value targets you are getting.

1.9 Summary

The failure of projects (especially large, complex software delivery projects) is an endemic problem in the IT industry. Even when projects 'succeed' there are often huge doubts about the realization of promised benefits, creating senior business management dissatisfaction and disillusionment with IT product and service delivery.

There is often a tacit conspiracy between the business sponsors of projects and the IT supplier to develop IT solutions that are unlikely to actually deliver the benefits promised. This 'conspiracy' is typically founded on the justification of projects being based on unrealistic assumptions and the subsequent focusing of management attention on the delivery of the solution rather than the delivery of the promised benefits. To optimize the value of IT to the business the focus of IT management activity and IT performance improvement activity must be on those practices that optimize *outcomes*.

2	Defining goals

'When *I* use a word,' Humpty Dumpty said in rather
a scornful tone, 'it means just what I choose
it to mean – neither more nor less.'

Lewis Carroll – *Through the Looking Glass*

In my Introduction I made the case for focusing our approach to
the management of IT product and service delivery on *outcomes*
in order to maximize the value derived from IT investments. So
what does our 'idealized', high value-adding IT environment
look like? Presumably this would be the much vaunted 'world
class IT' environment with a 'world class IT' IT function at its
'centre'. But what do we mean by 'world class IT'? Does it have
a specific, universally agreed, meaning – or does it mean just
what the speaker of the day chooses it to mean?

2.1 What is 'world class IT'?

Some time ago a client of mine, the CIO of a large food retailer,
asked me precisely this question. Although it is a term generally
much bandied about by consultants, it was one of which I have
fought shy, partially because it is linked in some people's minds
with a specific service offering of KPMG Consulting, but more
because I was unconvinced that it was particularly meaningful.
As far as I could see, 'world class IT' was something of a cross
between a chimera and a chameleon, a fabulously expedient
creature that mysteriously took the form of whatever IT panacea
was flavour of the month. This view was reinforced when I had
cause to use a niche IT benchmarking supplier who had stated
that the company peer group they had built to compare with my
client's performance was 'world class'. Looking at the list of
organizations included in this peer group quickly revealed that to
this supplier, 'world class' simply meant 'the most cost-efficient

organizations we happen to have in our database currently', irrespective of whether or not they were remotely comparable in market sector, size or complexity, irrespective of whether or not there were a thousand other organizations out there who were *more* cost-efficient and, more to the point, irrespective of whether or not *cost-efficiency* was the most reliable indicator of 'world class' status. Even if you could identify an IT function that, based on some amalgam of metrics, was universally agreed to be the world's most cost-efficient, it could still be hopeless at delivering value to the business it serviced; in which case, would it really be 'world class'?

Many years ago Robert Redford played the role of a fresh-faced up and coming politician in a marvellous (and hugely under-rated) film called *The Candidate*. At one point in the film he is asked by a posse of reporters for his policy on a controversial issue and then shocks them into stunned silence when he ingenuously and honestly replies that he hasn't really thought it through and so doesn't have a policy for that yet. It's a bit like management consultants (not). Over the years they have come to acquire a reputation (often richly deserved) for having an answer for everything, usually supported by 'business school' quasi-scientific, pseudo-academic (and crypto-agenda?) research (am I betraying my prejudices here?) which sounds superficially plausible but seems to run through your fingers when you actually try to apply it. The 'answer' is revealed in a (thinly veiled) sales presentation and generally will include a four stage 'maturity profile' that shows your organization to be at stage 1. Basically, it sounds great, but does it actually reflect how real (complex, contradictory, self-interested) people behave in the real world (and I don't just mean the real, tough, macho, manly world of business)? Over the years I have come to be increasingly wary of this and so increasingly follow the maxim that honesty (up to a point) really is the best policy, yes, even in business. Quite aside from the little matter of ethics, this is because even if you lose the battle (sale) in the short term by telling the client the truth, you will probably win the war in the long term by building a more lasting commercial relationship.

So, inspired by Robert Redford, my reply to the CIO's request to define 'world class IT' was, 'I have absolutely no idea'. Fortunately he knew well my reputation for being what I call 'a witty, iconoclastic, straight talking, man of the world' (and which some have been known to erroneously call, 'a sarcastic, cynical, tactless Scot'), so he simply laughed. However, he would not let me get away with this reply entirely. He asked me what a typical consultant would reply. I thought about it and proved that I had not completely forgotten my consultancy training by extemporizing the reply that 'world class IT' was 'a compilation of global, cross-industry, proven best practices in the management, delivery and running of IT solutions'. I thought this sounded appropriately pseudo-academic and superficially plausible and was therefore probably best described by one of at least two words beginning in 'b' and ending in 's'. So I was not surprised by his next question, namely, 'So what do you mean by the term "best practice"?' And that, I thought, was the key to the problem.

2.2 What is 'best practice'?

So what *do* we mean by 'best practice'? Here are a few definitions from others, with my comments in italics:

- 'Most excellent' (definition of 'best') 'habitual action' (definition of 'practice') (*Concise Oxford Dictionary*). [*And, of course the definition of 'most excellent habitual action' is 'best practice' – thanks a bundle Oxford University Press.*]
- 'A best practice communicates insight on the application of a process or the performance of a task. A best practice improves the outcome, diminishes the risk, increases the reliability, or improves the understanding of the process or task' (Gartner). [*I have an immediate liking for this 'definition' since, ironically, it quietly ducks the difficulty of actually defining what a 'best practice' actually is in favour of defining what a best practice should achieve. So it doesn't really help us recognize a best practice when we see one but does help us select one in preference to others on the basis that, to some extent, it delivers a better outcome, whatever an 'outcome' may be.*]
- 'Best practices are systematic processes – the marriage of applied behaviour and knowledge – that have been demonstrated and validated to yield competitive advantage [*this is certainly my idea of an improved outcome, although it is rather narrow*] for organizations that employ them. In order for a process to be considered a best practice, it must be replicable, transferable and adaptable across industries [*a good definition of the characteristics of candidates for a 'best practice' but again ducking the issue of telling us how to recognize one when we see one – maintaining your company's financial accounts with an abacus is replicable, transferable and adaptable across industries but probably isn't going to be regarded as 'best practice' – although a methodical set of instructions for how 'best' to use an abacus would*

presumably be a 'best practice']. Best practices require continual improvement and are, therefore, constantly changing' [*shouldn't that be, 'best practices are constantly changing and therefore require continual improvement'?*] (American Management Association)

- 'Best practices are those that have been shown to produce superior results [*once again, the 'better outcome' angle*], have been selected by a systematic process [*OK, but what process exactly?*] and are judged [*by whom exactly?*] as exemplary, good, or successfully demonstrated' [*don't you just love the tautology that best practices are those that have been judged to be good?*] (American Productivity and Quality Center)
- 'Best practices are good practices [*well that certainly clarifies that matter*] that have worked well elsewhere. They are proven [*i.e. it's not just theory – it actually works*] and have produced successful results' [*again, the 'outcomes' angle*] (GSA Office of Governmentwide Policy)
- 'Best practices are those disciplines that help prevent inexperienced staff from screwing up too badly and help prevent experienced staff from backsliding too far' (the author). OK, I just made that up (but then, so did the people who wrote the stuff above). This is my own, only slightly tongue-in-cheek, 'definition'. I suspect that the reason I like this 'definition' is that it brings people into the equation; and in my experience, if you want to do something that 'demonstrably results in a better outcome' you would invariably be advised to put your best staff on it long before you worry about best practices. When I (admittedly a long time ago!) ran a large programming group, programmer productivity metrics were rigorously maintained and my most productive programmers were not 10 per cent or 20 per cent more productive than my least productive programmers, they were around *1000 per cent* more productive, and produced much more reliable code to boot! And they did not achieve this just because they happened to follow the 'best practices' set out in the 'standards and procedures' manual.

I find it difficult to identify truly *common* themes in the above definitions, other than the fact that it appears to be impossible to define 'best practice' without becoming either precious and pretentious or tautological and trite. I would, however, distil the *key* themes as being:

1 Best practices must be methodical (i.e. an ordered set of steps that others can repeat systematically).

2 Best practices must be generally applicable (i.e. a 'best practice' that only works in your neck of the woods won't pass the, admittedly arbitrary, test of *our* definition of 'best practice').

3 Best practices must *demonstrably* be applicable in the 'real world' (i.e. a 'best practice' that is too complex to be understood and applied by most practitioners who might use it won't pass our definition of 'best practice').

4 For a best practice to satisfy our test of 'bestness', its *application* must *demonstrably* result in a better outcome, where by 'better outcome' we mean 'better' achieving the objectives of the task to which best practices are being applied. Note that this is not necessarily the best *commercial* outcome. So, for example, applying best practices to project management should *demonstrably* result in projects that are delivered more predictably to budget and schedule (among other things); applying best practices to systems development should *demonstrably* result in the delivery of applications of a more predictable quality (among other things). So if a new set of methodologies for project and systems development came along and we could actually prove that they delivered results more predictably than the existing 'best practice' methods we would have to 'demote' our existing 'best practices' to being just 'good practices' but *so* yesterday. This 'improving the *predictability* of results' is, I think, a critical characteristic of 'best practice'. Note again, however, that it does not necessarily mean that applying these best practices will optimally add value to the business.

To these I might add another criterion, which is not mentioned in our sample definitions above:

5 Best practices must be 'certifiable' (at a professional, corporate and product level, i.e. individuals must be able to be independently 'accredited', as must businesses and products that claim to be 'compliant' with the best practices). I shall not, however, apply this criterion from now on, simply because it is too limiting and, frankly, too anal for the pragmatic purposes of this book.

So these are criteria (or, at least, characteristics) by which we might identify 'best practices' and our hypothetical 'world class IT' IT function presumably epitomizes such practices. But there are surely a few things missing here. Our 'world class IT' IT function may indeed be highly effective (in terms of deploying highly engineered 'best practice' processes). But at what price (in terms of money and time)? And what about the issue of adding optimal value to the business? And do these 'best practices' actually result in the delivery of IT products and services of higher *commercial* quality (by which I mean 'necessary and sufficient quality for the price')? Do they result in more satisfied customers?

The major consultancy firms are awash with 'best practice models' ('methodologies' that have typically been hastily generalized from specific client experiences) for performing assignments to improve their clients' business performance (e.g. business process re-engineering, enterprise-wide cost reduction, business e-enablement, m-commerce, or whatever business panacea is flavour of the month). While such business performance improvement assignments are invariably *sold* on the basis of the consulting team deploying these best practices, I could count on the fingers of one hand the number of times I have ever seen such practices actually deployed anything like rigorously (if at all) once the job is sold. This is for the simple reason that no consultancy firm would win work in the highly competitive world of consultancy if it quoted for that work based on actually following its own best practice models – it would simply take far too long and cost far too much to either be acceptable to the client or even be in the commercial interests of the client. Note that this is not actually a criticism of my profession because consultancies *generally* largely staff such assignments with highly competent, highly experienced, highly intelligent, commercially shrewd people who 'carry the spirit of the best practice model' in their heads and who would often be *hindered* by the rigorous application of the method (all right, so I am the exception that proves the rule). Yes, it is also true that the general high levels of resistance to applying 'process' by consultants is rooted in arrogance; but there is good (commercial) reason for that arrogance! In short, management consultancies 'get away' with being 'inspired amateurs' owing to the calibre of their people. By *not* rigorously applying their own methods, consultancies increase their delivery risks (and, of course, the risk to the client in terms of predictable service delivery) but do so in the conscious understanding that the increase in risk is (generally!) more than compensated for by the increase in the value they can add (in terms of both reducing the cost of the assignment and delivering the benefits earlier than would otherwise have been the case). I'll let you judge for yourself whether or not this makes consultants blatant hypocrites, given that they spend most of their time telling their clients to follow rigorous processes!

Although this book is not about management consultancy best practices (perhaps that should be my next book!) but about IT best practices, the same commercial principles apply. For example, when you apply any systems development methodology it will almost inevitably (not just at first, but for *years*) result in development projects that cost more to deliver and take longer to deliver (not that those who sell these methods will rush to tell you that!). But you may choose this in preference to not applying a rigorous method because of the potential reduction in risk (i.e. the increase in the predictability of delivery), the potential increase in integrity of the deliverables (in terms of the match between the original specification and what was actually delivered), the potential increase in the reliability and recoverability of the delivered system and the potential reduction in support and maintenance costs over the life of the system.

It is generally not that difficult to get your 'best practice model' to pass the 'tests' of the first three 'best practice' criteria and even plausibly pass the fourth (i.e. demonstrably achieving the objectives of the practices – principally more predictable outcomes). Indeed, for my purposes in this book I am virtually assuming that this is taken as read. My concern here is with the additional points I have raised, principally the *cost-efficiency* of the supply of IT products and services, the *value-added* to the business by these products and services and the commercial *quality* of these products and services. In short, I want to find the practices that are the ones that not only optimize 'supply-side' (IT function) outcomes but also optimize 'demand-side' (business) *commercial outcomes* and which do so for the most palatable cost, i.e. I am seeking the best practices that don't 'just' result in the most predictable solutions delivery but those that result in the most predictable (and highest) *value-added* delivery, as cost-efficiently as possible.

I am effectively looking for the practices on which we should be focusing our limited time, energy, money and resources to get the 'biggest bang for our IT buck', without unacceptably compromising risk. My contention is that an organization that adopts and focuses on these practices will transform the value IT adds to the business. To put it another way, my contention is that an IT function that manages to consistently, predictably deliver IT products and services to the business is doing an outstanding job (in fact, it is probably unique in the cosmos!) but that is not actually the reason for the existence of the IT function. Its only justification is the delivery of *value* to the business, principally in terms of the commercial benefits achieved exceeding the costs incurred, and certainly exceeding the net benefits that might have been achieved if the investments in IT had been made elsewhere in the business (e.g. refurbishing a store, building a new warehouse, retooling a plant). Predictable solutions delivery is not enough – there has to be optimized value-added to the business by the IT function (by 'optimizing effectiveness', as set out in Chapter 3) and optimized cost-efficiency by the IT function (as set out in Chapter 4). It is about ensuring that management attention is first and foremost targeted on optimizing these two key aspects of the value equation.

2.3 Best practice models examined

Many IT best practice models exist. As I pointed out above, the big management consultancy firms (and many niche IT consultancies) claim to maintain best practice models for IT. For example, the PwC Consulting IT best practice manual (in which I should declare an interest, since I wrote it) provides best practice definitions for about 150 separate IT processes, Gartner Consulting have their TOP model, KPMG have their 'World Class IT' model, and so on. Most of these models would satisfy our first three criteria for 'best practice' and take a fair stab at our fourth (about which I will have more to say below), but few would satisfy our fifth (independent certifiability). In addition to these (very) proprietary approaches we have those that are in the public domain, in particular the IT Infrastructure Library (ITIL) and derivatives, such as the Hewlett-Packard Service Management Reference Model.

ITIL was developed by the British Central Computing and Telecommunications Agency (CCTA), currently known as the Office of Government Commerce (OGC). It provides a truly voluminous library (the hard copy books fill a bookshelf over a metre wide) of books focusing on best practice for different aspects of IT operational processes. Interest in ITIL is growing globally, particularly in the area of IT service management, where it could almost be called a *de facto* standard. Oddly enough, I have found that its greatest popularity generally is across Western European countries, but *not* Britain, its 'home', where it is often perceived as 'overprogrammatic' (or a clear sign of unwarranted British arrogance?). The OGC has also issued SSADM (best practices for systems development) and PRINCE (best practices for project management) so it has a lot of best practice to be responsible for.

A common characteristic of these various 'best practice' models is that they are rooted in the ethos of 'Total Quality Management', itself founded on the ideas and work of W. Edwards Demming in the 1950s. The central goal of these approaches is 'zero defects'. Zero defects as a goal is achieved by a philosophy of continuous process improvement. In an IT context this primarily means continually improving processes in a bid to eliminate bugs in the delivered solution. Obviously reducing, and ideally eliminating, bugs is a 'good thing'. But at what price (in terms of cost and time)? If you are writing the software for the Apollo 11 moonshot then 'zero defects' is certainly a goal worthy of your commitment, because human lives and national prestige are at stake. But software to improve the contracts management process has slightly different imperatives. My question here is about our 'definition' of 'quality'.

From a *commercial* standpoint the 'definition' of a 'quality product/service' might be 'a product/service that meets the most commercially critical needs of the customer, which is delivered in a timely manner and is delivered at a price the customer is prepared to pay'. It is, in short, about the '80/20' rule of using our limited resources, money and time to target the delivery of products and services that will realize '80 per cent' of the potential full benefits of a 'highly engineered', 'full function', 'defect-free' solution for '20 per cent' of the cost. Or, better still, 90 per cent for 10 per cent. The delivery of a 'perfect' system that cost a fortune to develop but does not actually deliver the promised benefits (and, anyway, was delivered so late that the business need has moved on) is a strange notion of 'perfection'. Implement a system with seriously compromised quality (i.e. defects) and you will almost certainly have some impact on realizing the full value of the solution. Implement a system with seriously compromised value and you have just wasted your time and the company's money. What we need is *necessary and sufficient* 'quality'. Where 'quality' is concerned, enough is enough. I am not suggesting that IT functions should not attempt to reduce defects in the systems they deliver by introducing more robust processes for systems development. All I am saying is that from the point of view of the business, from a *commercial* point of view, this is not where the game is at. The business first and foremost wants high *value* solutions. If the 'price' of this is somewhat compromised 'quality', so be it.

2.4 The cost and value of quality

Conventional best practice models are often justified on the premise that the cost of rectifying defects rises dramatically (potentially exponentially) as you pass through the systems development life-cycle. So, for example, the cost of rectifying a defect found in user acceptance testing of a system will be of the order of 10 times what it would have been had the problem been identified and corrected in system design. This assumption is important, valid, and is at the heart of the 'cost of quality' question. My point is that perhaps we need to shift our focus towards what might be called the 'value of quality' question. I believe (but could not prove) that a similar curve exists for value optimization, in that the later in the systems development life-cycle that you attempt to add value to your solution, the more difficult (and costly) it becomes. To look at it the other way, the earlier in the life-cycle you apply value improvement practices (which I will call 'best value practices'), the higher the value. For example, reducing the cost of service provision (service delivery) is going to contribute little to the business value of a system if the business case for the system was seriously flawed (systems development) and the system was poorly aligned to the priority needs of the business (strategy development).

So do any of these widely acknowledged best practice models meet our criteria of best practice set out above? To a greater or lesser extent they are all methodical, generally applicable, workable and, at least potentially, certifiable so they satisfy our first three (and, potentially, the fifth) characteristics. 'Best practice' in these models is principally about formality ('is it written down?'), coverage ('does everyone do this?'), completeness ('does it address all key needs?') and consistency ('does everyone who does this do it the same way?'). It is, in short, about compliance with *highly engineered* practices, irrespective of whether or not they are cost-efficient, value-adding, or even commercially appropriate. Having a highly engineered approach to IT security makes good sense if you are, say, the Pentagon but may be unacceptably expensive and commercially unnecessary if you are a food retailer. So our problem appears to lie with our fourth characteristic, 'demonstrably resulting in a better outcome'.

Let us say that an IT function adopts SSADM systems development practices and even that it does so within the quality management and improvement standards set down in ISO9000/15504. What this function should certainly be achieving is *repeatability* in its systems development processes. The way systems are developed will be highly formal, complete and consistent. But that is not the same thing as saying that it is going to produce a commercially preferable outcome. An organization could use developers who are inexperienced, technically unskilled and have poor commercial awareness and simply 'go through the motions' of compliance with an approach such as SSADM but almost certainly will not produce a 'quality' result, let alone a commercially preferable result. Note also that ISO9000 does not even require that highly engineered methods of working be adopted, only that what you do is written down, and you then actually do what you have written down. Theoretically, you could work in an idiotic way, document this thoroughly and then consistently comply with these idiotic working practices and still be ISO certified. Unfortunately, commercial pragmatism often seems to go out the window when 'best practice' methods come in. To paraphrase Hamlet, 'Though this be method, yet there is madness in it.'

2.5 Case study – worst practice, best outcome?

This was epitomized for me some years ago when I was employed by a group of venture capital backers who wanted me to give them reassurance about a substantial investment they were considering in a small, start-up credit card company. I travelled up from London to the English Midlands and found myself driving over a seriously pot-holed road onto a decidedly seedy and run down industrial estate (no 'business park' this!) where the cost of renting premises was presumably negligible. There I found that the credit card company (which was virtually entirely an IT operation) was run from what could only be described as a 'shack'. It included about 30 management and staff, most of whom I interviewed. What became very clear was that on any 'maturity profiling' of their processes against 'best practices' they were going to gain a minimum score, because virtually nothing was written down and there were no independent quality controls (how could there be – there was nothing against which to check compliance). I completed my review and ended up recommending strongly to the venture capital group that they *should* invest in the credit card company. Why? Because talking to these 30 people and reviewing their work and deliverables made it clear to me that they were a highly competent and highly commercially astute group. Most of them seemed to be related to one another (or at the least baby-sat for one another) and a strong 'family atmosphere' existed (I'm referring here more to the Waltons that the Simpsons, you understand!). In short, I decided that I would be willing to invest my *own* money in this company, despite the fact that they were as far removed from conventional IT 'best practice' as you might ever find.

Of course, there were risks, particularly if the three entrepreneurial leaders jointly left the company or died in a car crash. There were also considerable risks for me since I was basically saying to the venture capital backers that, despite the fact that I could not 'prove' it (with 'ticks' in the best practice compliance column), they were an excellent IT function. Their implementing, say, SSADM, PRINCE and gaining ISO9000 accreditation would almost certainly have produced a *less* commercially desirable outcome. Note that the IT *value-added* here was not 'just' the value-added to the business served. They *were* the business served and the value-added was a significant part of their gross margin. By adopting IT 'best practices' they would almost certainly have *reduced* the value-added so how can we say that these practices are 'best'? They certainly would not have been best for them! For them, conventional 'best practice' was in many ways (commercial) *worst* practice.

I fully accept that this little case study is an extreme example, and I am certainly not suggesting for a moment that we should just write off all IT best practice models just because a minority of organizations in specific circumstances find that they are commercially counterproductive. But I hope it makes the point that adopting 'world class IT' best practices is certainly no guarantee of commercial success; far from it. Every best practice must be examined to assess whether or not it really adds value, whether it adds the optimal value and whether the cost (in time, energy and money) of deploying that 'best' practice is commercially justified.

By the way, it is about 10 years since I conducted my review of the credit card company and I am happy to report that they are today one of the market leaders in their field. Sadly, I *didn't* invest in them. Instead I invested in Far East funds, thereby demonstrating my visionary powers of judgement.

A further point: ask your auditors if *their* IT staff or IT consultants in *their* management consultancy are ISO9000 accredited. I would be prepared to take a sizable bet that the answer will be that none of their internal IT groups are ISO accredited in any way and that the only IT consultancy group that *may* be accredited is the 'government services' group (who are only accredited because they would not make it onto the consultancy tender shortlist without accreditation). So the message is perhaps, 'do as your advisors do, not as they say!'

2.6 Is transfer charging best practice?

To help convince you of my point, let me give you another example of the need to be very careful about what we mean when we use the term 'best practice'. This is not an extreme example, but is one found in every internal IT function in which I have consulted. It is the issue of 'transfer charging'. This is about the internal IT function 'acting like' an ESP and, by one of a wide variety of means, 'charging' the internal customer for IT services consumed. My question is this: 'In these circumstances, is IT transfer charging a best practice for managing IT (irrespective of how it is actually achieved)?' This is a question I have been asked numerous times and a question I have asked even more times. I have found few IT management issues that inflame such strong opinions as this one. Many are ardent 'believers' in transfer charging, largely because this is a 'pseudo' commercial practice and conventional wisdom says that managing internal IT functions 'as though' they were an ESP is 'best practice'. These people, I have found, are generally young and inexperienced IT consultants or young and inexperienced CIOs. Many others are ardent 'non-believers', largely because they had tried it (or had seen it tried). These people, I have found, are generally grey-haired (or, more typically, no-haired) IT consultants or CIOs who have found that, while transfer charging may be *theoretical* IT management best practice, it cost a small fortune to deploy, caused endless aggravation with users as bills were disputed, decreased customer satisfaction with the IT function, drove users into the arms of ESPs (who would doubtless charge them *more* for the services) and failed dismally in the only real reason for its existence, namely, improving the commercial behaviours of users in their use of IT resources.

The 'best practice' transfer charging approach adopted may well have met our first three best practice criteria but certainly did not meet the fourth, of actually achieving the outcomes for which the initiative was implemented. Not only that, but it often did so at unacceptable cost. Let the record show that at the time of writing, I am neither young nor entirely bald (watch this space), but, based on my many sad experiences of witnessing attempts to implement transfer charging, I have historically fallen into the non-believers camp. *However,* I believe that it is surely not beyond the wit of man to devise an inexpensive approach to internal IT financial management that results in commercially optimized user behaviours. This may well seem to be a bizarre statement since I have clearly stated that the underlying ethos of this book is, 'If it works in the real world it's in; if it doesn't it's out.' So the reader has every right now to ask me just how many successful (in terms of outcomes) implementations of transfer charging I have seen between internal IT functions and the business. The answer is none. But I am *still* (with deep reluctance) adamant that transfer charging (*if correctly implemented*) is a key component of value transformation (for which I refer you to Chapter 3, where I set out the key success factors for achieving this). By the way, you may (reasonably) say that ESPs seem to be able to implement transfer charging quite easily (they call it 'billing') and you would, up to a point, have a good point. But remember that ESPs are not actually interested in our key desired outcome, 'commercially optimized user behaviours' – quite the opposite! As far as they are concerned, 'commercially optimized user behaviours' is getting the users (their customers) to spend as much money with them as possible (when an ESP says he will 'work with you in partnership', check your wallet).

My point here, however, is not to try to convince you of the benefits of transfer charging – I know that this is liable to be tough so I will leave that for a detailed exposition in Chapter 3. All I want to conclude at this time is that a 'best practice' must *at least* satisfy the first four criteria if it is seriously to be called 'best practice'.

2.7 The people factor

Just to emphasize how difficult it is to deploy best practices and deliver an optimally commercial desirable outcome, I give you another example. This concerns a highly challenging IT cost reduction consultancy project run in a major bank some years ago. I was the consultant responsible for the stream of work identifying cost reduction opportunities in the data centre. This data centre had an annual budget of around £110m ($165m), back in the days when that was a lot of money. My team was supposed to deliver at least a 15 per cent reduction in that figure. I reported to a very talented project manager who, had the manner in which he managed the project been subject to 'best practice' assessment, would unquestionably have scored poorly.

Detailed task plans and schedules monitored by in-depth analyses of progress against budget and schedule by task were not for him. Instead, his principal approach was to come by every few days and, never losing fierce eye contact, ask me deeply penetrating (and typically deeply uncomfortable) questions about whether each task in our work stream was actually achieving its objectives (i.e. finding a targeted level of cost reduction). And he would not take 'yes' for an answer. I had to absolutely *convince* him. If I could not entirely satisfy him that the task was still going to deliver its promised benefits (i.e. targeted reduced costs) then his response was simply to tell me to stop it immediately and reassign the staff working on the task to other tasks that actually *were* looking like winners. Basically he kept the entire team continually focused on delivering the maximum project benefits. Every member of the team knew that if any activity they were performing did not demonstrably add value then they had better have a damn good explanation ready. Now, you may think that he was a hard man, but after many years of working with him I knew that underneath that tough carapace beat a heart of stone. He succeeded by his robust, hands-on, pragmatic approach to project management, his focus on the commercial imperatives of the project, his demonstrably passionate commitment to obtaining a successful outcome and by the sheer force of his personality. Best practice? Well certainly not as ISO9000 would understand it.

2.8 The value goals

Value management as a concept goes way back, to the 1940s and 1950s, when Lawrence D. Miles pioneered value analysis techniques. But he was primarily concerned with product cost reduction. Since then value management has enlarged its view to also address increasing performance and improving commercial outcomes. So what 'value goals' will help drive an IT function to optimize commercial outcomes? To answer that I want to turn the question round and ask, 'What should we measure in order to get a balanced picture of IT performance that includes "commercial outcomes"?' Well, there are many ways of measuring the performance of an IT function (in the sense that we are using the word here – we are not talking about MIPs and MHz!) but in my experience most tend to focus on either or both of the following two key characteristics:

1 **Cost-efficiency**, i.e. how commercially appropriate is the level of spend with the 'IT solutions and services delivery factory'?

To put it another way, 'how economic is the IT function?' And how productive is the 'IT solutions and services delivery factory', i.e. how much output per unit of input/cost? That 'output' might be, for example, business system functionality delivered or mainframe resources delivered or laptops supported.

2 **Effectiveness**, i.e. how close to 'best practice' are the processes of the 'IT solutions and services delivery factory'? And do they *actually* produce a better outcome?

These measures should tell us a great deal about the performance of the IT function 'IT business' and are not *just* internal measures, i.e. they do tell us (potentially) something about the value of IT to the business since:

- the economy of running the IT function is a component of the total business overheads, so running that IT function at lower cost effectively ups your business profitability (*assuming* reducing the cost doesn't compromise efficiency or effectiveness);
- increasing the efficiency of the IT function should mean that more IT functionality is being delivered per unit time and/or per unit cost and since that functionality *presumably* has been commercially justified this should increase business value, in terms of revenue, profitability, market share, or whatever is relevant (*assuming* that the increase in efficiency is not at the expense of decreased IT economy or reduced solution or service effectiveness);
- improving the effectiveness of the IT product or services delivery practices should improve the predictability of systems and service delivery that, again, *presumably* deliver business benefit and so should increase business value (*assuming* that the increase in effectiveness is not at the expense of decreased efficiency or decreased economy).

Of course, the key words here (and where a good deal of the complexity lies) are in italics. There are an awful lot of *assumptions* and *presumptions*.

In the 'assumptions' lies the 'devil' of the typically adversarial inter-relationships between cost, productivity and quality. It is generally extremely difficult to improve the *effectiveness* of solution or service delivery without some degree (if only short term) of investment that will adversely affect *economy*. It is generally extremely difficult to increase *economy* without having *some* impact on the *effectiveness* of service delivery. And so on.

In the 'presumptions' lies the issue of whether or not all this work by the IT function is creating satisfied customers and actually adding maximum value to the business (e.g. are the IT solutions delivered optimally aligned with business priorities? Were they actually commercially justified originally? Did the finally delivered solution actually deliver the benefits promised?). In other words, we need to know if our IT function is *actually* adding maximum value to the business rather than simply being a highly economic, productive 'manufacturer' of high quality goods that don't actually justify the customers' investment and end up being quickly (and probably quietly) chucked in the 'corporate closet'. Therefore we critically need to add to our two 'supply-side' measures two further measures of business 'demand-side' value:

3 **Value-added**, i.e. how much value is the IT function adding to the business?
4 **Quality**, i.e. are the products and services of the IT function of the right commercial quality and are the customers of the IT function satisfied?

We can illustrate these 'poles' of value as the 'top level' of a 'value compass' helping to direct our commercial journey (see Figure 2.1). We will populate the compass with more detailed measures later.

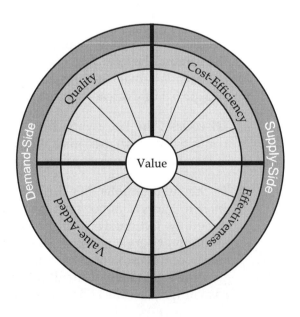

Figure 2.1

You will have gathered from the discourse above that the cost-efficiency and effectiveness quadrants can have a rather adversarial relationship. Further relationships exist between the quadrants:

A Improvements in cost-efficiency can improve quality because 'quality' here is *commercial* quality (i.e. necessary and sufficient quality *for the price*).
B Improvements in cost-efficiency can also improve value-added because improved staff productivity can reduce 'time to market' for projects (and their benefits) and because value is a matter of *net* benefits (i.e. the *cost* of IT product and service delivery is the 'flip side' of the *benefits* of the products and services supplied).
C Improvements in effectiveness by deploying systems and service delivery best practices (e.g. SSADM, ITIL) can improve the quality of products and services supplied.
D Improvements in effectiveness can also improve the value-added by products and services by deploying IT management best *value* practices (e.g. demand/portfolio management).

These relationships are illustrated in Figure 2.2.

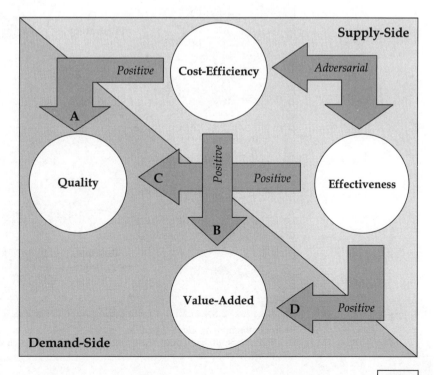

Figure 2.2

I have raised the issue of the rather adversarial relationship between the cost-efficiency and effectiveness quadrants. This begs the question, 'Which is the more important in *my* organization?' The answer to this question lies very much in the issue of the 'strategic alignment' of business and IT strategies. A useful model to explore this was developed in Harvard University by Henderson and Venkatraman. Their Strategic Alignment Model (SAM) is set out (in simplified form) in Figure 2.3.

Note that in SAM the term, 'infrastructure' is used in its broadest sense, i.e. it is meant to encapsulate not just physical (or technical) infrastructure, but also organization, processes and people. So 'optimizing the supply-side infrastructure' would, in SAM terms, be about optimizing the supply-side cost-efficiency/effectiveness quadrants.

The SAM model states that all four components are linked to one another but that the specific influences depend on the strategic position of IT supply in a particular organization. Four key perspectives are identified, namely, IT function as a cost centre, IT function as an investment centre, IT function as a profit centre and IT function as a service centre.

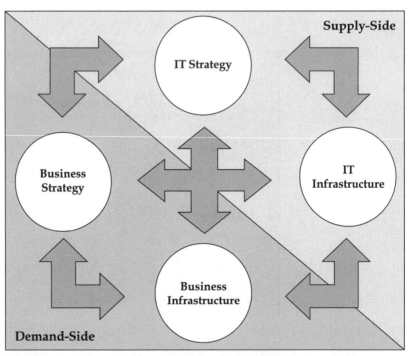

Figure 2.3

(from *Transforming Organizations*, edited by T. A. Kochan and M. Useem, © 1992 by Sloan School of Management. Used by permission of Oxford University Press Inc.)

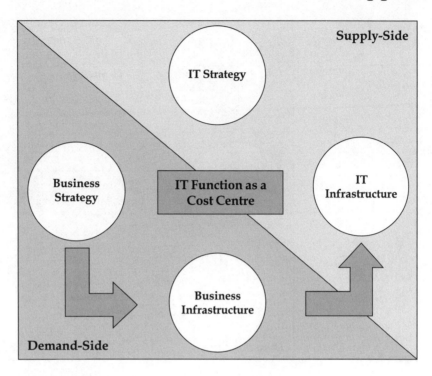

Figure 2.4

Where an IT function operates as a 'cost centre' (see Figure 2.4), the business strategy is used to shape business infrastructure, which in turn is 'serviced' by the IT function designing and implementing an IT infrastructure to support that business infrastructure. Here the focus of all IT function activities will be towards reducing the total cost of ownership (TCO) of IT. Therefore optimizing cost-efficiency is going to have a much higher business value than optimizing effectiveness.

Where an IT function operates as an 'investment centre' we see the opposite in terms of the relative importance of cost-efficiency and effectiveness. Here the starting point is the IT strategy, seeking ways to deploy emerging technologies that impact the business services and products, in particular seeking opportunities for competitive advantage from IT deployment. This is a classic Gartner 'Type A' organization. The name of the game here is innovation and time to market with IT solutions – so optimizing effectiveness for the addition of value to the business is paramount, even at the expense of cost-efficiency.

Where the IT function operates as a 'profit centre' the business strategy drives the IT strategy which in turn determines which technology solutions will best enable that business strategy. Here there is greater balance between cost-efficiency and

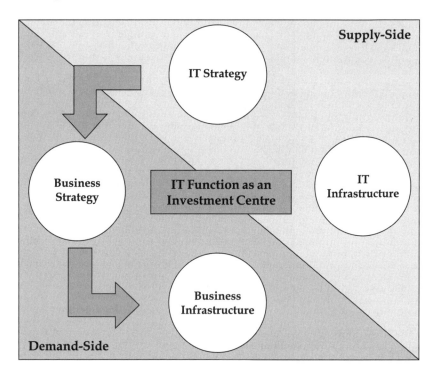

Figure 2.5

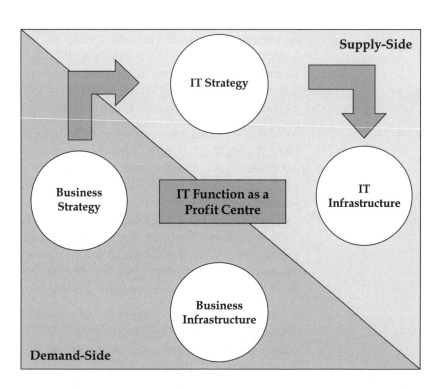

Figure 2.6

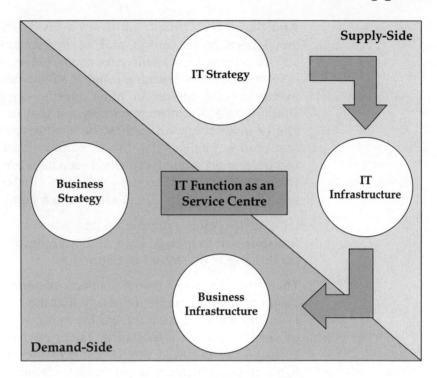

Figure 2.7

effectiveness priorities, although cost-efficiency is still clearly important because it determines the cost of service provision (and so the 'margins' on the services and products of the 'profit centre'). Of course, if the IT function is a *zero* profit centre', the relative importance of cost-efficiency may diminish somewhat.

Where the IT function operates as a 'service centre' IT is regarded as a corporate resource and no single business strategy can be identified. Here the focus is on developing an IT strategy that provides cost-efficient shared IT infrastructure services to support the business infrastructure. Therefore, here cost-efficiency may be more important than effectiveness.

Generally speaking (*very* generally), the 'IT function as a profit centre' and 'IT function as a service centre' will tend to make more sense for *ESPs* while 'IT function as a cost centre' and 'IT function as an investment centre' will tend to make more sense for *internal service providers*. Of course you may opt for the 'IT function as a *zero* profit centre' route. Note that in any one organization at any one time, more than one 'SAM positioning' of IT will very probably apply.

Over the years I have found that the vast majority of IT functions with whom I have consulted have been run (from a business finance/management point of view) as cost centres.

And they have virtually all (from a SAM positioning point of view) been profit centres and/or investment centres and/or service centres. I have only once consulted in an IT function that is (from a SAM positioning point of view) clearly and predominantly a cost centre. In other words, organizations whose strategic role is almost invariably *not* that of a cost centre are almost invariably managed by the business as though they *were* cost centres. I believe that this is significant and a key source of the 'disconnect' often (typically?) seen between the business and IT agendas. If the CIO could explain this dichotomy to the CEO and CFO they might all get along much better!

I found a typical example of this when I consulted in an IT function within a large food and clothing retailer whose SAM positioning is illustrated in Figure 2.8.

They were in every material effect managed and run by the business as a cost centre, implying that the cost-efficiency of the IT function was paramount and the value-added to the business of very secondary importance. Taken on face value, then, the message the business was sending to the IT function was to focus on cost-efficiency improvements rather than value-adding effectiveness improvements. However, since it was the case that business value-added from IT was in fact critical to the business and cost-efficiency very much secondary they were actually predominantly an investment centre and least of all a cost centre, and should be focusing on their effectiveness (in order to maximize value-added to the business).

In the next two chapters I will set out the IT practices and initiatives that I believe potentially optimize the two supply-side quadrants in order to optimize the demand-side quadrants (i.e.

SAM positioning	IT function's SAM positioning	Value-added importance	Cost-efficiency importance
Cost centre	Actual positioning / Implied importance	LOW	HIGH
Profit centre		MED	MED
Investment centre	Actual importance / Implied positioning	HIGH	LOW
Service centre		MED	HIGH

Figure 2.8

44

which practices and what form these practices need to take if they are to add most value to the business). I will also describe *how* these practices need to be implemented if they are to realize their potential benefits (i.e. the benefits of optimizing *business* value). Chapter 3 deals with the effectiveness quadrant and Chapter 4 with the cost-efficiency quadrant.

My contention is that a *truly* 'world class IT' organization would (minimally) have to demonstrate 'best *value* practices' (relative to the strategic role of IT – its 'SAM positioning') in all components of the cost-efficiency and effectiveness quadrants. In fact, from now on I am going to stop using the highly ambiguous term 'world class IT function' and instead make our target the creation of a 'value-driven IT function'. *That* is our goal.

2.9 The need for business buy-in

Note that 'achieving' this goal will be significantly outside the remit of the IT function to address in isolation. 'Best value IT practices' are not just about the practices of the IT function – in fact I would argue that it is *impossible* for any IT function to optimize value to the business without the full co-operation and buy-in of the business. This is absolutely key to understand because in my experience many (read 'most') key stakeholders in the business whose co-operation is crucial to successfully implementing best value practices will not readily understand *why* their co-operation is key. They will often take the attitude that what they perceive as 'an IT issue' has nothing to do with them. ('This isn't my job – I've got a business to run – it's the IT function's problem. Let them sort it out. Lord knows we're paying them enough.') Additionally, many key stakeholders will actually *actively resist* best value practices because they do not see them as being in their own parochial best interests. ('Let me see if I've got this right. You think you're going to charge me directly for IT when I used to get it free. And I'm supposed to want this? Sorry, I must be missing something here. And you think you're going to adjust my budgets to reflect the financial benefits I said we would get from this system? You're kidding, right?') Remember that everyone has an agenda and it will often not be remotely aligned with the company's commercial agenda.

2.10 Best practice trends

I must have conducted over 50 'IT performance diagnostic reviews' in my years in IT consultancy. And the results of assessing client IT practices against the 'best practice' models have been astonishingly consistent. What is even more astonishing is that over the last 18 years I have seen virtually no change. The things IT functions were relatively bad at in 1985 *still* seem to be the things they are relatively bad at. Almost invariably, the top practices are in the areas of data centre management (principally the effective operation of computer equipment and the management of systems and network performance) and technology management (principally the effective selection and implementation of technology and subsequent maintenance and support of that technology). Almost invariably, the bottom practices are in the areas of quality management (principally effectively defining quality standards and assuring work performed against those standards), project management (principally the effective estimation, planning and tracking of projects) and systems development management (principally the effective definition of systems requirements, through testing to implementation).

As a generalization, therefore, I would say that the 'IT industry' continues to be relatively good at the things that are relatively unimportant (from a value perspective) and relatively poor at the things that are relatively important (from a value perspective). Basically, we have focused our energies on getting right the things that we find easiest to get right and with which we are most comfortable (generally effectively managing physical assets) and repeatedly duck the really tough but truly important things (generally effectively managing people – because that is what the effective management of quality, projects and systems development ultimately comes down to).

The traditional recommendation to address these weaknesses is to initiate an IT performance improvement programme that essentially sets out to develop and implement 'best practices' in quality management (usually heading in the general direction of ISO accreditation), project management (usually heading in the general direction of PRINCE, or one of its many proprietary derivatives) and systems development management (usually heading in the general direction of SSADM, or one of its many proprietary derivatives). The results of these endeavours are then entombed in the (now unliftable) 'standards and procedures manual' and a group of 'quality management' people (often, in my experience, sad, anally retentive guys who never did quite fit in, are approaching retirement and who needed to be found something to do in the meantime) trek around with clipboards and checklists policing the level of compliance with said standards. Suspects/victims subjected to compliance review put up with all this (because they have to and it is politically unacceptable to say that it is largely a waste of time), while secretly wishing the 'police' would be put out of their misery (but I exaggerate, of course). As Terry White beautifully puts it in *Reinventing the IT Department*, 'The step between rigour and rigor-mortis is a small one.' So, 'astonishingly', these initiatives typically fail to cure the problem. Why? Well, where should I start and how long have you got? Suffice it to say that it fails because the focus is *still* on the relatively easy bits, implementing the 'best practices' that increase the formality, completeness and consistency of working practices without taking proper account of the cost and value of quality and without focusing on a 'best *value* practices' framework that will truly add maximum value to the business. It also engenders a mentality of 'keep your head below the parapet and protect your backside' rather than one of trust and empowerment. In short, it fails fundamentally because of the focus on more predictably delivering 'better' *outputs* rather than more predictably delivering better (commercially more advantageous) *outcomes*.

For example (and admittedly at risk of grossly oversimplifying the matter), best practice for project management may well be about adhering to strict disciplines for developing project charters, deploying PERT and CPA techniques, developing project plans, analysing project risks, tracking progress against plan etc. But the best *value* practices are rooted in the more difficult areas of project governance (basically, managing business case change and managing the risks of the solution not delivering the benefits, things that require us to focus on the outcomes of project management, rather than the processes of project management, and things that require both IT people and business people to change their behaviours). In fact the *real* challenge in value-adding project management is little or nothing to do with processes at all – it is about effective project leadership and team management. But that is a separate issue that is beyond my remit here!

2.11 The need to focus on best value practices

In my widespread experience of reviewing large IT functions I have typically identified between 50 and 150 'key' opportunities for improvement (otherwise known less tactfully as 'weaknesses') in each IT function reviewed. You can't fix 50 to 150 problems, no matter how long you've got, because the problems will have changed long before you have fixed them. The fundamental difficulty for me has always been trying to identify what is *really* important, given the limited time, energy and money available for performance improvement and the immense difficulty of making *real* change happen in the typical organization. That is another reason why it is critically important to focus on the *best value* practices. The trap that many (in fact, every organization in which I have consulted has fallen into this trap) IT functions fall into is trying to tackle too many problems in too short a timescale with a wholly unrealistic understanding of the huge difficulties of changing people's behaviour. They want to 'solve world poverty' in a week when they would actually ultimately achieve more by tackling, say, three to five *key* incremental improvements, over a realistic timeframe (a year is a good starting point for demonstrating real change) with the sponsorship, leadership and energy commitments that will be required. This is one reason why I have become increasingly disillusioned with 'IT transformation programmes'. They are just too difficult (as I hope to illustrate in a major case study of just this in the next chapter). It is also why this book's title is not the hubristic *Transforming the IT Function*. I am not trying to transform the IT function. I 'just' want to help you transform the business *value* you deliver from IT by becoming a value-driven IT function. This is likely to be a *realizable* goal in a realistic timeframe. And I do not believe that there are 50 to 150 things that IT functions must critically do well to achieve value transformation – my contention is that there are just half a dozen critical success factors (CSFs – that I set out in the next chapter) that will at least address the key aspects of adding value.

2.12 Advisors' agendas

We live in a world in which no one (over the age of 10) asks what a politician stands for. We know what he stands for, namely, being re-elected. As Cecil B. De Mille said, 'Those are my principles, and if you don't like them then I've got others.' Democracy is essentially a popularity contest. And so the name of the game is basically to tell people what you think they want to hear, burying the unspeakable news and dressing up and animating the corpse of the unpalatable. My point is simply that just as every utterance of politicians should be examined carefully through the murky haze of their political agenda, so every utterance of management consultants must be seen in the radiant light of their commercial agenda. They will also tell you what you want to hear ('*Together* we can solve this problem') and will then whack you with a big invoice, rather in the manner of Groucho Marx wooing Emily – for the benefit of those readers not entirely word perfect with the scripts of the films of the Marx Brothers, Groucho said, 'Send two dozen roses to Room 424 and put "Emily, I love you" on the back of the bill.'

While, of course, a key selling point (what used to be *the* key selling point when I started out in consultancy) of management consultancies is that they are founded on the principles of independence and objectivity, these things can easily be contaminated by self-interest. Real 'independence and objectivity' is a very, very rare commodity. For example, have you ever taken advice from an Independent Financial Advisor, only to subsequently find that the financial product recommended just happened to have the highest commission rates for the advisor? Let me give you another example, this time of professionals whose judgement and recommendations really are, of course, beyond reproach, namely, medical consultants. I have undergone two operations recommended by (and then conducted by) highly auspicious Harley Street consultants (you know, the ones who rent the cachet of their business address by the hour) and both of those operations, which I would *never* have obtained on the National Health Service (NHS) achieved precisely nothing. No, I'm lying. They did achieve something. They took up valuable theatre time that could have doubtless been used for an NHS operation that *would* actually have helped someone and they doubtless put a new set of tyres on the consultants' Porsches, but that was about it.

So what about management consultants? Anyone who has worked in a management consultancy knows that it is not so much that you are only as good as your last job – it is more that you are only as good as your *next* job. Consultancies (like pretty much all ESPs) make their real living from getting a foot in the door of a client and then broadening and deepening their penetration of that client, ideally making the client's management team as dependent on them as possible. It is called 'sell-on', and consultants are trained thoroughly in looking for the *next* assignment the moment they begin their *current* assignment. The people who become partners in management consultancies do so largely because they are opportunists who have mastered the art of sell-on, not because of their hard work and general intellectual brilliance.

My point is that consultants are highly incentivized to find a wide range of problems in the clients they review, particularly if the consultancy business happens to have an 'off-the-shelf' methodology, or solution, for those problems. It is not in their self-interest to tell you to focus on just half a dozen key value-adding improvement initiatives (as I propose in the next chapter). I am not seriously impugning the integrity of management consultancy businesses here. I am simply saying that they have an agenda like any outside supplier and that *caveat emptor* must apply. Their recommendations are designed to help you – but they are also designed to help them. Large, complex implementation programmes are loved by management consultancies – they can minimally sell in a programme manager to oversee the programme and ideally they can pull in below him or her a range of specialists in each of the performance improvement areas. They will also try to bring in change management specialists. And best of all they get to hang around your business for longer, make more contacts, find more problems and potentially sell on even more work, broadening and deepening their involvement and increasing your dependence on them. Basically, they are selling or they are failing.

Try to picture the (career limited) consultant who says to a CIO, 'Actually, although we found about 100 problem areas when we reviewed your IT function, I believe you should focus for the next year on addressing just a few key issues which, if addressed well, should transform the value you add to the business – and you should be able to do this with minimal or no consultancy support.' Not easy to picture, is it? Conversely, our hapless consultant is not going to say, 'Here are 100 things you need to change to transform your approach to IT management, but, frankly, there is absolutely no point in our two firms working together to tackle them because thanks to your mutually distrustful relationship with the business, poor leadership skills and a complacent management team who are largely incapable of understanding the compelling need for change, you haven't a hope in hell of succeeding and all you will end up doing is spending a small fortune with our consultancy firm to little or no demonstrable effect. It's been a real pleasure working with you and goodbye.' Both of these responses may be true but they will hardly do. Instead our consultant will tell the CIO that 'Although you do indeed find yourself with a wide range of demanding challenges, I have every confidence that they can certainly be met. In fact they should really be regarded as key opportunities for you to make your mark as the man who transformed the IT function. Having said that I do understand the enormous pressures both you and your entire management team are working under so I suspect that you will need external support to make it happen. Oh, and by the way, it would be remiss of me not to mention the fact that my firm would be delighted to work in partnership with you, bringing to bear our global best practice methodology and toolset for IT transformation and an interdisciplinary team of internationally recognized experts who have had extensive experience of solving just these problems in other comparable organizations . . . '

In the examples above I am obviously not talking about *your* organization and I exaggerate wildly, of course, but you get my drift! I am reminded of a favourite Dilbert cartoon. Dogbert, the consultant, says, 'If you give a man a fish he will eat for a day. But if you teach a man to fish he will buy an ugly hat. And if you talk about fish to a starving man then you're a consultant.' Think about it.

2.13 A hierarchy of value

Which brings me to a further important point, namely, that implementing best value practices will not alone turn you into a true value-driven IT function. High value IT is about more than practices. It is also about people (highly intelligent, highly competent, highly mature, widely experienced, trusted, customer focused and commercial shrewd staff) and organization. Indeed, if I had to create a hierarchy of importance for these, I would have no hesitation in putting people at the top (high calibre people, especially at the top of the IT function, can achieve far more in value delivery than best value practices alone can deliver; conversely, poor calibre people, especially at the top, will almost certainly guarantee poor value delivery). If you cannot attract, incentivize and retain the very best IT staff because of restrictive or outdated HR policies then change your policies! Trite but true. Next in the hierarchy I would put working practices, followed finally by organization structure.

When you consult for any length of time with a particular organization you spot the 5 per cent to 10 per cent (maximum) of people who are sharp, commercially aware and quite passionate about their work. These are the people who actually *could* make a real difference, the people who really *care*. The common characteristic that makes these people easy to spot is the fact that they are visibly frustrated (and often very angry) with the pace of change and resistance to change that they see in their colleagues, and even more so in their so-called superiors. They are also typically inadequately financially rewarded because the corporate human resources regime is designed to address the needs of the 'toe the line' proletariat, rather than recognize, single out and *seriously* reward excellence. These people are the 'silver lining' of the organization. And yes, you are way ahead of me, every silver lining has a cloud, this being the corporate cloud of complacency and conservatism. These people are often perceived as 'loose cannons' and will tend either to be smothered into the submission of corporate conformity or, sooner or later, leave and move on to more dynamic, progressive, commercially exciting companies that are not hamstrung by Victorian reward mechanisms. Alternatively they become management consultants (or, occasionally, drop out and acquire a Harley-Davidson and a ponytail). These are the people who are the pains in the ass who ask the difficult questions – but, in my experience, it is facing up to the difficult questions that almost invariably yields the most valuable outcomes (not to mention being the most fun!). Admittedly they are often their own worst enemies because they lack the political finesse to win over their superiors and convince them that the changes were really all their idea.

By the way, I would be less than honest if I failed to point out that just as consultants quickly spot the 5 per cent to 10 per cent 'who really count' in an organization, so they tend to spot quickly the typical 10 per cent to 20 per cent who are, frankly, a waste of space (if not actually *counter*productive). The same corporate cultures and HR regimes that fail to adequately recognize and reward the excellent also fail to recognize and 'punish' the inept. People who would long ago have been thrown out of a truly commercial organization can hang on for decades in the corporate environment, often, in my experience, with a spectacular lack of self-awareness of their inadequacies. Basically, my message is that a commercially successful organization will not so much espouse the cliché that 'people are their biggest asset' as *truly* recognize that '*certain* people are their biggest assets'; they will *also* recognize that *certain* people should be their most expendable assets. Speaking as someone whose job was kept open for him during the 13 months it took to recover from a serious accident, I entirely applaud humane HR practices. But this isn't about applying humane practices for those in times of temporary adversity. It is about applying commercial practices for those who are never likely to be value-adders to the organization. Of course, if you don't accept that wealth creation must precede job creation I don't suppose you will agree with me!

When I first considered this 'value hierarchy' I put a thing called 'culture' at the top (if the underlying culture of the organization is essentially uncommercial it is *immensely* difficult to optimize IT value). But things like 'culture' and 'values' are amorphous, 'tree-hugger' terms. Like Hermann Goering, I tend to reach for my metaphorical revolver when I hear these terms used in business. If your company has a documented set of 'corporate values' (which doubtless were produced at great cost by some management consultancy), can you actually remember them (without looking them up)? More to the point, do they actually cause you to behave differently? Like 'mission statements', they doubtless serve some role (if only to fill white space on the cover of the annual company accounts) but rarely actually have any affect whatsoever on people's behaviours. In fact, when the stated values are obviously at odds with the *actual* culture it just engenders cynicism and so is counterproductive (e.g. a corporate value of 'honesty and integrity in serving the needs of the customer', when everyone knows the name of the game is basically to take the money and run – in Scotland we say, 'Yeah, that'll be right'). Culture is essentially a fancy word for 'how people behave'. The fastest and most effective way to change your culture is to change your people, especially those at the top, because people below will take their lead from their example. Having said that, the practices I will propose in this book (in Chapters 3, 4 and 5) are precisely designed to incentivize commercial behaviours. Therefore I believe that if organizations embraced these practices, organizational behaviours (i.e. corporate culture) would almost inevitably change to create an environment that is much more commercially astute and much more open to the cultivation of commercially astute people (and the growth and retention of such people). Despite my instinctive discomfort with the word 'culture' I will be obliged to use it repeatedly in this book because it *is* at the apex of my 'value pyramid'.

Unfortunately, the things that most readily tend to be changed by companies seeking to improve IT value fall in the exact opposite order to my hierarchy, i.e. change to organizational structure and roles (which will generally tend to have the least impact) tends to be the first (and repeated) initiative undertaken. The next most frequently attempted initiatives tend to be in process improvement, often in selecting and implementing a systems development methodology (despite the fact that, as I have indicated above, this is very unlikely indeed to be a major 'value-adder'). Very occasionally organizations will actually gather up all their courage and replace some or all of their commercially challenged IT management team with people of real business talent, but although this would very probably be the single biggest source of value improvement (and it is relatively 'easy' and cheap to achieve), few have this courage (or they will hide behind 'humanitarian' or cultural shields).

I have my reservations about the 'management sciences'. I find that they have a tendency to combine simplistic generalizations of how businesses work with often pretentious, pedantic, pseudo-academic theories that somehow never quite seem to correlate how normal people actually behave when you place them in an office. However, one 'business theory' that I certainly would sign up to is the so-called 'Peter Principle'. This essentially states that corporate man is promoted up to his level of incompetence and there he stays (to death or retirement, whichever comes first), ineffectual, self-justifying and probably quite miserable. It is an endemic corporate problem that is actively fostered by the typical policy of 'promoting from within', a laudable policy only when it results in the promotion of people who commercially excel at the job, not because it is 'Joe's turn' for promotion or because Joe has basically toed the corporate line for years. And once there they promote under them people who are very much like them, people who won't make them feel too inadequate. I have never seen a survey of the average length of service of senior IT managers in corporations so I can only go on my own experience. My experience may be skewed by my extensive exposure to the retail industry with its extremely paternalistic roots but this tells me that it is quite frightening the proportion of people in such positions who have percolated up through long service and little, if any, exposure to any other business than the one they joined decades ago (often directly from school or college).

What about the aspect I put at the bottom of my 'value hierarchy'? I appreciate that I may be open to the charge of being curtly dismissive of organizational change as a means of adding business value, without any closely reasoned argument. All right, I'm guilty. But in my defence I have watched with wry amusement as client after client have changed their 'organizational philosophy' from one of centralization to one of decentralization (and then back again); from insourcing to outsourcing (and then back again); from role based to project based to process based (and then back again). I've seen clients who have gone through these cycles *several times* over the years. Didn't someone say, 'History repeats itself, first as tragedy then as farce.' I've seen specialization and generalization. I've seen vertical and I've seen horizontal. I've seen groups form, empires grow, disband and reform (under another name). And all to generally little avail (other than huge disruption and a fun time had by a select few who jostle for the plum jobs in the latest, greatest reorganization). I'm afraid that as far as value delivery is concerned I cannot get very excited about organizational change. But if you remain unconvinced then I refer you to a Gartner Research publication called *The Five Pillars of IS Organisational Effectiveness* (Andren, Furlonger, Magee and Mingay) which does an excellent job of exploring these issues. I am not suggesting that organizational issues are irrelevant. I do have (not particularly strongly held) views that I will share with you later. I am simply saying that organizational issues are *relatively* unimportant when the imperative is business value delivery.

Basically, in my experience, senior IT managers (and organizations as a whole) tend to undertake performance improvement initiatives with which they are most comfortable, which don't force them to face up to their own inadequacies and which don't force them to take difficult decisions. The most fatuous and often risible example of this is companies spending millions (I'm not talking Turkish lire here) on rebranding, as epitomized by Consignia (aka the British Post Office, now, courageously, re-re-branded The Royal Mail). They will also often give the responsibility for effecting performance improvement initiatives to consultants, partially in an attempt to transfer responsibility (and risk) away from themselves. Creating a corporate environment in which risk aversion, deference and conservatism is seen as the way to seniority is self-perpetuating. By all means call it circumspection, conformity and prudence (a rose by any other name still has thorns). In short, senior managers can often end up being decisive about the irrelevant but in denial about the real problems (because they seem just too difficult to address and tackling them may well make their own shortcomings only too visible). If you are a senior manager and are offended by this then I apologize for my lack of risk aversion, deference and conservatism. But then maybe you are in denial.

In this book I focus almost entirely on optimizing IT processes and practices rather than addressing people or organizational issues simply because getting companies to tackle the people issues head-on is too difficult for me to address (and anyway largely comes down simply to the will of senior management to bring in fresh, talented, broadly experienced, commercially astute blood) and organizational structure optimization is, in my experience, *relatively* unimportant in trying to optimize IT value. Furthermore, as I suggested above, I do at least come at the people problem obliquely, by tackling head-on the people *behavioural* problem.

To return to the example of management consultancies, they are almost devoid of 'best practices' (in terms of how to deliver consultancy assignments). Yes, as I noted before, they are awash with such 'methods' but virtually no one actually uses them. Organizationally they are generally in a state of constant flux as they reorganize themselves now around industry facing lines, then around product lines, then around technical disciplines, then globally, then nationally, then regionally, and so on, trying to dynamically stay focused on the market need of the moment. I have never, ever, seen an organization chart for a management consultancy firm (despite spending most of my career in them), which is an indicator of what management consultants think of conventional hierarchies. However, if you *were* to draw a conventional hierarchy structure chart for a large management consultancy it would include a blur of dotted lines, the typical sign of unsatisfactory organizational compromises. Yet management consultancies have been enormously commercially successful. Why? Because in our 'value hierarchy', while they may be seriously deficient in organization and practices, they do generally have highly commercially focused, first rate staff.

In fact, management consultancies are *not* generally seriously deficient in organization because they recognize that they are essentially *project* driven organizations (as, note, are IT functions) and this is something they *do* tend to get right by structuring projects in such a way as to get the best results, largely irrespective of the seniority of the staff assigned. Therefore, generally speaking, the most competent (available) group of people are brought together to tackle a particular problem and are structured in whatever way will achieve the best result. The person who works for you on one project may well be the person you work for on the next. So, once again, perhaps we should do as consultancies *do*, rather than as they *say*? You should not, however, extend this to the IT functions within management consultancies which, in keeping with the principle of 'cobbler's shoes', often are excellent models of *worst* IT practice. This is not, by the way, to say that 'if these people cannot put their own house in order why should I trust them to put *my* house in order?' Again, consultancies are archly commercial and they will not put their top IT consultants onto the job of transforming their internal IT service when they can be out there with clients generating profits for the firm's partners and directors.

2.14 Confusing busyness with business

In conclusion, only when all these people (leadership, behaviours, competency) and organizational components come together with best value practices can we say that we have truly been delivered into the promised land of value-driven IT. Changing entrenched behaviours, in particular, is not at all easy. Most of my IT industry experience and subsequent IT consultancy experience have been in the retail industry, which is not noted for its lack of hard-edged commercial realism. Yet I have found that IT functions in these organizations tend to display highly *uncommercial* behaviours. It is not *just* that their typical focus is on solution delivery rather then value delivery. Underlying this is often a fundamental lack of grasp of commercial realities. It is as though the money they are spending is somehow less real because it is the 'company's money'. In the last consultancy firm in which I worked before starting my own business, the directors (one step below partners) were, at that time, charging out their time at £500 ($750) per hour. No, it's not a mistype. It's not per day. Although I have seen the odd raised eyebrow, I have never once heard a client say the choice and robust words he surely might say if this money was coming directly out of *his* pay cheque. Frankly, I can think of few people who would pay that sort of money for an entire *night* with Liz Hurley/Hugh Grant (delete as applicable), never mind an hour with a middle-ranking management consultant with an agenda. By the way, directors are well rehearsed in what to say if they are challenged on their outrageous rates – I call it the 'L'Oreal defence': 'Because we're worth it.'

In my final corporate job before I became a consultant I managed about 80 IT development staff and spent my days racing from meeting to meeting. The rare times I wasn't in a meeting I was probably at an IT industry conference. On the even rarer times when I wasn't at a meeting or at a conference I was probably on a course (usually a time management course, if I recall correctly). The culture was such that to *not* be invited to a meeting that had even the most tenuous connection with your responsibilities was taken as a personal affront. Of course, I couldn't possibly attend all the meetings I was invited to so I had to delegate down and swamp the next layer of management's diaries too. Certainly, my diary was permanently packed – *ergo* I was really, really important. In fact I am ashamed to say that for a short while I think I conned myself into actually believing that. In short, I was endlessly confusing *busyness* with *business*, a crucial distinction. I was 'corporate man', with wall-to-wall, back-to-back diary commitments for weeks ahead. As Richard Yates put it back in 1961 in his outstanding novel *Revolutionary Road*, '"I'm afraid I'm booked solid through the end of the month," says the executive, voluptuously nestling the phone at his cheek as he thumbs the leaves of his appointment calendar, and his mouth and eyes at that moment betray a sense of deep security. The crisp, plentiful, day-sized pages before him prove that nothing unforeseen, no calamity of chance or fate can overtake him between now and the end of the month. Ruin and pestilence have been held at bay, and death itself will have to wait; for he is booked solid.' In short, I was not embracing change and risk – I was embracing stability and security. I was held in 'respect' principally because of my seniority, not because of my essential value to the company. I was extremely busy, I was extremely hard working and I was essentially a commercial waste of space. I even found myself living on a suburban 'executive housing estate' in a semi-detached, accountant-designed, quiet-desperation house built in the character-free vernacular, where, to the best of my recollection I did indeed wash my company-supplied car each Sunday morning. It was really only a matter of time before I took up golf.

Having eventually decided that I was enjoying a very slow, but natural, death, I launched whole-heartedly into a precocious mid-life crisis-lite (I was 30 at the time) – I quit my corporate job and the 'burbs and moved to central London to become a professional gigolo to the young, beautiful, bored wives of old, ugly, rich, workaholic city executives. All right, that last bit wasn't entirely true. Actually I became a management consultant.

I initially experienced a deep 'culture shock' to find myself suddenly, overnight, going from rajah to rookie, from overlord to underdog. From there being no requirement whatsoever to account for how I spent my time I was immediately required to record and account for my activities every 10 minute unit of my day (and explain myself when any of those 10 minute periods were not adding value to the firm, i.e. being billed to clients).

From having nothing whatsoever to do with selling I was required to generate value-adding activities (i.e. literally sell myself and others and convince clients of the patently preposterous proposition that a week of my time was worth them paying the price of a family car). I went from having 80 people to delegate to, to having zero people to delegate to and from being treated with deference to being treated with deprecation (which was fair enough because I was clearly way out of my depth). Additionally I went from a situation of having my own office and a secretary shared with two other managers to a situation where there were on average eight consultants to each desk in the office (i.e. a 'hotdesking' approach, where you book a desk somewhere in the building each day you are in the office – a major incentive to be on a client site earning fees) and each secretary 'supported' on average about 100 consultants. Basically you were on your own and expected to be self-reliant. I went from attending internal meetings as a way of life (in fact, my *raison d'être*) to the expectation that if you held an internal meeting you held it outside business hours (effectively in your own time). I went from a 'requirement' that you spent at least 10 days a year on training courses to one where you only attended training that was truly indispensable for a sold assignment (and for which a client was paying). As for industry conferences: in my 16 years in consultancy firms I attended precisely one. Why? Because all these activities (even going on holiday) depressed your billable utilization (basically, the hours you billed to clients), the key criterion that determined your remuneration and prospects. When you work in a management consultancy you are in no doubt whatsoever that every minute of the day you are in the business of generating revenue and maximizing profits, and just happen to be doing this by providing advice to clients. After the comfortable, controlled, mollycoddled, routine busyness of being a corporate manager, I found that exposure to 'real' business, with its constant focus on selling, its unpredictability, need for constant focus, enormous resilience and self-reliance, sustained high energy levels, working much of the time at the very limit of your ability, thinking on your feet and hourly accountability for value-added to the business, was, frankly, frightening. In fact it was so frightening that I resigned after six weeks (with no job to go to) and had to be persuaded back by the one partner who apparently had some faith that I was not beyond redemption. It was only some time later, after I had adapted to working in such a commercial culture that I made the rather banal discovery that fear and excitement went hand in hand and that having complete clarity about how well you were doing (what you were billing) engendered a clear sense of personal worth (or, of course, worthlessness). This was a quintessentially commercial culture, light years removed from the culture of the IT functions in which I had worked. I will have much more to say about the essential differences between uncommercial and commercial cultures in Chapters 4 and 5 and how to establish practices and measures that will help to commercialize the typical corporate IT function.

I have found that most who work in large IT functions, even at very senior levels, still *at heart* think of themselves as working in the IT industry and are far removed from thinking of themselves as being, say, retailers, let alone thinking of themselves as revenue and profit generators. They are in the 'business' of delivering IT systems and services rather than the business of delivering value (ultimately flogging more baked beans). But you've got to sell a *lot* of cans of baked beans to buy one IT system (in fact, assuming a modest £500 000 system and a generous 1 per cent profit margin, you've probably got to sell about 100 000 000 cans of beans, rather more than are consumed in my home in an entire year).

In the next chapter I will set out the 'best value practices' for the effectiveness quadrant of our 'value compass'. These are basically about *how* we achieve our key value-adding goals.

2.15 Summary

'World class IT' is a much abused (and ill-defined) term. Its most common characteristic, however, is the deployment of 'best practices'. Best practices are characterized as being methodical, generally applicable, workable and resulting in more predictable outcomes, outcomes that do not, however, necessarily result in the optimum value being added to the business. In fact, rigorously applying best practices will often result in the increased predictability of product and service delivery at the expense of increased cost, delayed delivery and/or reduced value. Therefore the 'best *value* practices' we seek must not only satisfy the characteristics of 'best practices' (by being highly 'effective') but must also result in the most predictable (and highest) value-added delivery of quality products and services as cost-efficiently as possible. The 'best value practices' cannot be successfully deployed by IT functions in isolation – they need the full co-operation and buy-in of the business.

This leads us to a more complete picture of the value of IT as encompassing cost-efficiency and effectiveness on the 'supply side' (the IT function) of the 'IT business' and value-added and quality on the 'demand side' (the business served) of the 'IT business'. Cost-efficiency and effectiveness often have an adversarial relationship, their relative importance being largely determined by the strategic role of IT in support of the business.

The IT industry has a long history of being relatively good at doing the things that are relatively unimportant (from a value point of view) and relatively poor at doing things that are relatively important (from a value point of view). With the (sometimes cynical) encouragement of its advisors, it has also tended to be overambitious in its performance improvement initiatives and failed to focus adequately on the deployment of best *value* practices. The priority has, in fact, tended to be on the improvement of organizational structures first, practice improvement second and people improvement last, despite the fact that the highest value would be added by reversing these priorities. Even in otherwise highly commercial organizations, IT management and staff often display highly uncommercial behaviours.

3

Optimizing effectiveness

A man may be very sincere in good principles without having good practice.

Dr Samuel Johnson

This chapter is about optimizing the effectiveness of the IT function's working practices. 'Effectiveness' is a key indicator of the perceived 'professionalism' of the 'IT products and services delivery factory'. This is principally about the rigour of the working practices adopted, largely embodied in the methods adopted. In my experience IT staff will almost invariably profess their support for the methods in place across their IT function. This is partially, of course, because it is not politically correct to say otherwise. But I believe it is also because they really support the 'principle' that 'methods are a good thing', in the same sense that 'virtue is a good thing'. It does not mean that they necessarily actually apply the 'best practice' methods with any degree of rigour in everyday practice.

Effectiveness is optimized by establishing these 'best practices' across the IT function, where 'best practices' are as I have characterized them in Chapter 2, namely:

1 Best practices must be methodical.
2 Best practices must be generally applicable.
3 Best practices must *demonstrably* be applicable in the 'real world'.
4 For a best practice to satisfy our test of 'bestness', its *application* must *demonstrably* result in a better outcome.

In order to identify key areas that would benefit most from the adoption of best practices, a 'diagnostic review' of strengths and weaknesses would typically be conducted on the existing IT practices. This would also be used to help prioritize required practice improvements. The IT function would then optimize its effectiveness by developing improved practices based on best practice 'standards' and/or 'selecting' appropriate 'best of breed' IT industry best practice models and creating a programme of work to 'bridge the gap' between its existing practices and those set out in the models. Typical models selected from the public domain might be SSADM for systems development, PRINCE for project management and ITIL for service delivery.

By adopting best practices in the effectiveness quadrant we achieve the principal outcome of improved quality (as assessed in the quality, demand-side, quadrant of our value compass). However, I am going to say little more about adopting best practices because, as I hope I made clear in Chapter 2, my key concern is with the 'best *value* practices'. By adopting best value practices in the effectiveness quadrant we achieve the principal outcome of improved value-added to the business (as assessed in the value-added, demand-side, quadrant).

In this chapter I will propose how to achieve 'value-adding' transformation by focusing the limited time, money and energy available on defining and implementing value-adding 'best value practices'. I will set out six key value-adding CSF opportunity areas, describing best value practices for each. It is by focusing here on these half dozen CSFs that I hope to help IT functions avoid the 'solving world poverty' problem of trying to make the '100 effectiveness improvements' I discussed in the previous chapter.

Note that this book is not meant to be a 'procedures manual'. I can only give guidance on the nature of the actual procedures an organization may wish to implement because these will be unique to each organization's circumstances and existing practices. Nevertheless, I believe that the 'leap' from my proposed practice framework to organization-specific, documented procedures should not generally be a large one. I have also tried to keep my framework simple. However, as Einstein said, 'Everything should be made as simple as possible but not simpler.' I am a great believer in designing and implementing simple solutions that actually 'take', in preference to designing and implementing 'clever' solutions that may indeed comply with best value practice characteristics (as we defined it in the previous chapter) but don't 'take'. Conversely, if you *over*simplify the problem, quietly trying to ignore real life complexities, then the 'simple' solution will also fail. The devil is almost invariably in the detail. To try to resolve this conundrum I have probably erred on the side of complexity in specifying my 'best value practices' below but on the understanding that organizations will extract the *necessary and sufficient* subset that is commercially applicable to them.

3.1 The transfer charging debate

Before I begin to set out my proposed best value practices I need to 'get out of the way' an issue that underpins many of the practices I am about to discuss. That issue is 'transfer charging'. As I said in the Introduction, this is a very emotive issue, with those who are strongly 'pro' ranged against those who are strongly 'anti'.

Those who are 'pro' are typically so because they maintain that it is virtually impossible to develop a genuinely commercial mindset in the relationship between the business and the IT function (or, indeed, an ESP supplying IT services) *without* a 'commercial' transaction taking place. Without this the business mindset is that 'IT is free' and the central issue for the user of IT services is negotiating the biggest slice of the IT cake he can get (since 'someone else' is paying for that slice). Note that when I state that the business mindset is that 'IT is free' I am not talking about *senior* business management. They know only *too* well that IT is anything but free. But they are not the point of 'IT consumption' (which is typically some considerable distance lower in the pecking order).

Those who are 'anti' are typically so because they have seen the immense difficulty of successfully implementing a 'transfer charging regime'.

For the 'pros' it is an almost axiomatic assumption that to charge the business directly for IT services is 'inherently better' than to not do so. This is based on the assumption that (generally speaking) the more an internal service provider (IT function) 'looks like' an external service provider (ESP), the better (in fact, this is a highly dubious point of view that I will take up in some detail in Chapter 6). And ESPs charge for their services, don't they? And transfer charging is a common 'first step' in moving away from an IT function that acts as a monopoly supplier to opening up IT services supply to the business in a 'free market' model. And (anti-capitalist demonstrators and French farmers aside) we all believe in free markets, don't we? I will risk a contentious political parallel here by saying that making an internal IT function act as an ESP is similar, in the context of 'United Kingdom plc', to making a National Health Service hospital 'pay its way'. Is this a 'business' with the overriding goal of 'paying its way' or 'making a profit' for itself or is this a service with the overriding goal of meeting customer needs cost-efficiently and effectively? As I shall explain in Chapter 6, running an organization to make a profit and running an organization 'commercially' are emphatically *not* identical, especially when that organization is an internal service provider.

In the last chapter I made clear that despite my very negative experiences of internal transfer charging I was, in fact, in favour of it. This sounds like hypocrisy, in as much as I am apparently preaching the deployment of something that has demonstrably repeatedly failed. But the crucial point is *how* transfer charging is established. In my experience the failing has not been so much in the concept as in the typically deeply flawed implementations. I know from experience that it is virtually impossible to engender commercial attitudes in either the business user or the IT function without some form of transfer charging. Equally I know that it is immensely difficult to achieve this without establishing a 'transfer charging regime' that is complex, costly and generates aggravation. It reminds me of the Will Rogers quote, 'Communism is like prohibition; it's a good idea but it doesn't work.' Basically I am *pro* the principle but *anti* the *typical* implementation.

Continuing the capitalism/communism simile, let me quote the old Polish joke, 'Capitalism is the exploitation of man by man; Communism is the reverse.' Whether you charge back or not, you will potentially have some serious negative consequences. Generally I have found that those who evangelize transfer charging are arguing the unassailability of the theory; those we demonize transfer charging are arguing the ineffectuality of the (typical) implementation. Between these two extremes are the 'fellow travellers', publicly saluting the concept of transfer charging, just so long as they don't have to actually live under its yoke.

3.2 The objectives of transfer charging

So what are the *theoretical* objectives of transfer charging for IT products and services between an IT function and its business users (and are those objectives actually realizable when the supplier is *internal*)?

1 To make the cost of IT service provision more visible to the business and so incentivize users to modify their behaviours and/or usage of IT services, so potentially reducing (or at least better controlling) IT costs. This typically has to be *the* key objective.

2 To allow business users to move their IT spend to a more variable cost base under their control (although in *internal* charging this will potentially simply result in other users having to bear the 'displaced' costs from the organization's fixed IT costs).

3 To incentivize the IT function to meet its service level agreement (SLA) targets by means of various penalties (service credits or 'financial' penalties) on its failure to hit those targets (although in *internal* charging any 'financial' penalties will almost certainly be 'wooden dollars' and therefore of questionable value as a sanction).

4 To allow the IT function to demonstrate its commercial competitiveness by demonstrably successfully selling IT services to third parties at the same price as set internally. Note that, minimally, transfer charging should help foster a 'measurement culture' in the IT function and provide an unprecedented understanding of cost-intensive resources and activities (as a possible basis for IT cost-efficiency improvement initiatives). This can also assist in making service sourcing decisions.

5 To allow the IT function to 'commercially segregate' a particular IT service with a view to subsequently comparing price and service levels with third party suppliers (and so potentially outsourcing that service).

6 To help 'commercialize' the culture of the IT function and so help establish, or improve, a culture of customer service.

3.3 The principles of transfer charging

There are two 'poles' of transfer charging implementation, namely, the *cost recovery* model and the *market-based pricing* model (in practice, implementations typically fall between these extremes).

A *market pricing* model begins by assessing the components and scope of the IT service and the total costs of providing that service over its lifetime (depending on various assumptions about the future price/performance of equipment and the amount of service that is likely to be taken). It then builds up a tariff per 'service unit' (considering the risks in delivering the service and its reinvestment needs). This is the 'commercial' model that an ESP would adopt. Different tariffs might be set for peak and non-peak usage times in order to provide financial incentives for the user to perform more work at off-peak times and so help to reduce the total capacity requirements (and so overall hardware costs). Similarly, different staff tariffs might be set for delivering and supporting standard and non-standard services in order to incentivize the use of standard services. Note that this use of variable tariffing to incentivize more commercial user behaviours is a key tool available to both the internal IT function or an ESP (but consider for a moment what incentive the ESP has to deploy such tools). There are various methods of pricing, including standard cost, cost-plus, target return and market pricing (or 'going rate'). The price of the service is then the 'service unit' tariff multiplied by the amount of 'service units' consumed by the user. Readers who are paying attention may reflect that despite the logical and concise description of market pricing that I have set out above, it ain't simple.

A *cost recovery* model sums up the cost of delivering a service and on some more or less reasonable basis apportions and passes these on to a user. This is a tad simpler than market pricing.

The key difference between the two models can be likened to the key difference between charging a householder for water usage based on metering (i.e. payment by actual usage multiplied by tariff) and charging based on the rateable value of the house. Both approaches recoup the cost of supplying water but the former incentivizes the user to control or reduce usage. Where transfer charging is applied between an *internal* IT service supplier and the business, the 'charges' will effectively be 'wooden dollars', or based on a system of service credits and debits.

The main underlying goal of *effective* internal IT transfer charging is typically to ensure that commercially appropriate behaviours are achieved by *both* the IT function and the business. This is encouraged by ensuring that business users of IT services understand the 'true' commercial cost of service provision and are able to 'take control' of IT costs and optimize them. By 'optimize' I mean ensuring that *enough* IT service is provided to meet commercial business needs but that this service should not *exceed* commercial business needs (i.e. *necessary and sufficient* service levels).

Implementing a *market pricing* model should achieve fair and accurate transfer pricing and ensure that the business user is 'charged' for his service based on the actual volume of the service taken (such as: number of SAP seats; number of programmer days; CPU consumption; number of network nodes; number of portals) and the agreed service level taken.

This should (in theory) provide him with the ability to manage, on an ongoing basis, his IT costs by changing the volume of service taken and/or changing the service level selected and/or changing business behaviours (e.g. changing shift patterns to make high IT workload occur outside prime tariffing hours on the CPU). For example, the business user might choose to reduce his IT costs over the next year by reducing the number of complex online queries or by requesting a reduction in service levels from, say, sub-second average online transaction response times to sub-four second response times.

What is required is a psychological and fiscal 'connect' between the amount of service consumed, the service level selected and the true cost of that service provision. This is what market pricing should give you. In principle at least, a further benefit of implementing a market pricing model is the increased ability to compare internal charges with the outside marketplace (and so assess more objectively the opportunities for outsourcing). The market pricing model is typically relatively (oh, all right, very) complex to implement (compared with the cost recovery model) and relatively expensive to administer and to run the supporting systems.

For example, in a cost reduction study performed for a major insurance company, I found a 'classic' transfer charging regime in place. It had been implemented to address a recommendation made in an *earlier* cost reduction exercise, i.e. transfer charging had been introduced with a key objective of reducing IT costs. I computed the total cost of running the transfer charging regime was about 3 per cent of the IT function's budget. Since it clearly was dismally failing to achieve *any* of the six objectives set out above my recommendation was to *terminate* the transfer charging regime as a key cost reduction opportunity. In other words, significantly reduce costs by removing the cost reduction initiative! Interestingly, they both accepted my recommendation and quietly buried it. As far as I could gather, this was because it was too embarrassing to admit to the business that the fortune they had just invested in developing the transfer charging regime had been wasted. I have long suspected that the single biggest barrier to maximizing business value is pride.

Further complexities arise in trying (by a combination of capacity planning and equipment price/performance trend prediction) to set tariffs that will *at least* recover all IT costs based on assumptions of the volumes of service to be taken and the service levels that will be selected. This can lead to conservative assessments that result in over-recovery of costs (typically leading to 'rebates' to the business at year end often accompanied by budgetary control chaos when the 'business books' don't balance). It can have other unwelcome 'side-effects', such as adversely 'skewing' cost/benefit cases for IT developments (since the costs used in the business case were actually excessive). Note that tariffs relate to the *anticipated* costs, to enable the user of the service to budget for the forthcoming period and enable the supplier to ensure that all costs are covered by income from the user. Tariffed services are typically described in an IT service 'catalogue' with a price list (or in SLAs), with different tariffs according to the level of service requested.

An implementation based on the *cost recovery* model will typically be intrinsically less objectively equitable and less accurate (in terms of charging based on the actual volume of service taken and the service levels achieved) but has the key benefit of simplicity (and reduced implementation and running cost) compared with implementing the pricing model. Note that Gartner research shows that IT functions with highly sophisticated transfer charging strategies (in particular, government contractors or aerospace enterprises) can consume as much as 7 per cent of their IT budgets running these regimes. Yes, you read right, *7 per cent*.

Both models can be associated with SLAs 'with teeth' (i.e. with the IT function incurring financial penalties or issuing service credits if they fail to achieve agreed service level targets and attracting incentives if service level targets are exceeded). Without 'SLAs with teeth' *and* an implementation of transfer charging it can be difficult to create effective incentives to achieve *necessary and sufficient* levels of service. A recent Strategic Analysis Report from Gartner stated that 'the overwhelming majority of our [i.e. Gartner] clients report that financial penalties are needed to reinforce the IS supplier's commitment to the SLA. More than half tell us that their suppliers are more likely to respond in a timely manner to services that are tied to performance penalties than those services that are not.'

It should be noted, however, that this Gartner assertion related to *external* suppliers of IT services. It is certainly open to debate whether the same would hold true for *internal* suppliers, when the penalties or incentives are typically less tangible.

3.4 Transfer charging in practice

So that was the theory. But does it work in practice? I have already cited above the case of the insurance company failing to achieve any of the key objectives of transfer charging. To help illustrate further some of the difficulties of successfully implementing transfer charging I set out below my experience with a British clearing bank. You will hear much more about my friends at this bank in the case study in the next chapter.

The IT function at this bank had developed a very complex algorithm that collated literally hundreds of metrics to build a sophisticated market pricing model linked to various levels of SLA ('Gold', 'Silver' etc.) for mainframe and network services. Development services were charged on a simple per diem staff rate basis. All IT staff time was factored into the tariffs by a sophisticated activity-based costing model (e.g. CPU tariffs included a certain amount for capacity planning staff, perform-ance monitoring staff etc.). The cost of 'central services' (e.g. security management, strategy planning) and overall IT manage-ment were factored into the tariffs on an allocation (cost recovery) basis. No incentives or penalties were included in the process (although the success of the IT function in meeting its SLA targets was widely publicized).

So was this complex implementation of transfer charging a success and, if so, at what cost? Well, 34 staff were required to administer the tariffing/billing system and the application sys-tem that collated the usage data and computed bills was costing several hundred thousand pounds per annum to run. I think in most people's language this would be regarded as a costly regime. But, cost and complexity aside, was it a success in terms of achieving the objectives of transfer charging? In summary:

- the bills (of which there were many from the different parts of the IT function providing the various services) were extremely long, complex and 'IT-centric' and were generally poorly understood by recipients (and few in the IT function!); this resulted also in typically long, arduous and divisive negotia-tion of bills between user departments and (proliferating) IT account managers;
- the SLAs were not 'end to end' (i.e. including all underlying IT service components required to deliver each user service) and so it was very difficult for users to relate the part of the service they were being billed for (e.g. the network) to the actual use of the service as they perceived it;

- although the SLA targets agreed with the users *appeared* challenging to the naive IT user (e.g. typically 99 per cent + mainframe availability) they were actually absurdly easy to achieve with modern technologies;
- the costs were borne by the user department at a high level, and as such were essentially 'invisible' to the actual user managers whose own budgets were not directly affected (which resulted in almost all users selecting the 'Gold' service level for all IT services);
- the IT function was being run as a profit centre (with all 'profits' being passed back to the business at year end) and with IT management bonuses strongly related to profit levels. This arguably incentivized the IT function to actually *increase* charges (and hence 'profits'). Please note that when a consultant uses the word 'arguably', it is his way of tactfully saying, 'it bloody well does – you know it and I know it, even if it is unacceptable to say it'.

The upshot was that user behaviours were generally *not* commercially altered (or, at least, not altered commercially *advantageously* from the bank's point of view). This was as a direct result of 'technology service focused tariffs' (rather than 'business service focused tariffs') coupled with arcanely complex bills that were largely incomprehensible to the users coupled with the inability of the users to understand what they could actually do to affect future bills coupled with bills being 'paid' at a higher level in the business organization. In other words, 'I don't understand what I'm paying for, I haven't a clue how they arrive at the frightening figures billed, I haven't a clue what I can do about the size of the bills in future and, anyway, why should I care when someone upstairs actually pays.' In this case not only does the key objective of transfer charging fail, it actually just creates work, cost and aggravation all round. On the basis of this evidence I found it difficult to regard this implementation of transfer charging as a complete success (who says I can't be tactful?). Other implementations I have seen have revealed similar problems.

3.5 CFFs and CSFs for transfer charging

But this was just one example. What are the most *common* pitfalls when implementing a transfer charging 'regime'? In other words, what are the critical *failure* factors (CFFs)?

- Introducing IT transfer charging without any clear understanding of (or communication of) its objectives, how it is going to achieve these objectives and the difficulty, complexity, costs and risks associated with it. ('ESPs do this and we want to be seen to be more like an ESP, don't we.' The word 'duh' comes to mind.)

- Not allocating the *entire* cost base to the services sold or cross-subsidizing services or simply not allocating costs accurately to services, resulting in users not having a true picture of the cost of service provision. This may be done consciously by the IT function for services that are readily comparable with those of ESPs to make them *appear* as though they are competitively priced. ('Please don't outsource us because, look, we are competitive in the marketplace.')

- Not making provision in the pricing structure to fund such costs as infrastructure refresh, product development, research, disaster recovery infrastructure etc. ('I didn't ask for any of those things so I'm not paying for them.')

- Defining chargeable services in such a way as to be 'easy for IT to measure' rather than defining them in an 'end-to-end' way that relates to the user's experience of the service, e.g. billing for utilization of the WAN/LAN, mainframe MIPS etc. rather than billing for the number of business transactions processed over the infrastructure. ('I didn't ask for any WAN, whatever the hell that is, so I'm not paying for it.')

- Creating costing and pricing models that are generally not understood by the business users. Note that Gartner Research report this as *by far* the single biggest complaint about transfer charging mechanisms. Similarly, a 1998 survey on this topic conducted by IDC revealed that only about 70 per cent of user respondents claimed to understand the basis of their IT charging mechanism. ('I should be charging the guys in IT for the time it takes me to get my head round these gobbledegook bills.')

- Setting tariffs that under- or over-recover IT costs. This can result in inappropriate business decisions being made based on artificially low or high prices. Note that users will often underestimate the quantity of service they intend to take in the coming year and IT will tend to make conservative assumptions about the level of service that will be taken in order to ensure that, whatever happens, they do recover all their costs; these can combine to produce tariffs that greatly over-recover costs and result in a (not necessarily welcome, from an accounting point of view) rebate being made at year end to business users. ('I've just spent the last year in a seemingly endless debate over the bills I get from the guys in IT and now they send me this whopping rebate! What are they playing at?') Alternatively, of course, 'over-recovery' can be regarded as 'contribution' or 'profit' or used to fund infra-structure refresh, R&D etc.

- Frequently materially changing tariffs to try to meet cost recovery targets. This can create great difficulty for user planning and budgeting. ('How am I supposed to keep track of prices? They're all over the place.')
- Not reflecting the fixed nature of certain costs in the tariff structure. This can result in over-recovery of cost if volumes are higher than budgeted and under-recovery if volumes are lower than budgeted. ('Oops, we are going to have to ask for a financial top-up from the business.')
- Billing the business at such a high level in the organization that the *actual* user is *still* not incentivized to change behaviour; the bills must hit the user 'above the line', not below it. ('Why should I care – after all, IT is still free.')
- Billing users for IT services without giving them the choice to purchase their services elsewhere or giving them effective levers (e.g. selecting lower service levels) to manage down their costs. ('I'm stuck with my monopoly internal IT supplier so why are they wasting everyone's time playing at being a competitive supplier – they're kidding nobody.')
- Not directly linking price levels to service levels. ('It doesn't cost me any more so I'll have more of that please.')
- Failing to validate and justify internal charges by benchmark-ing prices against other comparable organizations and/or ESPs. ('I'll bet I could buy this cheaper on the open market.') Alternatively, performing price benchmarking, but in such an 'unnormalized' way that it does not have credibility with the business. Note, however, that making true 'like-for-like' service and service level comparisons can be extremely difficult. And making true 'like-for-like' price comparisons with ESPs is virtually impossible, since ESPs are not just looking to recover the costs of their services, or even just working on a cost-plus basis. Instead they are examining IRR, cashflow, risk, contract growth potential, potential to sell on other services, length of contract, market penetration etc. with a view to their long-term revenue stream. *And* they will routinely cross-subsidize services and work to low (or even negative) margins at the start of deals in order to 'get a foot in the door'. I will go into these difficulties in more detail in Chapter 5.

On a more positive note, then, what are the critical *success* factors (CSFs) for implementing transfer charging? To put it

13 CSFs for transfer charging	
1	Agree and state the objectives clearly
2	Implement a 'pricing model'
3	Keep the pricing model simple
4	Keep the bills simple
5	Ensure that the prices/tariffs set are precisely those that appear in project business cases
6	Implement timesheets for development staff and record the actual costs of projects
7	Package products and services in such a way that they are both 'end to end' and clearly understandable to the user
8	Make users directly *accountable* for the costs 'billed'
9	Ensure that different cost vs service level SLA packages are offered to users
10	Make prices 'honest'
11	Don't be tempted to sell IT services externally
12	Don't 'financially' penalize IT for failure to achieve SLA targets
13	Don't make service sourcing decisions based solely on comparing internal and external tariffs

Figure 3.1

another way, what is 'best value practice' for transfer charging? These 13 CSFs are summarized in Figure 3.1.

1 *Do* agree and state the objectives clearly and remember *why* you are doing it. In many significant ways you do *not* want your IT function to be like an ESP. If your relationship with ESPs is 'traditional' then they, frankly, are in the business of screwing you and you, frankly, are in the business of screwing them. Is that the nature of the relationship you want between your internal IT function and the business it serves?

2 *Do* implement a 'pricing model' (because you will fundamentally undermine the value of the 'best value practices' of IT I am about to set out without it!). I'm afraid that without a pricing model it will be *extremely* difficult to change user (and IT) commercial behaviours.

3 *Do* keep the pricing model simple, even if that means it is not scrupulously accurate, objective and consistent. Use simple per diem prices for development and support staff with, say, three cost tiers for permanent staff, and one for contractors. Use simple apportionment of costs for 'capital' costs. Pricing infrastructure and support costs will be *much* easier if these 'post-implementation' services (e.g. WAN, LAN, portal, web) are offered in a standardized form for which the total

cost of ownership (TCO) is clearly understood (and can be input into project business cases, as well as used for post-implementation transfer charging).

4 *Do* keep the bills simple. The supplier in this case is internal. Start from a position of trusting that the bills are fair (unless proved otherwise).

5 *Do* ensure that the prices/tariffs set are precisely those that appear in project business cases (which should, as we shall see, include the TCO of all 'assets' consumed over the project deliverable's life) so that commercially astute decisions can be taken on projects (and those decisions will be reflected in the 'actuals' later).

6 *Do* implement timesheets for development staff and record the actual costs of projects. When I say 'actual costs' I mean the actual *billable* costs. Having to record the time you actually put into a project (and having to reconcile that with the price the user is prepared to pay) commercially concentrates the mind wonderfully. And please don't say that your staff wouldn't stand for it or that it would imply that you don't trust them. *Everyone* who works in any professional services firm (or ESP) fills in timesheets and is held accountable for the contents, from the most junior to the most senior, generally accounting for (and accountable for) 10–15 minute units of time. This is what commercial people do. (Virtually) no one is too 'important' to fill in a timesheet.

7 *Do* package products and services in such a way that they are both 'end to end' and clearly understandable to the user (i.e. 'price of bundled product/service' – the user will be very unlikely to understand a bill for his 'percentage' or measured utilization of a LAN but should understand what a 'desktop' is, as a 'package deal').

8 *Do* make users directly *accountable* for the costs 'billed', i.e. directly adjust their bottom line budgets to reflect IT resources (equipment or people) consumed. This *must* be at the point of 'IT consumption' if it is to have the desired effect.

9 *Do* ensure that when SLAs are being negotiated for production services that different cost vs service level packages are offered so that the user can influence his IT production costs, but ensure that this is *before* the service is offered so that it is *initially* implemented with *necessary and sufficient* service levels. Changes afterwards must be possible but this will be much more difficult to effect (since, for example, all you are doing, at least in the short term, is squeezing one user's costs

onto other users. If everyone suddenly decide to move from the 'Gold' service level to the 'Bronze' level everyone's bills would still be the same, at least in the short term.)

10 *Do* make prices 'honest', i.e. do not stack the odds in favour of 'making a profit' or 'avoiding making a loss'. The IT function is *not* a separate business. They are not going to have to file for bankruptcy or Chapter 11 protection if they fail to recover all their costs. And the shareholders are not going to vote you 'CIO of year' if you make a whopping 'profit' (because the IT function doesn't have any share-holders – other than the business, of course).

11 *Do not* be tempted to sell IT services externally. It will just take your eye off the ball (serving *your* business) and will tempt you to dark and evil practices (cross-subsidizing external work from internal work, to name but one); and, anyway, you will fool no one.

12 *Do not* 'financially' penalize the IT function for failure to achieve SLA targets. It is just an expensive administrative game involving 'wooden dollars'. Instead simply ensure that this is clearly measured and reported (see Chapter 5) and that there are serious *personal* consequences for failure (and, incidentally, serious rewards for success), i.e. start from a position of mutual trust but make people truly *accountable* for their actions.

13 *Do not* imagine that with such a transfer pricing regime you can fairly and meaningfully compare your internal tariffs/ prices with ESPs and make sourcing decisions on this basis. You can't. In fact, you very probably cannot even with the most sophisticated transfer pricing regime. It is much harder than that (and I will explain why in Chapter 5). Now readers who are concentrating may at this point want to remind me that only a few paragraphs above I cited the failure to benchmark the price of services as a critical *failure* factor. And here I am now suggesting that you shouldn't bother. I'm afraid it is rather a case of 'damned if you do, damned if you don't'. Understanding that what you are attempting to do is virtually impossible but cynically doing it anyway (because it is the only way to get the CFO off your back) is one approach. Refusing to do it and explaining clearly why to the CFO is another. The latter approach is certainly preferable (perhaps when the CIO is brave and the CFO is highly IT literate).

So what might we conclude about the virtues and vices of transfer charging? To *successfully* meet *any* of the six objectives set out at the start of this chapter depends generally on implementing transfer charging *and* SLAs 'with teeth'; to meet *most or all* of the objectives would almost certainly require implementation of the market pricing model and SLAs 'with teeth'.

Establishing the market pricing model and SLAs 'with teeth' successfully *should* greatly improve the commercial account-ability and culture of the IT function and control (and potentially reduce) IT costs. However, it is generally perceived to be time consuming and expensive to implement, maintain and admin-ister and, in the internal market, can prove politically divisive unless extremely well implemented, administered and managed.

The costs of developing and implementing charging mecha-nisms, administering the mechanisms, accounting and billing, software purchases to monitor user utilization and prepare bills, monitoring software running/licence costs, and so on in themselves can drive up costs. Indeed, in the case of one of my clients, 30 per cent of the mainframe was being used on average to run the monitoring and cost allocation systems. Therefore it is essential to have clear, agreed, documented objectives for implementing such a system and a clear understanding of both the potential benefits and potential costs and implications. A system that is expensive to run and administer, is little understood by users, does not engender appropriate user or IT behaviours, which would be expensive and complex to redesign and which is not actually mandated by the business, might better be simply avoided. But *without* transfer charging, how do you convincingly develop a commercial culture and commercial behaviours?

Because it underpins several of the value-adding CSFs set out below (in particular, 'optimize projects value' and 'optimize benefits realization') and many of the cost-efficiency practices set out in the next chapter, I will from now on *assume* that 'best value' transfer charging practices are in place.

3.6 IT governance

There is one more issue that I must 'get out of the way' before I set out the value-adding CSFs. That issue can be summed up in the word 'governance'. Just as *effective* transfer charging is an essential prerequisite to the success of a number of value-adding and cost-efficiency improvement practices, so they will not succeed without effective IT governance.

'IT governance' is a vogue and much bandied-about term with no clearly agreed definition or boundaries. I have heard it used in a wide variety of ways ranging from what I would call project direction and control, through financial direction and control to IT business management as a whole. For my purposes I am saying that it is about the relationship between the IT function and the business and how, specifically, the business manages and controls all its IT investments. Essentially I am saying that it is about establishing mechanisms to agree between the business and the IT function:

1 the IT function's funding levels in the context of business profitability and market/competitor trends;
2 the IT function's budgets for operating plan projects, discretionary projects (not identified in the operating plan), infrastructure projects/upgrades, enhancements (including work to develop feasibility studies), R&D/continuous performance improvement, and 'zero-based' legacy infrastructure and systems support and maintenance;
3 the IT function's policies, 'strategic role' (e.g. cost/investment/service/profit centre) and operating principles (consistent with fulfilling its agreed strategic role);
4 the IT function's competency development requirements (and/or strategic alliances to redress competency shortfalls);
5 the long-term applications strategy and technology strategy;
6 the IT function's objectives, in the context of the business's objectives;
7 the projects to be approved, delayed or rejected, balancing project priorities and investments *across* the business (and assessing them against other *non*-IT investment requests);
8 the ongoing projects to be continued, rescoped or terminated;
9 the production systems to be replaced or terminated;
10 the extent to which the IT function is hitting quality, value-added, cost-efficiency and effectiveness targets.

The final point, the measurement of the success of the IT function from a value delivery point of view, I will deal with at length in Chapter 5. The rest of this chapter is principally concerned with optimizing points 6 to 9 because I contend that it is here that the greatest opportunities exist for maximizing business value-added.

The mechanisms to achieve these 10 points will require a combination of organizational groups, processes, systems and controls. In particular, it will almost certainly be necessary to establish at least two 'IT governance' committees, one meeting relatively infrequently to address major investments and programmes and strategic issues (this group is sometimes called the 'Office of Enterprise IT', and would typically include the CIO and business division heads), and one to meet more frequently to address the review, approval and monitoring of smaller investments (typically including business departmental managers and their corresponding IT manager). Major programmes or projects might also require 'standing committees'. A specialist committee focused on technology direction would almost certainly also be required.

On the subject of IT budgets I have found that many organizations (in particular, the CFOs of organizations) balk at the idea of the 'discretionary budget' I suggested above. But what are they suggesting? That no one is going to come up with a business idea during the year that needs IT funding and didn't happen to be in the operating plan? And anyway, in my experience typically 10 per cent to 15 per cent of the IT function's operating plan budget is unspent at year end because of delays in starting projects or simply changes of mind. So it will probably all balance out in the end. In fact, this is what CIOs tend to do (on the quiet, of course) anyway. So why not do it honestly? Remember (CFOs), that it is not so much the beans that are spent which is important – it is the value *derived* from those beans. So just say to your CFO bean counter, '*Chill*, man'.

3.7 CSFs for optimizing business value-added

So, *assuming* that value-added is a key goal (which, recalling the SAM model set out in the previous chapter, will be very much the case where the IT function operates as an investment centre, less the case where it operates as a profit centre or service centre, and least the case where it operates as a cost centre) *generally* what are the things we most critically need to do most effectively in our IT function in order to optimize business value-added, i.e. what are the CSFs for optimizing business value-added?

These CSFs affect various IT practices. I am contending that improving value-add to the business can typically best be achieved by focusing practice effectiveness improvements on:

- **Optimizing IT function alignment:** optimizing the strategic alignment of the IT function with the business it serves (so they share common commercial goals).

- **Optimizing competitive advantage:** optimizing the identification of IT opportunities that will yield the highest business competitive advantage.
- **Optimizing portfolio alignment:** optimizing the alignment between the products of the IT function and the priority needs of the business units that they support (so they facilitate the business unit achieving *its* commercial goals).
- **Optimizing portfolio value:** optimizing the value (alignment/cost/benefit/risk) of the planned project portfolio.
- **Optimizing value delivery:** *sustaining* the value-adding imperative throughout the process of developing projects in the portfolio.
- **Optimizing benefits realization:** optimizing the realization of promised project benefits.

Is there any evidence to suggest that addressing these CSFs should increase the probability of project success and benefits realization? Well, in Britain, the House of Commons' Committee of Public Accounts issued a report in 1999 examining the delivery of government IT projects. This concluded that the key root causes for the many troubled public sector projects were:

- lack of senior management commitment and involvement [IT governance with respect to all 6 CSFs];
- failure to focus on key business and end-user needs [Optimizing alignment and competitive advantage];
- failure to break complex projects into manageable, separately contracted units [Optimizing value delivery];
- poor and unimaginative project management ('project management by numbers') [Optimizing value delivery];
- insufficient focus on user education to extract the benefits [Optimizing benefits realization].

The text in square brackets sets out the correspondence between these root causes and my proposed CSFs for optimizing IT product and service delivery effectiveness in order to optimize value-added.

Turning more to the private sector, the IBM book *Troubled IT Projects* (ISBN 0852961049) includes in its list of root causes very similar issues:

- lack of senior management commitment [IT governance];
- unrealistic business case [Optimizing value delivery];
- failure to define clear benefits [Optimizing value delivery];

- failure to break complex projects into smaller projects [Optimizing value delivery];
- poor project management, planning and execution [Optimizing value delivery];
- poor change control [Optimizing value delivery];
- failure to undertake project reviews and take decisive action [Optimizing value delivery];
- inadequate user training [Optimizing benefits realization];
- failure to measure benefits delivered [Optimizing benefits realization].

Basically, these value delivery problems are endemic across the IT industry.

3.8 CSF exclusions

Now I appreciate that many of you may have reacted with some shock to my six 'value-adding CSFs'. Maybe you are saying, 'But what about optimizing systems requirements specification? What about optimizing system design? What about optimizing testing? What, for goodness sake, about optimizing quality management?' Look, if you were right I would be the first to agree with you. Sorry, but these systems development management practices simply do not make the cut when the key criterion is *business value-adding*. With the arguable exclusion of rapid application development (RAD) best practices, systems development management 'best practices' are principally about increasing the predictability of systems delivery, increasing the reliability of the delivered system and reducing post-implementation maintenance and support costs. It is secondarily about improving the functional quality of the system delivered. And it will almost certainly cost more and take longer to deliver systems using these practices. This is not my idea of 'high value-adding', at least not relative to the CSFs I have set out. Please understand that I am not (entirely) attacking the 'waterfall' approach of conventional structured systems development methods *per se*. If you are developing a huge, complex, interdependent suite of systems of the likes of SAP or Peoplesoft then you are going to need this level of structure and formality. On the other hand, if you are developing a huge, complex, interdependent suite of systems of the likes of SAP or Peoplesoft, why aren't you buying SAP or Peoplesoft (or whatever)? Are your needs *really* so unique, or so business transformational, as to justify a development that very probably has a low chance of success and will anyway cost a multiple of what a package addressing your main needs will cost (and take many times as long to deliver)? As to best practice quality management, this is typically concerned with assuring compliance with documented processes (best practice or otherwise). Compliance with a process is not at all necessarily value-adding (or even necessarily quality adding – unless you disregard the cost of quality).

I'm sure you would pay serious money for me *not* to repeat all the arguments I set out in Chapter 2 for why I believe that 'conventional best practice' is wholly inadequate where value-added is the imperative. So let me just briefly relate one of my more instructive experiences of 'conventional best practice' in systems development. This came some years ago when I was responsible for the IT best practice model in one of the 'Big 6/5/4' management consultancy firms. Our consultancy teams performed 'diagnostic reviews' of IT functions, assessing their strengths and weaknesses against the model. This required us to capture and analyse literally thousands of items of information, including typically hundreds of questionnaires. This was extremely time consuming and error prone. Therefore we made the business case for largely automating the process of data capture, analysis and graphical report production. For the first, and only, time in my life, I was then the project sponsor, the user, on an IT project being performed by our consultancy firm's internal IT function. Suddenly I was a gamekeeper turned poacher. The developers were required to comply with the 'SSADM-equivalent' internal systems development methodology, complete with its requirements specifications, sign-offs and scope controls. The system was developed as a Visual Basic front end on top of an Access database.

The experience of this development was a nightmare for all concerned. Although the algorithms required for questionnaire analysis were very well defined, we, the users, had little idea of the form of the graphic outputs that would best illustrate the results to the client. Our ideas changed rapidly as we saw early outputs from the system. We also had little understanding of the strengths and (extensive) limitations of VB and so (as it turned out) ended up shaping the requirements in such a way as to be extremely expensive to design and develop the solution. For their part, the developers clearly knew a lot about VB and absolutely nothing about how a management consultant worked. The user interface on the first release of the system was absolutely appalling. After a series of acrimonious emails I eventually insisted that the IT project manager come up from his remote 'lair' to London for a day to work through our problems. When he arrived I immediately sat him in a room and placed in front of him a box of questionnaires from a previous diagnostic review and told him to process them through the system. After an hour of this he was going quietly mad with frustration at the use of his own system. That was a turning point in the relationship and the system. Basically, the traditional 'waterfall' systems development 'best practices' simply did not work for such a development in which the requirements were extremely fluid, the users had little understanding of the limitations of the technology and the developers had little real understanding of how the business practitioner actually worked. But isn't that a description of many/most IT projects? I use this example simply to help illustrate why I am thoroughly unconvinced that systems development 'best practices' generally optimize commercial outcomes, whatever their arguable merits in the predictability of solution delivery.

Basically, everyone within a particular IT discipline will doubtless have a particular axe to grind. The only axe I am grinding here is the value axe, and I'm grinding it ruthlessly. To help illustrate the 'axe grinding' problem, let me briefly cite a task I was once given to develop a comprehensive activity dictionary for IT functions. I started by asking consultancy colleagues from a wide variety of IT disciplines to give me their list of the 10 top level activities of the typical 'full service', insourced IT function that I could then generalize and subsequently break down into lower levels of detail. One colleague gave me a list that included nine network management activities and then, almost as an afterthought, squeezed in 'develop applications' at number 10. Yes, he was a consultant specializing in network management in whose mind the essential reason for an IT function's existence was the provision of the telecommunications infrastructure. *My* definition of the essential reason for an IT function's existence is the delivery of business value.

3.9 Defining the effectiveness improvement goal

Improvements in effectiveness (on the supply side of the value compass), by deploying best practices, will improve the quality of products and services supplied (on the demand side). Improvements in effectiveness (on the supply side), by deploying best *value* practices, will improve the value-added by products and services (on the demand side). Therefore my goal in this chapter is to optimize the value that IT adds to the business by focusing on deploying key 'best value practices' in support of the six value-adding CSFs set out above. The way in which these are achieved is essentially about creating 'value portals' through which solutions must pass if they are to continue to be developed or run.

Note that just as the cost of rectifying defects rises dramatically (potentially exponentially) as you pass through the systems development life-cycle, so I believe the value of adopting 'best value practices' is at its highest at an early point in the life-cycle, because the earlier we focus on high value-adding work and the earlier we choke non-viable work, the better. Therefore let's first look at the issue of 'strategic alignment', at the start of the life-cycle.

Over the years I have interviewed numerous senior business managers to determine their views of their IT functions. The single most common quote is words to the effect of, 'They have their agenda and we have ours.' The typical perception of senior managers is that the IT function does not truly understand the needs and priorities of the business and often substitutes its 'technology-driven' view of needs and priorities, not because it has any desire whatsoever to undermine the business but just because this is a worldview with which they are most comfortable. The next most common quotes (I am obviously paraphrasing and generalizing, but with justification) are:

- 'Not only do they not have a customer service culture, they don't even really understand what that looks like.'
- 'They know their tekky stuff but they are not commercially focused.'
- 'They are generally not proactive – they are basically reactive to who shouts loudest.'
- 'They have a poor leadership team.'

If the last quote applies to your IT function there is, frankly, not much I can do to help here. But this book can help to address the other criticisms. At their root is a lack of alignment between the IT function and the business, a lack of 'proactiveness' by the IT function in identifying and promoting value-adding IT solutions and the creation of 'strategic portfolios' of IT solutions that are often driven more by internal political games than by commercial priorities. These are addressed by the first three value-adding CSFs.

3.10 The issue of alignment

The Institute of Value Management states that a root principle of value management is 'a focus on objectives and targets before seeking solutions'. This is about 'alignment'. The goal of IT and business alignment is to focus the limited IT resources on maximizing the delivery of value from IT product and service delivery by focusing on the priority business needs. Alignment can be effected at different 'levels' from the 'strategic' (e.g. aligning specific programmes of projects on the long-term priority needs of senior management) to the 'tactical' (e.g. aligning specific projects on the short-term priority needs of specific business units). Balance is typically required. Excessive focus at the strategic level may compromise customer satisfaction at the business middle-management level while excessive focus at the tactical level may compromise customer satisfaction at the business senior management level. Note also that the 'strategic' and 'tactical' can overlap and can extend beyond the boundaries of the business, as when synergy benefits are identified across business units, suppliers or business partners.

IT/business alignment can be viewed as a four-dimensional model, the first three of which are illustrated in Figure 3.2. The fourth dimension is time (which I will come to presently).

The business executive team will typically be most concerned with 'strategic alignment' issues (perhaps thinking two to three

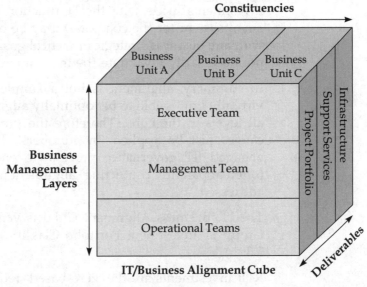

Figure 3.2   *Source*: Gartner

years forward), the management team will typically be concerned with aligning the portfolio with their immediate (one year forward?) business unit priorities, while the operational teams will typically be most concerned with 'tactical alignment' issues ('is my system meeting my priority needs today?'). The executive team will typically be prepared to sacrifice tactical goals in pursuit of strategic goals. Where insufficient guidance is given to the IT function as to the strategic direction of the business served, the focus of the IT function's work will tend to be on tactical alignment (and meeting the priority needs of middle management). The place in which the tensions between strategic and tactical alignment are debated and resolved is the governance process, set out above. The business operational teams are typically most concerned with IT service delivery (including the quality of the delivered systems, services and support). 'Alignment' here is principally about supplying commercially *necessary and sufficient* quality products and services.

The fourth dimension on the IT/Business Alignment Cube is time. This reflects the fact that different layers in the model are focused on alignment in different timeframes and the fact that it is difficult to say *at any one point in time* whether or not an IT function and its products and services are optimally aligned because business strategic (and tactical) priorities change with time and the IT function cannot respond instantaneously (especially if its applications and/or technology infrastructure is 'locked into' the supply of products and services that will not optimally meet new strategies). Note also that infrastructure investments made with the IT function (e.g. to implement an email system for the company) may be only tenuously aligned with any business strategic or tactical goal. But that in itself does not necessarily invalidate the investment.

In summary, alignment is not a simple issue. Basically, it is virtually impossible to be 'optimally aligned' at all times and at all levels in the cube. Therefore the practices I set out below cannot just be applied 'by numbers'. It will require a fully engaged 'IT governance process' to ensure that the various (often apparently conflicting) alignment needs are balanced and addressed.

The IT/Business Alignment Cube is very similar to the Meta Group IT Investment Portfolio Classification set out in Figure 3.3.

RTB investments are the 'zero-based' requirements to keep the business running. GTB investments expand the products or

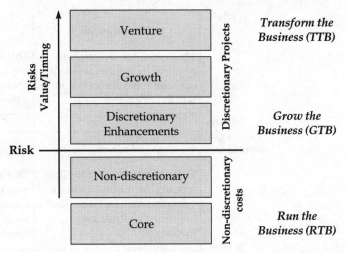

Figure 3.3

Source: Meta Group – 'The Business of IT Portfolio Management' (02.02)

services of the business. TTB investments involve moving into new markets. A 'balanced portfolio' of projects will typically include a range from RTB to TTB. If the IT function is (from a SAM alignment point of view) predominantly a cost centre then RTB projects will tend to take precedence. If the IT function is predominantly an investment centre then TTB projects will tend to take precedence. As with the 'IT/Business Alignment Cube', the portfolio mix will vary over time as business objectives and economic conditions change. The overriding goal, however, will tend to be to maximize cost-efficiency in order to minimize RTB costs and maximize the effectiveness of portfolio management practices to maximize value-added to the business and so support GTB and TTB goals.

A further simple but powerful technique for debating the strategic alignment of the portfolio is to place each proposed solution on the McFarlan grid (Applegate, McFarlan and McKenny, 1996), as illustrated in Figure 3.4.

A 'balanced portfolio' of projects will typically include initiatives ranging from support to strategic. 'Cost centre' IT functions will tend to focus on support projects to reduce business costs while 'investment centre' IT functions will tend to focus on strategic projects to support/drive business profitability.

Below I set out key practices (best value practices) for optimizing IT/business alignment. However, please note that the key driver of good IT/business alignment is arguably personal

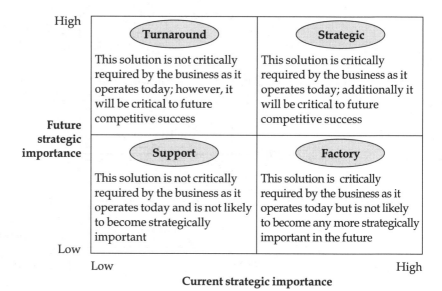

Turnaround	**Strategic**
This solution is not critically required by the business as it operates today; however, it will be critical to future competitive success	This solution is critically required by the business as it operates today; additionally it will be critical to future competitive success
Support	**Factory**
This solution is not critically required by the business as it operates today and is not likely to become strategically important	This solution is critically required by the business as it operates today but is not likely to become any more strategically important in the future

High — Future strategic importance — Low

Low — Current strategic importance — High

Figure 3.4

relationships rather than any formal process. A CIO whose role is integral to the business senior management team, is well respected by the business and has a close relationship with his peers will very probably 'intuit' well-aligned products and services (and so have less critical need for the practices I set out below).

First, we want to design best value practices that will help to ensure that the IT function and the business are 'singing to the same song sheet'.

3.11 Optimizing IT function alignment

Our objective here is to ensure that the IT function 'as a business', and the business it serves, are strategically aligned, so helping to optimize the value that the IT function as a whole adds to the business. Basically we want to move way beyond the typical 'IT strategy' which can be characterized by the business dictate, 'Do this for me, and don't screw up.'

To achieve this we need first to ensure that the business agrees *specific* objectives for IT product and service delivery from the IT function. These will typically be focused on the delivery of (the IT part of) specific business projects in a specific time frame (e.g. develop and implement *that* system by date X, roll out *that* system across American sites by date Y, roll out XP to all desktops by date Z). They may also be focused on the performance of specific IT 'internal' projects in a specific

timeframe (e.g. implement *that* systems development methodology by date *P*, implement transfer pricing by date *Q*, build and
commission disaster recovery data centre by date *R*). They may
also be specific IT function cost-efficiency objectives, typically in
terms of reducing costs (e.g. reduce proportion of contractors,
reduce data centre operational costs, reduce support budgets).
They may even be specific business value-adding objectives,
typically in terms of helping the business achieve 'competitive
advantage', reduce its business overhead costs, increase revenues or increase margins.

A 'good' (i.e. 'balanced') set of IT function objectives agreed
with the business will cover aspects of *what* is to be delivered
(e.g. specific systems), *how* it is to be delivered (i.e. practices), *at
what cost* it is to be delivered, *what quality* is to be delivered and
what value is to be added, i.e. it will set out and agree both product
delivery objectives *and* value delivery objectives (if only by
phrasing the product delivery objective in such a way as to
clearly define also the outcomes/benefits expected).

All these IT function objectives need to be rigorously tested to
ensure that they are articulated in such a way as to be truly
SMART (i.e. Specific, Measurable, Achievable, Relevant and
Timebound). This is essential if we are going to able to measure
success (as set out in Chapter 5). They also need to be
challenging and they should be selected on some rigorous basis
that helps to determine which *specific* objectives will contribute
most to the achievement of the high level business key
performance objectives. They may also be weighed to reflect, for
example, the relative priorities of cost-efficiency and effectiveness (as suggested by the 'SAM positioning'). Note that I am
assuming that the business actually *has* a set of high level
objectives. I am also assuming that they are much less banal and
much more specific than the typical 'visionary' type of clichéd,
motherhood objectives of 'pic'n'mix' management jargon that
read something like, 'Maximize shareholder value by being a
customer-led, innovative, world class market leader in the
provision of extruded plastic gnomes to the global
marketplace.'

This mapping between business and IT function objectives can
be achieved quite simply by constructing a matrix of the
business's objectives against the objectives proposed for the IT
function and then rating each intersection with something
like:

–1 = actively hinders the achievement of business objectives (so why are you even thinking about doing it)

0 = no direct contribution to the achievement of business objectives

1 = no direct contribution to the achievement of business objectives but supports another IT function objective that contributes to the achievement of business objectives

2 = does not directly contribute, but is a prerequisite to another IT function objective that contributes to the achievement of business objectives

3 = does not directly contribute, but is a prerequisite to another IT function objective that directly achieves business objectives

4 = directly contributes to the achievement of business objectives

5 = directly achieves business objectives

This simple approach can also profitably be used to help agree 'weightings' on each IT function objective (according to the extent to which it supports business objectives). In the traditional 'management by objectives' manner, the high level IT function objectives must then be cascaded down through the IT function management structure to set specific performance objectives for 'all' IT management and staff. Measures (key performance indicators – KPIs), and KPI targets, to assess the extent to which the objectives are being achieved, should be set at all levels and reviewed periodically. So, for example, if one of the IT function's internal objectives is to implement a specific systems development methodology by year end, a 'downstream' KPI might be, 'Has it been implemented?' This is an example of a very bad objective and KPI! Why? Because it tells us nothing about *why* we wanted to do this in the first place, i.e. it tells us nothing about the outcomes/benefits we were presumably seeking. Better would be an objective to implement the methodology *in order to* achieve a Software Engineering Institute (SEI) Capability Maturity Modelling (CMM) rating with, say, a KPI target of achieving CMM Level 2. Better still would be measures that directly reflect the *value* of the objective, in terms of cost-efficiency improvement or business value-adding improvement (e.g. reduce systems support budgets by 15 per cent year-on-year). Indeed the greatest benefit of the entire objectives/KPIs development process is precisely in forcing you to really think through the value of what you are planning to do, and its real priority. 'Objectives' and 'CSFs' are often confused (or just plain thought through lazily). Objectives should as far as possible be phrased in a manner that sets out the achievement of a benefit. CSFs set out the things you most critically have to do well in order to achieve that objective. 'Achieve benefit X' is a good objective. 'Do thing Y in order to achieve benefit X' is a good CSF. For example, 'Implement XP across all desktops' is really a CSF. It only becomes an objective if it is accompanied by the benefits that are sought by performing this activity.

Note that the likelihood of the company's objectives being stable over the period of a year is probably negligible. Therefore there must be the ability to amend the IT function's objectives, KPIs and targets throughout the year. There is a great deal more to be said about creating a good set of KPIs but I will leave that until Chapter 5, 'Measuring success'.

Many IT functions today deploy similar approaches to this objectives setting regime (although typically without even the '−1 to 5' ratings scheme). However, in my experience they often are poor at actually achieving the 'mutual alignment' goal (as is evidenced by the senior management quotes I set out at the start of this chapter). One of the typical reasons is that objectives are often 'visionary' (sometimes my euphemism for 'lazy and useless') rather than being truly SMART, i.e. they are not thought through in a disciplined, rigorous way to ensure that they will make a *real* difference to people's behaviour. Another is that the objectives are often focused more on delivering specific projects than genuinely achieving business performance goals, i.e. they are essentially phrased as CSFs rather than outcome/benefit delivering objectives. However, I believe that the key reason for the often poor delivery of alignment is *lack of accountability*.

The obvious mechanism to use for setting management and staff objectives and measures is the annual (or, sometimes, bi-annual) staff performance review (and, again, I am *assuming* you actually *have* such reviews and that they are conducted rigorously and without exception). Even when business objectives-driven individual performance objectives are set, they will rarely pass the SMART tests (which they *must*, even though it can take considerable ingenuity to phrase the objectives in such a way that they do) and there are rarely any serious (or even significant) consequences for failure to meet objectives and achieve targets (or, conversely, positive consequences for meet-ing or exceeding targets). Basically, the management and staff collude in a game in which they go through the motions of 'cascaded objectives' without there being any real, disciplined commitment to the spirit of the process. It's got to be serious or it is worse than pointless.

My own experience is interesting here (and I strongly suspect not atypical). When I worked for one of the big management consultancy firms, I found myself in the position of changing managers on average every year for a period of many years. This, I'm afraid, is an endemic problem in the dynamic world of consulting where people tend to move around quickly. I played a little game at each annual performance appraisal in which I agreed a personal development objective with my manager and then pointedly did absolutely nothing about it. At the end of every year either the fact that the objective had not been met was simply ignored or was simply 'registered'. Every year we then reset the same objective. It was a joke, but not a very funny joke because if the process is so obviously just a game it actually is not only not value-adding, it is positively value-reducing because of the time wasted and the cynicism engendered. Once again, it's got to be serious. If you are not going to do it seriously, don't do it at all. By the way, the personal development objective I ignored every year was, 'To complete the "Selling to the Board" training programme'. I (silently) refused to attend this on the grounds of my experience attending the predecessor course, 'General Selling Skills'. This recommended the technique called 'SOFTEN', a six letter acronym that had the one virtue of being quite memorable. It told you that the way to sell consultancy to someone was to Smile a lot, use Open gestures, lean Forward in rapt attention to what the client was saying, find opportunities to Touch him/her (lawyers please note!), maintain Eye contact at all times and repeatedly Nod your agreement with whatever nonsense the client is saying. Our syndicate having learnt this valuable lesson on the course, I was then selected (big mistake) to represent my syndicate and stand on a platform before the other course attendees and 'sell' the SOFTEN approach to them as part of a role-playing exercise. I did this by applying *all* the SOFTEN techniques simultaneously. Try it. It's hilarious (well everyone in the room, apart from the instructors, cracked up). So the next time you see a management consultant having a fit, don't worry, it's OK, he's just trying to sell you something. Seriously, people buy from people they trust (provided they can afford it) – you don't have to 'soften' them up with sleazeball sales techniques (such as faking sincerity). An underlying goal of this book is get the relationship between the IT function and its internal customers onto a basis of greater trust so they positively *want* to 'do business' with each other.

Even in the best (i.e. best practice) implementation of personal objectives setting I have seen (in a major IT function serving a 'semi-privatized' government agency) in which the extent of achievement of objectives was fed into an algorithm that computed a performance related bonus, the bonus was so laughably low as to be utterly irrelevant in terms of conditioning behaviour. Basically, if you were inept and hopelessly failed to meet your performance objectives you could, in theory, get a zero bonus. If you wildly exceeded your objectives (in which case they were probably not exactly 'stretch' targets) then you could theoretically get 100 per cent of the available 'potential bonus per person' pot. The trouble was that the 'potential bonus per person' pot was less than 3 per cent of base pay! So the attitude of the staff was, of course, 'what's the point?' That was one of the *best* implementations I have personally seen (although I'm told companies in the USA often fare better). In the typical implementation the only 'connect' between the achievement of performance objectives and reward is the much more subtle (and far less effective) one of the 'jam tomorrow' of promotion. Furthermore, the world will almost certainly have moved on since the performance objectives were originally agreed and this is often used as an excuse for the current irrelevancy of the measures when they come round to be assessed (usually a year after they were originally agreed). Worst of all is where the reward mechanism is not tied to *individual* performance but overall *company* performance. This is fine (and necessary) for establishing the size of the 'reward pot' but is quite hopeless as an incentive because it will not condition individual behaviour. Basically, 'best value practice' for optimizing IT function alignment must include *serious consequences* for both success and failure *at an individual level*.

Note that if any of this is to succeed then senior business management must commit the time and energy to the disciplined objectives/KPIs setting process and pay much more than 'lip service' to these 'IT governance' responsibilities. I last attempted this at a client whose senior managers had moaned repeatedly about their IT function 'having its own agenda'. Consequently an 'IT governance' inaugural meeting was convened with the directors of all of the six business divisions served by the IT function, initially to address the 'agenda issue'.

A presentation had, of course, been prepared explaining the process of the agreement of objectives and KPIs for the IT function. This presentation also set out the case for the importance of this process in aligning the business and IT function agendas. The meeting started (and stopped) with seven people in the room, the CIO, five members of his management team, and me. After around 15 minutes of sitting around drinking cups of excellent coffee and discussing the previous night's television we had received calls from the secretaries of three of the divisional directors sending their apologies. They had suddenly found other (more important) things to do. After 20 minutes, the remaining three directors bustled in and one immediately said that he had another meeting to attend but would try to get back later. The remaining two sat fidgeting for around 15 minutes (one openly replying to emails on his laptop) before announcing that they too had other meetings to attend. And then there were none. Basically their attitude was that they asked the IT function for systems, the IT function told them what it would cost and then they told the IT function whether or not they could afford it. Then, because the total cost was typically twice the budget set for the IT function, a bun fight would be conducted while the divisional directors shouted one another down in order to get the biggest slice possible of the IT cake for themselves. And *then* they complained about the fact that the IT function didn't understand their agenda! Actually, they quickly got the agenda message – shut up and just get on with doing what I tell you to do. Once again, tacit (if understandable) collusion in a deeply flawed process.

Either business managers have to understand the need for a clear agreement of common goals or the process has to be mandated from on high. Otherwise it will either not happen at all or, as was the case above, the IT function has to 'guess' the agenda on behalf of the business, which makes a farce of the entire process. Senior management cannot have it both ways. They cannot both complain about the IT function's agenda *and* not contribute to the shaping of that agenda.

Next, we want to implement 'best value practices' that will help to ensure that the IT function identifies solutions that enhance the competitiveness of the business.

3.12 Optimizing competitive advantage

Our goal is to ensure that the information systems architecture and plans reflect (and exploit) technology capabilities and directions, so helping to optimize the value that the IT function as a whole adds to the business. Note that I am not concerning myself here with how long-term (three to five years) business and strategic systems planning as a whole are performed. This is obviously important but does not pass my 'test' of being 'key value-adding', i.e. with a limited budget of time, money and energy, improvements in 'best practice' in this area will be unlikely to add high value to the business. If you want business strategy, talk to people like McKinsey or Bain. And all of the major management consultancy firms have methodologies for how to perform strategic systems planning to develop a three to five year plan. Such methodologies typically include business vision development, strategic business analysis, business modelling and strategic risk assessment with a view to developing strategic systems, technology and data architectures. The key time for such formal approaches is when you are in a complex, changing business situation (such as a merger or acquisition) or when your current approach is little more than a 'bottom-up' collation of system requirements agreed with each business division (resulting in a 'wish list' which is subsequently debated for IT budgetary planning purposes). No, my key value-adding practice is concerned with working with the business to identify competitive advantage opportunities from IT.

These opportunities will often be raised during the annual process in which the IT function's operating plan is agreed (primarily in order to agree the following year's budget for the IT function). The objectives of such work are typically to:

- develop an understanding of the business and its immediate plans;
- develop an understanding of the current and future role of technology within the business;
- position the business against the external environment, its competitive threats, market trends, and regulatory or political constraints;
- identify potential business opportunities where technology can be used to enhance that position (by growing or transforming the business).

Through this (short-term strategic systems planning) process the IT function (in collaboration with the business) must identify opportunities to:

- create defensive entry barriers (i.e. make it more difficult for competitors to arise);

- increase customer switching costs (i.e. make it more difficult for customers to switch suppliers);
- increase retailer switching costs (i.e. make it more difficult for retailers of your products to switch suppliers);
- change the ground rules of competition;
- change business competition from being cost based (i.e. a commodity) to being based on sustainable product differentiation;
- help build links (and lock in) suppliers;
- help generate new products and services;
- help establish new product distribution channels;
- help facilitate or establish business collaborations or joint ventures;
- help improve the image of the business.

This needs to be done in the context of an understanding of the strategic use of IT by competitors (and the IT industry as a whole).

Potential opportunities could be assessed (a 'competitive impact' assessment) for their 'competitive advantage potential' using a simple scale such as:

–1 = the solution would actively hinder achieving competitive advantage

0 = the solution would deliver no competitive advantage

1 = the solution would not directly deliver any competitive advantage but should deliver operational efficiencies that deliver a degree of competitive advantage

2 = the solution would not deliver any competitive advantage but supports other solutions that should deliver a degree of competitive advantage

3 = the solution would not deliver any competitive advantage but supports other solutions that should deliver a high degree of competitive advantage

4 = the solution should directly deliver a degree of competitive advantage

5 = the solution should directly deliver a high degree of competitive advantage

Competitive advantage opportunities are not always technology driven. However, organizations that make extensive use of technology to gain competitive advantage are commonly called

Gartner 'Type A'. They are often willing to risk using immature technologies (and often at an expensive point in their life-cycle) to gain the desired edge. 'Type B' organizations only adopt technologies after they have been proven (in which case their competitors may have stolen the edge). 'Type C' organizations are risk averse and are usually the last to adopt newer technologies. Remember that although we are focusing on the value-added quadrant of the value compass here and are therefore seeking 'Type A' opportunities, the cost-efficiency' quadrant must be considered too, namely, the inevitable increase in IT costs (and risks) associated with such an approach.

3.13 Optimizing portfolio alignment

Next, we want to implement 'best value practices' that will help to ensure that the planned portfolio of IT solutions will effectively support business processes and are aligned with business strategy, i.e. ensure that delivered IT solutions actually contribute optimally to the achievement of the performance targets set for the business units using them (or information provided by them). This is about optimizing the value of the project portfolio as a whole, i.e. defining the 'best' portfolio from the point of view of early delivery of the highest benefits. If this portfolio is derived from a 'strategic systems planning' exercise that attempts to look three to five years into the future, then great. I am very happy for you and wonder what kind of business you are working in that can possibly look with any confidence that far into the future. It is more likely that the 'default' portfolio reflecting the IT priorities within business units will be agreed annually (as part of the agreement of the IT function operating plan, as discussed above) and then used to shape the project portfolio that actually emerges with time. Projects that are identified during the subsequent year obviously cannot be ignored 'because they are not on the list'. But new requirements must be validated against the list to ensure that their priority is seen in context.

The ITIL library's book *Application Management* says this about systems portfolio alignment: 'The biggest challenge for IT in today's rapidly changing business environment is in accurately aligning IT projects with well-understood business objectives. In many cases the IT projects themselves are ill-conceived and/or the business objectives are poorly understood.' Our goal here, therefore, is to optimize the alignment of the systems portfolio with business objectives. This can be performed quite simply by constructing a matrix of the business unit performance targets against the IT solutions proposed to support those business units and rating each intersection using a simple scale, such as:

–1 = would actively hinder the achievement of business performance targets

0 = would make no direct contribution to the achievement of business performance targets

1 = the solution would not directly contribute to the achievement of business performance targets but should deliver operational efficiencies that deliver a degree of support for business performance targets

2 = would not directly contribute, but is a prerequisite to another system that should contribute to the achievement of business performance target

3 = would not directly contribute, but is a prerequisite to another system that should directly achieve business performance target

4 = should directly contribute to the achievement of business performance target

5 = should directly achieve business performance target

Note that this 'strategic impact' evaluation may have to be conducted at different levels in the 'strategic alignment cube' to build a 'balanced portfolio' that meets the priority needs of different levels of business management with different time horizons. Note also the *assumption* that each business unit actually *has* an agreed set of objectives/KPIs.

We now want to construct the highest value-adding portfolio of potential IT solutions. This will build on the strategic foundations we set above in optimizing the portfolio alignment.

3.14 Optimizing portfolio value

The traditional approach to authorizing and prioritizing investments (not just in IT) has been to focus on ROI (return on investment) rather than 'value' in its broadest commercial sense, including ROI, competitive advantage, alignment and risk. As Terry White puts it in *Reinventing the IT Department*, 'A simple

ROI equation – net income divided by net assets – has led us astray. Because it is always easier to measure and manage the denominator (assets, capital employed, costs, headcount, etc.) than to take a position on the numerator (income, new business, etc.). Because nearly everything in the denominator is internal to the organisation – and in general in the past – while the numerator deals with the creation of value, of risk-taking, of abandoning the old and taking on the new. Ask any executive where his or her information needs really lie. It is in the numerator, in the external, in the future. Then ask the average IT person where they spend their efforts.' This is why I emphasize assessing and prioritizing the project portfolio on a range of value measures, not just ROI. But you certainly cannot ignore costs, benefits and risks. Therefore here (in *addition* to the competitive impact and strategic impact raised above) we want a high level assessment (the 'economic impact') of the likely return on investment (ROI) for each proposed project, scoring each solution proposed on a simple scale such as:

–1 = likely costs exceed likely benefits (over the life of the anticipated solution)

0 = likely costs equal likely benefits. No payback

1 = marginal positive ROI

2 = positive ROI, but probably not above the organization's hurdle rate (i.e. the level of ROI necessary to gain approval for investment)

3 = positive ROI, approximately at the organization's hurdle rate

4 = positive ROI, probably exceeding the organization's hurdle rate

5 = positive ROI, very probably exceeding organization's hurdle rate by more than 100 per cent

These rather crass assessments of ROI are probably as good as can reasonably be expected at this early 'work request' stage (given that the requirement is still very probably ill-defined and the means of delivery also ill-defined). Clearly, however, if more accurate ROI data is available (as might be the case where a package solution has been 'pre-selected') then this should be input to the process. Note that I am using 'ROI' as a generic term here. Your organization may use other economic valuing techniques, such as sustainable cashflow return on investment

(CFROI), economic value sourced (EVS), economic value added (EVA), risk-adjusted net present value (NPV), return on net assets (RONA), market value added (MVA) or, indeed, a combination of these. I fully accept that there are certain projects for which ROI is virtually undeterminable (such as implementing an email system, and other such 'infrastructural' changes) and which will be justified as 'acts of faith'. Fine, but be very, very careful before you allow too many eggs to be dropped into this basket.

We can also make a high level assessment (the 'management information impact' assessment) of the extent to which the potential solution will provide management information support of core business activities. This can be evaluated using a simple scale, such as:

−1 = the solution could be expected to provide inadequate, misleading or out-of-date management information

0 = the solution is not intended to provide new management information

1 = the solution is not intended to provide new management information, but does provide some information on functions that directly support core business activities

2 = the solution is not intended to provide new management information, but provides information on functions that directly support core business activities

3 = the solution is not intended to provide new management information but provides essential information on functions identified as core business activities

4 = the solution will be essential to providing key management information in the future

5 = the solution will be essential to providing key management information

We now have four key 'value' assessments of each candidate IT solution in the total potential project portfolio, namely, the competitive impact, the strategic impact, the economic impact and the management information impact. These are four key inputs to the information economics approach to selecting the commercially optimum (highest value) portfolio. The information economics approach sets out high level criteria for assessing competing potential IT solutions on a more objective basis than the traditional 'shouting match'. I do not suggest that you simply award scores and the biggest numbers 'win'. But it is an excellent way to help think through the way alternative portfolios might add optimum value to the business. Note that some of the criteria contribute positive value and others negative value.

Business domain factors

Economic impact: (+) The indicative ROI

Strategic impact: (+) The degree to which the project is aligned with corporate strategic objectives

Competitive impact: (+) The degree to which the project should deliver competitive advantage

Management information impact: (+) The degree of management information provision for key corporate activities

Project risk: (–) The degree to which the initiative is dependent on new or untested management capabilities and experience

Benefits realization risk: (–) The degree to which the initiative is likely to face significant barriers to actually realizing the benefits promised

Competitive response: (+) The corporate risk of not undertaking the project

Technology domain factors

Definitional uncertainty: (–) The degree to which the technical requirements of the project are ill-defined

Technical uncertainty: (–) The degree to which the project is dependent on new or untested technical skills, hardware, software or systems

Strategic IT architecture: (+) The degree to which the solution is aligned with the technology strategy and architecture

Infrastructure risk: (–) The degree to which investment in new technology infrastructure services/products or environmental facilities is required

By agreeing a 'score' for each of the 11 factors (and, potentially, weighting each factor appropriately), a total value can be placed on each IT opportunity in the portfolio.

A useful model for conducting portfolio analysis is to classify projects into four categories:

1 'Early successes' (high payoff with low risk).
2 'Easy successes' (low payoff and low risk).
3 'Glittering prizes' (high payoff but high risk).
4 'Back burners' (low payoff and high risk).

The finally agreed portfolio (the 'balanced portfolio') will probably be a mixture of solutions from these four categories.

In order to compare the merits of alternative portfolios, an 'IT governance' group, as set out above, will be required to assess the *relative* merits of different portfolios *across* the business (i.e. not just within individual departmental/divisional 'silos') and authorize and prioritize appropriately. Ideally, this should also be assessed against *other* potential corporate investments (i.e. non-IT investments) that may provide higher value. The 'name of the game' here is to get away from 'emotionally-driven' project portfolios which are predicated on 'decibel management' (he who shouts loudest and has most political clout) to more 'objective' selection and prioritization.

The information economics approach set out above is a powerful and simple way of *assessing* the value of a proposed entrant into the project portfolio. But what are the CSFs for such an approach to succeed?

The first key to success here is breaking projects in the portfolio down into 'work packets' that can each be assessed on a comparative value basis. The objective is to identify the functionality that will offer the highest business value for the lowest development and implementation cost (applying the '80/20 rule') and phasing the development of work packets to reflect these commercial priorities. In fact I would argue that there is often great benefit in 'budget boxing' work packages, especially when the potential tangible benefits are reasonably well understood but the requirements are ill-understood and/or effort (cost) is hard to predict with any accuracy. By 'budget boxing' I mean determining how much you can reasonably spend before the costs exceed the cost/benefit 'ROI hurdle' and then *stopping*. This acknowledges the reality of the situation and focuses the mind on using the available budget to largest benefits effect.

The second key to success is to ensure that all non-trivial work is defined as project work and is fully costed. By 'fully costed' I mean that it includes:

- the cost of the development staff to be assigned to work on the project based on their *actual* cost of employment, not just a nominal figure averaged across permanent staff (and *definitely* not ignoring the dramatically higher costs of contractors) – note that how a project manager chooses to staff the project is essentially his or her concern, whether it be with a large number of inexperienced (and inexpensive) trainees or a small number of highly experienced (and expensive) contractors – but the cost (i.e. the real cost) is the business's concern;
- the cost of technology/infrastructure that will have to be purchased to develop and test the system (or the cost of the use of installed infrastructure);
- the cost of technology/infrastructure that will have to be purchased to run the system (or the cost of the use of installed infrastructure);
- package licence costs (and subsequent maintenance payments);
- consultancy costs;
- project management costs;
- technical support costs;
- user costs (e.g. specification, testing);
- the costs of operating, maintaining and supporting the system once it is implemented (and to the anticipated end of its life). These would include, for example, first, second and third level problem management staff/costs, operations staff time, applications support staff time etc.

At the time of the creation of the initial business case the probability is that most of the figures above will typically be, at best, estimated with an accuracy of ±50 per cent. It is generally pointless attempting to estimate with a greater accuracy than this given the relatively ill-defined nature of both the problem and the potential solution at this stage. The ± accuracy will converge with time and understanding. In my experience the best (best value) way of estimating such figures is the simple Delphi approach, namely:

- ask a respected colleague to estimate the work *completely independently* and then compare your figures and his/hers;
- ask senior members of the proposed project team to estimate the work *completely independently* and then compare your figures and theirs.

This has several benefits, namely:

- it does not pretend to be based on any pseudo-scientific approach that will almost certainly lead to a 'brick polishing' exercise;
- it helps gain buy-in to the finally agreed figures by the staff who will have to deliver against those figures;
- significant discrepancies in the numbers are typically fascinating because they usually reveal a wildly different interpretation of the nature of the problem or the difficulty of the solution – this is an excellent way of clarifying the articulation of the problem.

If you already have in place function point (see Chapter 5) metrics databases from which you can extrapolate potential costs, or you have in place a systems development methodology that has estimating factors built in, then fine. Use them. But *still* go through the Delphi process.

Once you have arrived at agreed figures (±X per cent), *stick* with them. Do not be tempted to 'massage' them because 'it just *can't* cost that much'. Nothing sinks projects faster than wishful thinking. I understand this only too well thanks to my appallingly consistent record of wildly optimistic estimation decimation. You would think that I might just have spotted a pattern in my behaviour here and, like an intelligent animal, learnt from it. But no. In fact underestimation of projects is my very worst fault (I write this in the sure and safe knowledge that my wife will not read this book).

The third key to success is user accountability for the costs predicted. If a project sponsor signs off a business case for a project then *his* budgets (not five levels above him) must be adjusted to reflect the costs, either by direct transfer charging of project costs as they are incurred or, at the least, taking the final project costs and deducting that figure from his ('above-the-line') budgets. The crucial point is *individual* accountability for the cost of the project. It is easy for a user to fight for a project when he regards it as 'free'. Having to recover the costs from his own budgets concentrates the mind wonderfully (and helps make all parties focus on the 80/20 rule of getting the big payoff items first). If the solution crosses departmental/divisional boundaries then the costs must be apportioned across them (based on the anticipated apportionment of benefits).

The fourth key to success is ensuring that the project benefits (*and underlying assumptions*) are as objectively defined as is practicable. The tangible (i.e. quantifiable) financial benefits would include:

- reductions in existing IT systems costs;
- reductions in other business costs;
- savings from reduced business investment;
- additional business revenues or improved cashflow;
- business revenue reductions avoided;
- business cost increases avoided.

The tangible non-financial benefits (e.g. improvements in the quality of outputs) should also be quantified and performance measures identified. All 'intangible' benefits (e.g. the 'competitive advantage' list above, improving staff working conditions, improving image etc.) ultimately should be resolvable to tangible benefits, albeit the accuracy will typically be problematic. Note that it is essential to identify and agree the baseline from which benefits improvements will be measured. Once the benefits have been quantified and valued it is also essential to specify *how* these benefits will be achieved, what *assumptions* are to be made about the delivery of benefits (remember our case study in Chapter 1 where £200m of benefits were predicted based on wholly unrealistic assumptions) and *when* the benefits are to be delivered (i.e. the benefits delivery plan). There also needs to be a clear definition of *which* project deliverables will deliver *which* benefits and precisely *who* is going to be responsible for realizing those benefits. Note that some projects will be 'must dos' and have no benefits for the organization (e.g. regulatory or legal compliance). For more detail on such benefits management techniques I would refer you to Chapter 10 of *Goal Directed Project Management* by Andersen, Grude and Haug, published by Kogan Page.

If this all sounds like hard work, you are right. But it is essential because it is the sole justification for the work being proposed. The greatest benefit of it is arguably in the process itself because the harder you find it to pin down benefits, the more you must ask yourself about the true commercial justification for the work. Common sense must prevail, however. Do not waste time and money 'brick polishing' what can only ever be intelligent 'best guesses'. I saw a project team (the project was to implement improved benefits management processes!) spend literally weeks trying to pin down the financial benefits of an improved benefits management process, principally by 'auditing' several years of previous IT systems delivery projects and attempting to assess the increased benefits that would have been achieved (and the reduced wasted effort that would have been achieved) through improved processes. It was a well-meant exercise that the team thought was in compliance with the very processes they were developing but which hopelessly lost sight of the commercial spirit of the exercise.

Note that the importance of the cost and benefits assessment process is so great (and the temptation to skimp on detail or 'massage' numbers so great) that independent assurance of both sets of numbers (and the assumptions, baselines and benefits delivery plan) will almost certainly be required. The accuracy and completeness of the financials and baselines would typically be assured by the internal finance function. The reasonableness of the assumptions and benefits delivery plan would typically be assured by a central 'Programme Management Office' (which would also be responsible for tracking the project business case throughout the development and measuring and reporting benefits realized against the benefits delivery plan post-implementation).

The fifth key to success is user *accountability* for realizing the benefits predicted. If a project sponsor signs off a business case for a project then *his* budgets (not five levels above him) must be adjusted to reflect the benefits. So, for example, if the business case predicts that the proposed system will save the business department £2m ($3m) per annum, ensure that in the year in which the system is to be implemented the project sponsor's budgets are adjusted to reflect these savings (pro rata). This will concentrate his mind wonderfully on the *actual* value of benefits he is prepared to sign up to (and will typically result in a *much* more realistic and realizable level of predicted benefits). The crucial point is *individual* accountability for the benefits of the project. It is easy to fight for a project when you don't believe that you will be held accountable for realizing the benefits. If the solution crosses departmental/divisional boundaries then the realization of the benefits must be apportioned across them. Whether or not the benefits are financial or non-financial, the realization of them must be built into the performance targets set in the performance reviews of individuals identified as being responsible for delivering benefits. There must then be *material* benefits (or sanctions) for those individuals to incentivize them appropriately.

The sixth key to success is to ensure that the preparation of project terms of reference and business cases is separately funded (from a budget agreed at year start) and that project work *cannot* commence without the allocation of a unique project code (to which time and costs will be booked). That code will only be assigned if the project's business case is approved.

We have now addressed the 'cost' and 'benefit' parts of the business case. This leads us to the remaining seventh key to success, 'risk management'. Any truly commercially managed organization examines each work request critically from a risk point of view. Our value-driven IT function should be in just the same position. It should not be 'forced' to deliver projects that it regards as unacceptably risky and it should be able to charge on a basis that reflects the inherent risk. Project risk assessment will include an evaluation of:

- the project type (small enhancement through to major bespoke/customized);
- technology type (established and proved through to 'bleeding edge' and unproved);
- project management and technical skills required, and available to the project (established skill base through to new skills required);
- development time (short through to long);
- immovability of the delivery deadline (as epitomized by the year 2000 projects);
- development cost (low through to high);
- anticipated life of system (short through to long);
- anticipated user involvement (minimal through to team secondment);
- anticipated frequency of use (ad hoc through to constant);
- number of interfacing systems (none through to many).

Benefits realization risk assessment will include an assessment of:

- project sponsor commitment (negligible through to leadership);
- project stakeholder commitment (negligible through to leadership);
- anticipated business impact (low through to major, from one business unit to all business units);
- anticipated business impact of non-availability (low through to mission critical);
- benefits accountability (negligible through to total);

- benefits size (low through major);
- benefits delivery speed (long term through short term);
- benefits tangibility (low through to high);
- benefits constraints (few through to major, e.g. union resistance);
- benefits assumptions (few through to major assumptions).

Once the overall risk is understood, this can be used by the IT function to decide how, if at all, to 'bid' for the work, namely:

- fixed price quote for low risk work;
- time-and-materials for medium risk work;
- decline high risk work (or rescope down to lower risk or outsource to an ESP who *will* accommodate the risk, albeit at a price).

As we will see later, this risk rating will also be used to help us decide what 'tolerance' in business case variance we will accept during the development process before critically re-examining the case for allowing the project to continue.

I have found that IT functions increasingly perform (with varying levels of formality) project risk assessments. However, they are almost invariably 'one off' exercises (i.e. the risk profile is not maintained throughout the project), risk mitigation actions are rarely effectively 'seen through', the level of risk does not inform the ability of the IT function to decline the project (or otherwise protect itself) and the risks assessed are almost invariably only *project* risks, i.e. the risks of the project 'failing', rather than including *benefits realization* risks, the risks of the project failing to realize the benefits promised.

My point above about the IT function 'declining' work may look a little shocking – since when could an internal IT function turn down work the business asked it to do? But it is just a foot in the door of treating the internal customer like a 'true' customer and enabling a much more 'commercial culture'. This is what Terry White has to say about 'internal customers' in his book *Reinventing the IT Department*: 'There is no such thing as an internal customer . . . there is only one customer – the person who pays for goods or services.' He goes on to say, 'A true customer–supplier relationship has a number of factors which are particular to it. But the most telling one in connection with the IT-business relationship is that both parties are able to fire each other: the customer can look elsewhere for their services, and the supplier can withdraw their services from the customer if he or she becomes uneconomical to service. Usually this is not possible in in-house business-IT relationships.' It certainly isn't usual. I've never seen it. But why not? The practices I suggest here are not going to turn the 'internal customers' into 'true customers' – that is not the underlying goal. If you want 'true customers' you are not going to *be* an internal IT function any longer, you are going to be an ESP. But the practices should increase the commercial behaviours of both the 'internal service consumer' and the 'internal service provider', the demand side and the supply side.

In order to compare the merits of project 'value cases', an 'IT governance' group will be required to assess the *relative* merits (value) of each project *across* the business (i.e. not just within individual departmental/divisional 'silos') and authorize and prioritize appropriately. Ideally, this should also be assessed against *other* potential corporate investments (i.e. non-IT investments) that may provide higher value. In practice, it is likely that several levels of 'project governance' would be required, depending on the level of expenditure proposed. For example, work estimated as incurring less than, say, £30 000 ($45 000) in development expenditure might be classified as 'minor works' and *by definition* not be 'project work'. Such work (like support and maintenance work) would be funded from separately negotiated budgets and authorized by the business unit manager. Work with development costs above the threshold would have to be authorized by a group of business managers from across the business, their seniority (and the frequency with which they met) typically being dependent on the importance (or spend level) of the project proposed. A project will only be authorized if it is 'must-do/compulsory' (e.g. required for legal/regulatory compliance) or, for discretionary projects:

- has clearly defined ownership, scope, costs, benefits, plans, resources, risks and issues;
- meets a clearly articulated business need;
- is clearly aligned with business strategy;
- is clearly aligned with IT technology strategy;
- is technically feasible;
- is affordable (potentially as a result of another lower value, or non-viable, project's ejection from the portfolio);
- is in the IT function operating plan (i.e. the 'strategic' project portfolio agreed at the start of the financial year) or, if not, is sufficiently convincing to take funds from the discretionary budget or substitute for a lower valued project in the plan;

- does not carry unacceptable project risk;
- is likely to realize its promised benefits;
- can be scheduled into the work load (or outsourced);
- has a convincing (and quality assured) business case;
- exceeds the information economics (or equivalent) valuation hurdle set.

This decision on the viability of the proposed project constitutes our first 'value portal'.

Note that for a project to be 'compulsory' (and so 'side step' these value controls) it must *really* be compulsory. In a company in which I recently consulted almost every project in the portfolio was categorized as 'compulsory'. However, not a single one was compulsory in my sense. They were only 'compulsory' in the sense that the project sponsors 'demanded' that they be done! However important the business may perceive these projects to be (or however important the project sponsor may think he is) they are still *discretionary* and need to pass the 'value tests'.

Note also the importance of being *absolutely clear* on the definitions of work (and so the budget from which they will be funded and the level of control that will be commercially appropriate):

- project work (work that adds/changes functionality and whose cost exceeds the agreed spend threshold – funded from the operating plan budget or, if not in the operating plan, the discretionary budget. If it has a sufficiently persuasive business case and cannot be funded from either of these sources then the business sponsor may directly fund the project from *his* operational plan budget);
- minor work (work that adds/changes functionality and whose cost is less than the agreed spend threshold – funded from the 'minor works budget');
- support and maintenance work (work that exists to simply sustain the existing 'legacy' portfolio of systems/infrastructure *without adding functionality* – funded from the 'support and maintenance budget'). This is often called the 'zero-based budgeting' cost of IT, i.e. what it costs to 'keep systems ticking over'. Note that should a piece of 'support and maintenance' work exceed the 'project cost threshold' then it must be managed and controlled as 'project work', even though it is being performed by 'support and maintenance' staff and funded from the 'support and maintenance' budget. This

prevents those in systems development project groups being suddenly hit with unplanned 'project' costs that have not been built into their budgets.

Note that in order to discriminate between different 'types' of work, separate budgets will almost certainly be required to discriminate between work being performed 'directly' for the business, internal IT function R&D/continuous performance improvement work and 'infrastructure upgrade' work that is not directly attributable to particular business projects or business units (e.g. upgrade of the mainframe, upgrade of the WAN, installation of a company email system).

Our next value-adding CSF is to optimize the size and speed of business benefits delivery at the time of systems development (i.e. after the project has been approved).

3.15 Optimizing value delivery

The key to success here is actively reviewing the value of all projects at all key milestones during the development process (e.g. the completion of requirements specification, the completion of systems design and pre-implementation) and on any 'significant' change in circumstances (e.g. changed business priorities, changed scope, changed understanding of the complexity). 'Significance' here is a product of two things, namely:

- the extent to which the changes will impact the delivery dates, the delivery budgets or benefits planned; and
- the risk assessment of the project.

So, for example, a project categorized as 'high risk' might only tolerate a 10 per cent variation in budget, schedule or benefits before 'tripping' a project appraisal. A project categorized as 'low risk' might tolerate a 30 per cent variation.

Note that my key concern here is controlling material change in the *value* of the project, rather than focusing on controlling changes in *requirements*. The vast majority of 'scope/change control' processes in systems development methodologies are focused on resisting changes in requirements after that precious 'requirements spec' has been signed off by the user. But requirements change is *good*, if it is going to result in a higher value-adding solution! Anyway, to resist changes in requirements is simply to fly in the face of reality. Users' understanding of what is possible and what they actually want will inevitably evolve with time, throughout the development process. So long as those changes will result in a better (higher value-adding) outcome then we should *embrace* them, not resist them (assuming, of course, that we can accommodate them). Requirements specifications are not there for the developer to hide behind (or to trap the customer – 'Gotcha! It's not in the spec!'). They are simply a starting point. A 'systems development methodology' that does not accommodate this reality is fundamentally flawed.

The business case (like the requirements) must be a living thing. Its accuracy will typically go from perhaps ±50 per cent at project initiation time down a 'funnel' to perhaps ±10 per cent at implementation time. Increasing accuracy comes with an increasing understanding of the nature and complexity of the business problem and increasing understanding of the nature and technical complexity of the solution and the likelihood of actually realizing the benefits. It also comes from an increasing understanding of the optimal delivery vehicle (e.g. package, bespoke/customized, RAD) and the specific staff assigned to the work. Note that we are not *just* talking about costs and benefits here. Throughout the development the project as a whole (or more typically particular work packets) may 'go negative' in terms of passing the 'value hurdles' (in terms of competitive advantage, ROI, alignment, risk). In this case the goal is to *terminate* the development of that functionality (or rescope to 'rescue' the functionality that will pay its way). The name of the game is to cease throwing good money after bad and stop non-value-adding work at the earliest time possible. Note that when I use the phrase 'throwing good money after bad' I do not mean to imply the money spent up to that time was ill-spent from the outset. It was only ill-spent *with the wisdom of hindsight*. Basically, my message is, 'Forget your pride – if you find yourself in a hole, stop digging.'

A project will only be authorized to continue (and continue to be funded) if it is 'compulsory' (e.g. regulatory compliance) or:

- continues to have clearly defined ownership, scope, costs, benefits, plans, resources, risks and issues;
- continues to meet a clearly articulated *current* business need;
- continues to be clearly aligned with *current* business strategy;
- continues to be clearly aligned with *current* IT technology strategy;

- continues to be technically feasible;
- continues to be affordable;
- continues to carry acceptable risk;
- can still be scheduled into the work load (or outsourced);
- *continues to have a convincing (and quality assured) business case*.

In order to compare the *ongoing* merits of projects, the appropriate 'IT governance' group will have to meet to *reassess* projects when there is a 'significant' change in the value of the project. Theirs, however, is now principally a 'watching brief'. The responsibility for focusing on only viable work (and prioritizing the most viable earliest) lies with the project manager and project sponsor. There is otherwise a great danger in projects being run 'to the beat of the drum' of the meetings of the appropriate 'IT governance' group (which might be every three months). The issue, once again, is *personal accountability*. Don't put bureaucratic barriers in people's way. Trust them to act responsibly. But as soon as they are found to have abused that trust, *there must be serious consequences*.

Bureaucracy is a real danger here. For example, a large government IT function at which I consulted had a well-intentioned 'pseudo-commercial' process in place such that it was not possible to get a time code to commence any piece of work (e.g. writing a specification, coding a program) until a long and tortuous process of quote production, quote authorization, quote acceptance and sales order entry had been completed. Whatever the virtues of this might have been for major projects, the fact was that the bureaucracy involved in this process often resulted in the process itself costing more than the value of the work it was authorizing. Since around *15 000* of these quotes were being issued each year (and almost all were then accepted), this was obviously a case of a well-intentioned piece of 'value-adding' best practice being compromised on the 'cost-efficiency' front and so failing to be a 'best value practice'. At the other extreme I saw a very similar process result in over 90 per cent of work quotes being rejected, resulting in huge wasted cost in preparing work proposals. Far more rigorous pre-qualification of work was required. The basic message is 'keep it simple' and trust people to behave responsibly (but come down on them like a ton of bricks if they abuse that trust).

Note that an implication of the business case monitoring is that if the costs rise above the original (or last agreed revised) budget, it will be necessary to go back to the business to ask for more funding, funding that must come directly from user budgets. It must *not* be 'quietly' stolen from support budgets or from other 'late starting' projects. Budgetary control is not a game in which numbers are shuffled around the board – it is real money we are talking about. The fact that there is a budget for the project in the IT function's operating plan does *not* mean that the money is 'real' and is available to be spent. It is *virtual* money, blocked out for budgetary control purposes. When you want to spend *real* money you must justify it (again and again). Note also that the above approach requires a much more dynamic authorization of monies from budgets than is often found. This also implies that the 'IT budget' is not 'carved up' between business divisions/units at the start of the financial year and that spending is then 'drawn down' from those budgets – instead, all projects continue to compete for funds throughout the year. Business unit X may be nominally allocated a percentage of the total IT spend planned at year start but it must then justify (and continue justifying) the actual release of funds to perform work. And if during the year the business case for 'its' projects fades while the projects planned for business unit Y increasingly shine, then budgets nominally allocated to business unit X may be reallocated dynamically to business unit Y. Note also that this entire system cannot meaningfully be applied to the 'IT bit' of business projects. If the business case for the 'IT bit' does not convince but the business case for the project as a whole is convincing then the IT function will not be thanked for stopping the project (in fact they will doubtless be told to stop being so stupid and just get on with the project). So the governance committees must take this 'holistic' view of the value of the entire project, not just the 'IT bit'.

This *ongoing* assessment of the viability of projects and sub-projects constitutes our second 'value portal'. Note that it is not a static portal! It moves with the project ensuring that functionality that moves into a 'non-viable' situation is rapidly terminated or rescoped.

The above practices are primarily about optimizing 'portfolio management', about which the Meta group had this to say in their report 'The Business of IT Portfolio Management: Balancing Risk, Innovation and ROI': 'IT portfolio management is the cornerstone process for maintaining dynamic alignment between business and the IT organization. Managing IT from an investment perspective – with continuing focus on value, risk, cost and benefits – has helped businesses reduce IT costs by up to 30% with a 2×–3× increase in value.' This report also, by the way, sets out the following results from its survey:

- 84 per cent of companies either do not do business cases for their IT projects at all or just do them on a select few projects;
- 83 per cent of companies are unable to adjust and align their budgets with business needs more than once or twice a year.

I am rather staggered by the 84 per cent number (because in my experience it is nothing like that bad) and I would like to know just how Meta measured the claimed two to three times increase in 'value' (and precisely what they mean by 'value'). However, scepticism aside, portfolio management is certainly key to successful value-added IT delivery but appears to have received remarkably little management attention.

Our final value-adding CSF is to optimize the actual realization of the project benefits after implementation.

3.16 Optimizing benefits realization

The key to success here is, once again, real user accountability for benefits realization and the cost of the production service, i.e. it is the *net* benefits we are worried about. This, of course, implies that the benefits achieved are actually being monitored and reported. Benefits monitoring and reporting must be an ongoing process (i.e. not just a 'one-off' post-implementation review – PIR). It must report the level of benefits being realized against the benefits delivery plan, actions that need to be taken to improve the level of benefits realization, any changes needed to benefits targets, delivery times and performance measures and any lessons that can be learned to improve benefits realization on future projects. As I suggested above, this is typically undertaken by a central 'Programme Management Office'. The results of benefits realization will be a key measure (in fact I would argue that it is *the* key measure) of the IT function and will feed the 'balanced scorecard' (discussed in Chapter 5).

Why is the typical project PIR not adequate for this? Many IT functions do indeed conduct PIRs (typically six to nine months after implementation) to try to ascertain whether or not the planned benefits have been realized. Unfortunately, my experience of reviewing a great many PIRs has been that while the benefits (as originally defined in the project justification) may have been dutifully 'SMART' (Specific, Measurable, Achievable, Relevant and Timebound), the PIR quietly ducked the specifics. A by no means atypical example of a recently reviewed project objectives document sets out an objective/benefit of reducing product returns by a very specific 7 per cent. The corresponding section in the subsequent PIR said simply, 'The project was delivered to schedule.' In fact, that was the *entire* text of the 'Realization of Benefits' section in the PIR! Furthermore, such PIRs are just a 'snapshot in time', not ongoing and they are essentially backward looking, not forward looking (in terms of seeking ways to ramp up benefits realized), i.e. they are perceived more as 'audits of failure' rather than 'facilitators of success' (which is why you rarely see a PIR being performed for a project that everyone *knows* was a disaster!).

The greatest problem with benefits tracking and reporting (whether a 'one-off' PIR or truly ongoing) is that by the time the benefits tracking begins so much may have changed, and so many other business or IT initiatives may have been applied, that it is very difficult to say if the benefits of the project have actually been delivered. For example, a project promises a 5 per cent improvement in superstore contribution as a result of the improved ability to range products to meet local customer and demographic needs. By the time of the post-implementation review on the pilot store, sales have indeed increased by 5 per cent. But in the meantime this store has been refitted, the (inept) previous store manager has been replaced, the nasty buyers have hammered the key suppliers with the threat of product withdrawal and pushed down product cost prices by 5 per cent and an executive housing estate has been completed nearby, bringing an influx of new, wealthy customers. So precisely *what* created the 5 per cent uplift? The key to measuring project benefits is 'ring-fencing' the IT benefits as far as is practicable and where full ring-fencing is not possible, apportioning the benefits in an equitable, independently assured, way.

The most successful implementations of the 'philosophy' of managing projects for benefits delivery include 'business change management' specialists within the business (either reporting to the business, or, more typically to the IT function). Their job is to drive out the benefits by whatever means necessary, be that 'occupational training', technical surgeries, user groups, maintaining FAQs (frequently asked questions), handholding, or whatever it takes. In some organizations these individuals will be the systems analysts who originally specified the requirements and prepared the original business case and who are now 'seconded' temporarily into the business to actually deliver what they promised. In other organizations these individuals are programme managers.

We have one further key 'value portal'. This is concerned with *terminating* functionality that has *ceased* to add value. This can be thought of as minimizing the level of 'service delivery wastage'. This is the post-implementation corollary of the best value practices to govern projects/subprojects in such a way as to terminate them if they become non-viable during development. I believe that this is potentially one of the big 'hidden costs' of IT service supply, especially with large IT functions with a long history. I have only once come across an IT function that had a clear plan for terminating increasingly redundant systems. I suspect (but cannot prove) that many IT functions would find that a material proportion of production functionality is either not used at all, or is being used but only by a few users or is being used but at a cost that far exceeds any benefits still being extracted. This was illustrated well for me many years ago in my time as a project manager at a major food retailer. This was in the old days when virtually all output came in the form of reports printed from the mainframe and distributed the next morning to the user departments. A situation arose where discarded reports were stolen from the company trash cans and found their way into the hands of our competitors. Yes, even food retailers enjoy a little bit of glamorous industrial espionage. As a result of this, our then CEO ordered that with immediate effect each business unit head would have to personally go to the computer room and sign out all his reports. You are probably way ahead of me now. Because, yes, at the end of 'day 1' the print room was knee high with unclaimed reports. By the end of 'week 1' you could barely *get into* the computer room let alone the print room, since it was stacked to the ceiling with unclaimed paper. Basically, we kept generating the stuff but around half of it no one was remotely interested in consulting any more (assuming they were *ever* interested in consulting it).

A project would be reviewed for its ongoing value at the 'traditional' PIR time (and then periodically). Terminating 'non-viable' functionality requires that those responsible for measuring benefits realization look periodically at the net benefits and flag the point at which the costs of running, maintaining and supporting the functionality are exceeding the value of the benefits being delivered. However, it is about more than *just* commercial viability. A (sub)system would be considered for retirement if it:

- no longer met a clearly articulated *current* business need;
- no longer was clearly aligned with *current* business strategy;
- no longer was clearly aligned with *current* IT technology strategy; or
- no longer was commercially viable (i.e. the costs of running and supporting the functionality are exceeding the benefits extracted).

This does not, of course, mean that the system (or subsystem) should immediately be shut down! There are still, presumably, users who depend on that functionality. But it does clearly flag the fact that this functionality should be carefully examined for replacement or termination and appropriate plans put in place. Of course, there *will* be circumstances (e.g. business group outsourcing, company divestments) where there really *are* no users any more (or, at least, few that 'matter'). This is similar to an application service provider (ASP) terminating an application delivery service that has become unprofitable. In the case of services, this is similar to an ESP terminating a service that has become unprofitable.

There is a strong parallel here with the 'traditional' recommendation that systems should have their reliability tracked over time, looking for the point in the 'reported incidents' curve at which the 'bathtub' turns sharply up, so indicating that the system may be at the point of replacement or termination. The 'bathtub' curve simply reflects the fact that *generally* when a system is implemented it will have a (hopefully known and understood) significant number of errors still present in the code (and many others that will only become apparent when the system runs 'in anger'). There will then be serious focus, in the early months, on removing these bugs (so the bathtub side drops downwards) and the system spends some years with relative stability (the bottom of the bathtub). Then, typically as a result of increasing code complexity, typically through ad-hoc bug fixes and small enhancements, coupled with the moving on of the staff with the greatest understanding of supporting the system, the 'other side' of bathtub is hit and the number of incidents starts to rise. I have three problems with this approach. The first is that I have never seen a single IT function that did actually track incident trends with a view to indicating system replacement or termination. The second is that even if does take account of the severity of the incident it does not take account of *when* the incident occurred (is it in the middle of critical month-end processing?) and the business impact of the loss (or degradation) of service. And third, for me it misses the really essential point, which is not the ongoing stability of the system but the ongoing *value* of the system.

Having said that, I am not for one moment suggesting that production stability is not important (it is a key component of the quality quadrant of the value compass). It is just that it must be seen in the context of the value added to the business from the implementation of the system. Of course, systems shouldn't *have* bugs when they are implemented, at least not if they have been subject to rigorous and complete systems testing, operations acceptance testing and user acceptance testing. But we are talking about the real world here and it is perfectly (commercially) valid to implement a system with known bugs *if* the trade-off between reliability and the early realization of system benefits has been considered maturely. This is typically *the* point of conflict between those responsible for systems development in an IT function and those responsible for service delivery post-implementation. The former group typically see themselves (with, in my view, considerable justification) as the 'value-adders' who want to get the benefits of the system out into the business as quickly as possible, and accept, pragmatically, as they see it, that a certain amount of system 'hand-holding' will be required in the early days to keep the system on its feet. They would claim to be operating in the value-added 'space' (although they are actually most probably just trying to find some way of delivering the system, or, well, key functionality of the system, to the agreed deadline in order to avoid embarrassment). Those responsible for service delivery, of course, are typically driven by the agenda of maximizing service and support quality (principally in terms of maximizing system stability and speed of recovery on an error) and so see themselves as the 'gatekeepers' to that hallowed turf, the production environment. Value-added is not their problem – they are operating in the quality 'space', specifically in the areas of system and support service level optimization (or, at least they are if you ignore the troublesome cost and value of quality questions).

And, of course, they are both right (and both wrong). Business value (demand-side value) is a product of *both* quality and value-added components. Therefore both parties need to take a mature, commercially astute look at the quality vs value-added trade-offs before taking a decision on implementation. Unfortunately, in my experience, this kind of commercial maturity is rarely found in large corporations, as developers self-righteously try to push into production systems that may seriously compromise the integrity of the production environment (because as far as they are concerned the primary objective is to deliver the system when promised, and so right is on their side) while those in IT 'operations' self-righteously try to resist the barbarian at the gate, insisting on near zero-defect, operationally acceptable and supportable code (because as far as they are concerned the primary objective is to provide a stable production environment, and so right is on *their* side). I have repeatedly seen those in development and operations functions take child-like 'positions' on these arguments (often accompanied, I'm afraid, by what can only be described as 'petulant management tantrums'), requiring senior management 'arbitration' to resolve deadlocks.

I have no sympathy for people's behaviours in these circumstances but great sympathy for the difficulty of the problem. Of course delivering the system to the business is critically important. Of course the integrity of the production environment is critically important. And, in my experience, developers are almost invariably fixated on (because it happens to most interest them) designing in business functionality. That is the 'fun bit'. Although they may not admit it, they may have little real commitment to, or focus on, designing in the dreary *non*-functional aspects of a system (operability, supportability, scalability, security, backup, recoverability etc.) that are not immediately visible to their customer (and who may well have a very limited understanding of the real business importance of these things – why should he?). And, of course, when the delivery deadline pressure is on and the development is running late (has anyone ever come across a development that was not squeezed as the delivery deadline approached?) the first thing to 'give' is testing. Couple this with the fact that if you graphed both the number of changes to the production environment and the service levels achieved in that environment in almost any data centre in the world I virtually guarantee you will see the two lines on the graph tracking each other (I actually did this once for a global IT provider and the correlation was uncanny). So, yes, both parties are right. But they have to see each other's point of view and behave with commercial maturity balancing the commercial benefits of implementation against the commercial risks. This is a key reason for my suggestion of the introduction of 'tension metrics' in Chapter 5 for both the developers and 'operations' such that the developers are incentivized (through the measurements system) to build in commercially acceptable (functional *and* non-functional) quality and those responsible for service delivery and support are incentivized to help developers get code of commercially acceptable quality into production.

That completes my 'half dozen' value-adding CSFs. However, there are a few other practices that, although not strictly 'best value practices' (because they are not designed to hit the value-adding quadrant) are still highly important in hitting the quality quadrant.

First, we want to optimize operational service levels (because we are certainly not in a position to realize system benefits if the system is not robust, is not available when we need it or is inefficient in use). Service levels come in two main shapes. First, there are *systems* service levels (e.g. system availability, transaction response times) which taken together for all systems represent overall service quality). Second, there are *support* service levels (e.g. service availability, service response times) which taken together for all systems represent overall support quality. Our key objective here is not to optimize service levels in terms of 'higher is better' because obviously higher service levels have a higher cost. Instead our key objective is to provide *necessary and sufficient* service levels to extract optimal *net* benefits from the service. Note that, as set out in my discussion of tariffing above, I am *assuming* the presence of a rigorous 'end-to-end' service level management approach and services packaged in such a way as to be readily understood by the user negotiating the 'service level vs cost' equation. I am also *assuming* that there is a cost/price (built from tariffs) for services and that the user negotiating the 'deal' has his budgets directly affected by whatever price is agreed (i.e. there is true business financial accountability for the level of service taken). These are *critical* assumptions and are set out in more detail under my 'CSFs for transfer charging' section above. If they do not apply in your organization then 'all bets are off' because you will simply not be able to optimize service levels for value delivered if the mindset of the user is that 'IT is free'.

As for achieving service level agreement targets, many (if not most) IT functions do indeed maintain such metrics. However, unless they are actually in a financial contractual relationship with their customers, these targets are often set (by the IT function) to be laughably easy to achieve on modern equipment. An annual availability figure of 99.8 per cent may sound extremely impressive to a naive user, but it would be remarkable if the IT function could generally *not* achieve such a figure (and has the user thought what 0.2 per cent outage means if it all happens at year end processing?). And then there is the definition of a 'service level'. Take even the simplest service level, 'availability'. I had a client a few years ago whose service delivery function proudly published 100 per cent system availability statistics for a week in which the WAN was out for a full day. As they pointed out, the network was the responsibility of the network services group, not them. As far as 'their' mainframes were concerned, the systems were 100 per cent available! Their users begged to differ. Although this is an extreme example, true 'end-to-end' service level agreements that encapsulate the entire service as experienced by the end user are, in my experience, very rare. But for our purposes, they are essential.

3.17 Portfolio management roles

The challenge of implementing the above practices effectively is considerable. Any team set up to help manage (and optimize) the value of the portfolio of projects and systems must position itself carefully to not be perceived as 'policemen' whose key role is to stop projects and terminate systems. Instead they must be perceived as offering a truly value-adding role by helping to focus projects on the 'value-adding core' of functionality and managing risks (especially benefits realization risks) effectively in order to *sustain* projects. In other words, they must be 'marketed' as a 'centre of excellence in value delivery', helping project/programme managers to maximize the value of their projects/programmes, not as 'value portal gatekeepers' trying to maximize the removal of *non*-value-adding functionality (although, of course, they are also trying to do this). This 'spin' may sound trivial but it is not. The ultimate success of value management may well depend on it.

Note also that the portfolio management 'value assurance' role is not for the faint-hearted. It will require highly mature, highly credible, business astute staff who will be comfortable asking what will often be deeply challenging questions to people who may be in very senior positions in the organization (and who are not, perhaps, accustomed to being challenged in this way). In my experience, the reaction of many such people to this type of challenge is, 'Who the devil do you think you are challenging the value of my project?', only in more robust language, typically accompanied by threatening gestures. It takes great courage and tact to carry off this role effectively. The skills needed to truly engage and challenge senior managers in a non-confrontational manner are essentially what I call 'consultancy skills' and any team trying to perform the portfolio assurance role will need them in abundance.

It will also be highly important to manage the portfolio 'by priority/impact' and 'by exception' because in the typical large company there may well be in excess of 100 projects at various stages of development at any one time. An IT governance committee that meets, say, once a month for two hours is obviously not going to be able to play any kind of a value-adding role in assessing all these projects as they pass through the value portals. Therefore care must be taken to only involve the more senior review bodies in the review and authorization of the high impact projects and those that appear to be going seriously 'off the value delivery rails'. Even then, the governance committees should be simply 'rubber stamping' decisions essentially taken before the committee meeting. The 'objective debate' (and the inevitable politics and wheeling-dealing that will accompany this) is a matter for the portfolio/value management team, the project/programme manager and the project/programme sponsor, not for the governance committees. On this basis a (simplified, generic) responsibility matrix might look something like Figure 3.5 below. The codes used are:

R   = Responsible for performing the activity
A   = Accountable for the success/failure of the activity
C   = Consulted as part of performing the activity
I   = Informed of the results of the activity
A&G = Advice & Guidance – plays an active role advising others on the performance of the activity, but is not actually responsible for performing it
QA   = Quality Assures the performance of the activity, *actively challenging* the quality of both the work and its deliverables
QC   = Quality Controls the deliverables of the activity (to ensure that they have complied with agreed standards and procedures)
Admin = Administers the activity

Activity	Group					
	Systems development areas	Systems support areas	Portfolio management team	IT governance committee	Corporate governance committee	Project sponsor
Value portal 1						
Prepare work request (including determination of project value)	R/A		QA/A&G/Admin			C
Evaluate work request – business transformation projects	C		QA/A&G/Admin	C	R/A	C
Evaluate work request – major projects	C		QA/A&G/Admin	R/A	C	C
Evaluate work request – other projects	C		R/A	I		C
Value portal 2						
Ongoing project value monitoring/reporting	R/A		QA/A&G/Admin			C
Project evaluation – business transformation projects	C		QA/A&G/Admin	C	R/A	C
Project evaluation – major projects	C		QA/A&G/Admin	R/A	C	C
Project evaluation – other projects	C		R/A	I		C
Value portal 3						
Ongoing system value monitoring/reporting	I	R/A	QA/A&G/Admin			I
System evaluation	I	C	QA/Admin	R/A	C	C

Figure 3.5

124

3.18 Implementing effectiveness improvements

The basic steps of implementing effectiveness improvements are set out below. I have tried to keep the process general (i.e. improving practices generally, whether they be 'practices', 'best practices' or 'best value practices') but I am obviously suggesting that a focus on implementing best *value* practices (at least initially) is almost certainly going to give you the biggest bang for your buck.

Figure 3.6

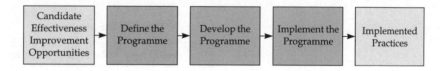

3.18.1 Defining the programme

Figure 3.7

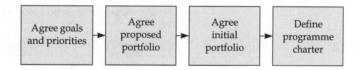

- Agree the goals of the programme (e.g. Primarily to improve delivered IT value-added? Primarily to improve the quality of IT products and services? Primarily to reduce the risk of IT outsourcing? Primarily to position IT practices in preparation for outsourcing?).
- Agree the immediate priorities for practice improvement (e.g. agenda alignment of the business and IT function? systems portfolio alignment? benefits management?). These priorities may have been informed by an earlier 'diagnostic review' of the effectiveness of existing practices in the IT function.
- On the basis of the goals and priorities, define the 'proposed portfolio' of practice improvement initiatives, i.e. those practices that you believe need to be implemented/improved in the foreseeable future (e.g. two to three years?).
- Agree the proposed portfolio with key stakeholders in the business (ensuring that they clearly understand the ramifications in terms of changed business practices and behaviours).
- Choose a subset of the proposed portfolio for an initial implementation – the initial practice set (generally the

'highest value', 'least cost to implement' set that require least change in existing IT processes and disciplines to be effected).

- Define the programme charter setting out the programme objectives, scope, sponsor, stakeholders, change leaders, deliverables, milestones, dependencies, business case, risks, assumptions, organization, roles and responsibilities, controls and plans.

3.18.2 Developing the programme

Develop the programme

| Develop new/enhanced procedures |
| Develop management reporting |
| Develop automation tools |
| Develop training and communications |
| Develop roles and responsibilities |

Figure 3.8

- Design and develop necessary enhancements and/or changes in procedures, practices and disciplines necessary to implement the initial new/enhanced practices.
- Specify and design the management reporting approach/processes for the initial practices.
- Specify, select/design/develop automation tools to support the initial practices and management reporting.
- Define training needs and develop training materials.
- Define communications needs (internally to the IT function and externally to the business).
- Define and allocate roles and responsibilities for supporting the initial practices (e.g. programme management office roles).

3.18.3 Implementing the programme

- Implement the initial portfolio of changes in practices and disciplines.
- Implement the reporting systems.
- Conduct training and communication.

Implement the programme

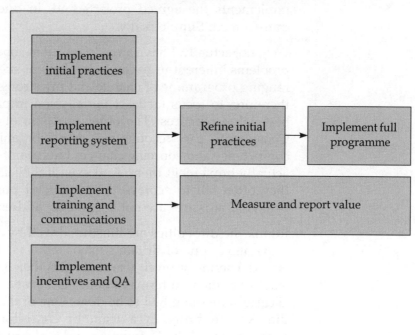

Figure 3.9

- Determine and implement incentives for staff to support the programme and act on its outcomes (and sanctions for non-compliance).
- Establish quality assurance of the delivery of the changes.
- Assess and refine the initial practices implemented, applying lessons learnt.
- Implement the full (proposed) practice portfolio.
- Measure and report the benefits realized (see Chapter 5).

3.19 Case study – implementing effectiveness improvements

My 18 years of experience in IT consulting has been focused almost exclusively on just one thing: helping IT functions to transform themselves into effective and cost-efficient performers, or, at the very least, achieve incremental improvements. The consultancy studies almost invariably start with an 'as is' diagnostic review to identify key strengths, weaknesses, opportunities and threats and so define a programme of projects that will leverage strengths and turn around weaknesses. These projects will typically include organizational improvements, process effectiveness improvements, competency improvements and sourcing improvements. The theory is that the client implements the agreed projects and, in due course, becomes transformed. Simple really.

Well, no, actually. I have already talked at some length about the problems inherent in trying to implement such a typically wide ranging programme of change and my strong recommendation, therefore, to focus (at least initially) on implementing the key best value practices. The other problem, of course, is people. Consultants can recommend many organizational, process, competency and sourcing changes but cannot 'force' the client to actually implement them. And even if they *do* implement them, they often fail to achieve their intended purpose because the behavioural issues are not adequately addressed.

I think the difficulties are illustrated well by a study I ran some years ago at one of Britain's major retailers. This company had issued a series of profit warnings and their key competitor had leapt over them in terms of both market share and profitability. Clearly something had to be done. One of the many things they did was to bring in a team of consultants to review the performance of the IT function and make recommendations for change. This duly happened and the 'traditional' 100-odd problems were found. The resolution of these problems was grouped into 26 key initiatives to improve the effectiveness of the IT function. These were incorporated in a major IT transformation programme of seven projects, focusing on improving the effectiveness of systems development processes, project management processes (i.e. the usual suspects), service management processes, staff management processes and benefits management processes (essentially defining and implementing 'best practices' for each). The programme was budgeted to cost £1.1m and take a year to deliver. In fact the programme took three years and, let us be charitable here, came in a tad over budget. Well, quite a large tad, actually. Nevertheless, was it a success? Well, we, the management consultancy, sold a load of consultancy business on the back of the assignment. So it was certainly a success for us! But did it actually demonstrably transform the IT function? To help answer these questions the original consultants were brought back to reassess the performance of the IT function on completion of the transformation programme (yes, more consultancy sell-on!). This was an extremely interesting development since it is almost unheard of for a consultancy to be brought back in to demonstrate that the changes they recommended actually made a difference! The consultancy partner responsible for the client was *extremely* anxious (and *not* because of the obvious conflict of interest issue inherent in our reviewing the success of our own recommendations).

However, this follow-up review showed clearly that in over 90 per cent of the areas addressed, process effectiveness (in terms of the establishment of improved processes and compliance with those processes) had improved substantially. So clearly the transformation was a 'success' (if you quietly forget the budget and schedule overruns). Or was it? About a year after this reassessment, the entire IT function was outsourced, and *not* because it was clearly regarded by the business as now being 'transformed'. Quite the reverse.

So what went wrong? How could the effectiveness of all these processes have improved so impressively and yet the outcome, in terms of the perceived performance of systems and service delivery by the business, was so poor? And, anyway, why *did* a one year programme take three years to complete?

In order to try to answer these questions we conducted a review of the transformation programme itself (yes, yet more consultancy sell-on!) and identified the following key problems:

- The 'bootstrap problem'. Improvement projects that were themselves designed to improve the effectiveness of programme and project management disciplines lacked effective programme and project management disciplines. This resulted in many problems, not the least of which was the absence of any credible 'objective' understanding of programme and projects progress. The bootstrap problem also occurred in change management, the historic focus having been on delivering technical changes rather than behavioural changes. The teams were accustomed to delivering a product; the selling of the vision behind the product was often well outside their 'comfort zone'. The transformation teams were essentially being expected to model the vision that they were trying to create, so it was hardly surprising that they had a challenging learning experience.
- The senior IT manager responsible for the transformation programme did not actually 'own' the transformation project teams. Instead they were on temporary secondment to the transformation programme. The staff on the teams worked out quickly that the name of the game was to keep happy the senior IT managers to whom they actually line reported (and who were responsible for their remuneration levels!). Therefore

129

their 'loyalties' lay outside the transformation team with the IT groups they were ostensibly trying to change. More to the point, they worked out quickly that when there was any disagreement between the transformation programme manager and their line managers (which there frequently was), the name of the game was to keep their line manager happy while *pretending* to push the messages of the transformation team. This was exacerbated by the fact that a culture of competition and distrust existed across the senior IT management team. When (frequent) differences of opinion occurred on the direction of the transformation programme or the nature of its outputs, the attitude was to indulge in 'ritual politeness' rather than honestly address and resolve the problems.

- Although, laudably, every member of the senior IT management team was nominated as a sponsor for at least one of the transformation projects, they were not held *accountable* for the success of the changes, instead regarding this as the responsibility of the senior IT manager running the transformation team. Basically, there was no clear ownership for realizing the benefits and the senior IT managers largely appeared to use their 'sponsorship' role to keep an eye on the changes being proposed and try to shape them to their parochial agendas. The nominated 'change leaders' out in the field were either *never* approached by the transformation project sponsors or were approached at most twice. Hardly the stuff of committed sponsorship, let alone 'change evangelism'.

- Senior IT managers, recognizing the long track record of failure at making real change happen within the company, generally assumed that if they gave their *verbal* agreement to change (but actually did little or nothing about it) and kept a low profile, the programme would, in due course, simply fade away, in the manner of all previous such initiatives.

- IT systems development teams historically worked 'in silos' and developed discrete methods of working of which they were generally highly protective. This resulted in a strong 'not invented here' attitude, with extensive resistance to anything that smacked of 'imposed' methods and a default reaction of 'well it certainly won't work here'.

- Practices defined by the transformation teams were essentially highly engineered 'best practices'. Many of these were indeed geared to address value problems – but they all appeared to be designed more to impress colleagues and management with the 'cleverness' of the transformation teams than to actually produce something workable. By the end of the programme there were around 1500 web pages on the company's intranet specifying the new procedures (and many of these pages simply pointed to other more detailed documents). In short, the transformation teams were justifying their existence and making an industry of producing procedures that few, if any, would have the time to read, let alone implement. The leap from current practices to 'bleeding edge' practices was daunting to many. Simple, pragmatic (best value) practices that instilled basic disciplines that were actually accepted and demonstrably worked would have been far preferable.

- As had been demonstrated clearly by an 'influence diagram' at an early point in the programme, the various transformation projects had a very high level of 'mutual synergy' (or, to put it another way, potential 'mutual interference'). However, the decision was taken to run the projects very much in silos and address the links, dependencies and influences by programme management 'from above'. This programme management did not happen and substantial time had to be taken to try to post-integrate the various practices delivered (with varying degrees of success).

- The programme was beset with the bureaucracy that seemed to be inherent to all activities in the company; transformation project managers were spending substantial time sitting at their desks completing project paperwork rather than actively leading and managing their projects and engaging with and influencing sponsors and stakeholders. At the best of times only 80 per cent of total programme activity was value-adding (creating outputs and gaining buy-in) and at worst it sank to just 30 per cent. One transformation project team was spending an average of 50 per cent of its effort on internal work (e.g. preparing plans, preparing progress reports, preparing scope variation documents).

- From day 1, project scope creep was endemic on all the transformation projects as the teams, with good intentions, increasingly tried to 'solve world poverty' and accommodate all the customization requests of the disparate systems development and service delivery teams, many of which were contradictory or incompatible.

- The historic focus of project justification had been to create 'cast iron' project business cases with pinned down numbers that set out an unambiguous economic argument for the project. For a conventional systems development project this would, of course, have been laudable (up to a point), and is, of course, very much in the spirit of 'best value practices'. However, this was not a conventional systems development project. This led to a well-intentioned effort to pin down the transformation benefits, with ludicrous levels of accuracy being sought in figures that could only be intelligent guesstimates at best. Furthermore, the benefits were not 'direct' (since the transformation projects were focused on improving the effectiveness of working practices that *themselves* should improve the delivery of benefits); instead they led *indirectly* to benefits for the business. For example, great effort and time was expended on attempts to quantify exactly how much more code would be delivered each year with improved systems development practices. Of course, this in itself did not deliver business benefits. So further (extensive – lasting *weeks*) effort was spent attempting to pin down how much more business benefit would be delivered through the earlier delivery of systems project benefits. Do you follow me so far? If not, don't worry, because few others did. It was an essentially abstract exercise that fell into a similar trap to that of any attempt to accurately quantify savings from infrastructure improvement projects (like implementing an email system). In short, time that should have been focused on delivering the transformation programme benefits were instead focused on essentially fruitless attempts to accurately quantify the benefits of the programme. This was not a case of the difficulty of pinning down the benefits being a warning sign – it was a case of the genuine pointlessness of trying to pin these extremely indirect benefits down (particularly in the light of the *cost* of trying to pin them down).

- Changes in working practices were focused almost exclusively on the IT function, despite the fact that many could *never* succeed without the active buy-in of key users. For example, the new scope control processes demanded that any new requirements identified during the development process must be commercially justified and that, if approved, either existing project budgets be increased, or existing deadlines be put back or other existing functionality requested be dropped. Up until then, the project teams had simply 'absorbed' new requirements, or brought in contractors to address them or 'stolen' budget from some other late starting project in order to address the new changes (all without any change in the cost or deadline or existing functionality to the user). The new working practices were (in theory) fine and very much in the spirit of 'best value practices'. However, quite aside from the bureaucratic nightmare of forms and signatures that accompanied these scope control processes, the users were horrified with this change in processes that they saw as being *against* their interests. They (understandably) wanted to retain the ability to keep their options open, and make changes and additions to their requirements, essentially without 'penalty'. The first time the practice was invoked and a systems project manager said to his business project sponsor, 'Sorry, but I can't do that – we've got to go through this scope control process and potentially agree more funds', the sponsor immediately had a temper tantrum and escalated the matter to business divisional management who put pressure on the CIO who leaned on the head of systems development management who told the project manager to immediately revert to the old methods of working. Day 1, cave in. So the message sent to both IT staff and users was depressingly clear – don't worry about all this benefits management nonsense, we are not really serious – just do what the users tell you to do. Similarly, attempts to introduce more rigorous service level management struggled with the fact that users were not directly charged for services taken and so continued to seek the 'biggest slice of the IT cake' and the highest service levels they could get. As far as they were concerned, 'IT was free', so why should they support measures that appeared to be designed to constrain their demand levels? All this is illustrative of why I have, with regret, stated at the start of this chapter that transfer charging is an almost certain prerequisite to implementing best value practices.

- Milestones in the transformation programme and project plans were routinely missed and moved without any serious (or any at all) negative ramifications, sending a clear message to the transformation project leaders and the teams that they were just engaged in 'a game'. The culture of the organization was to manage projects to the 'drum beat' of the next project steering group meeting. The very concept of 'managing to milestones' was alien. Decisions and sign-offs required, which 'just missed' a transformation programme steering group meeting, could (and did) delay the affected projects for weeks.

- The project culture of the entire organization was to 'deliver products' rather than 'deliver value'. This meant that the project leaders for the transformation projects (and *their* managers, right up to the top) primarily monitored and judged their 'success' by delivering what was in the original delivery plan (or as amended by the tortuous, change resistant, scope variation process), even when an outsider could immediately see that the deliverables as specified were not going to achieve the promised benefits. It was 'project management by numbers' rather than a dynamic and focused approach to realizing value. Basically, whatever their skills may have been at drawing PERT charts and performing critical path analysis, they were not following 'best value practices' for 'optimizing value delivery', our fifth value-adding CSF above.

- The CIO had, in a genuine attempt at 'empowerment', placed responsibility for the success of the transformation programme and projects with the transformation programme and project leaders. But the culture was so strongly hierarchic (even the most trivial decisions were routinely passed 'upstairs') with a deep culture of risk avoidance, saying the 'politically correct' thing and generally 'protecting your backside', that this was generally interpreted as a lack of commitment from the CIO *and* resulted in no one *really* feeling responsible for the success of the programme. Project staff told their project leaders 'what they wanted to hear'. Project leaders told programme managers 'what they wanted to hear'. Programme managers told senior IT managers 'what they wanted to hear'. And senior IT managers told the CIO 'what he wanted to hear', even when the real message was one of disillusionment or failure. This in turn resulted in it taking an unconscionable length of time before the problems of the transformation programme were recognized and acted upon. What appeared to be happening was that by the time the transformation project leaders had faced up to (or, at least, recognized) the fact that there *were* serious problems, it was becoming too embarrassing to share this openly with their superiors and so the attitude was generally to soldier on in the hope that it would somehow sort itself out in time.
- The transformation programme took so long that there were frequent changes of personnel along the way, resulting in changes in focus, changes in direction and repeated 'learning curves'.
- Once implemented, new processes were adopted largely by 'going through the motions', ensuring that 'all the control boxes were ticked' when the internal auditors came to check. People worked out quickly that the name of the game was first and foremost to be *seen* to outwardly comply, not to actually follow the commercial spirit of the new processes and genuinely add value. The end result was that often people were essentially behaving just as they had before, but now with *more* bureaucracy and *more* delays. No one (at least below CIO level) really understood why change was imperative. Basically, IT staff were 'in denial'; they did not treat the

changes as 'real' and did not commit to personal behavioural change.

Underlying all of this was a fundamental problem with the IT senior management 'leadership team'. I was trying to find a pithy way to characterize their behaviours when I happened to come across a paragraph in Terry White's *Reinventing the IT Department* that captured it superbly (and with a level of candour that not even I would risk). As he puts it, they 'operate as a boy's club and meet in their tree house to discuss secret things. They stick together and have secret codes and stuff ... Very often there is so much plotting within the "team" that their energy is largely directed away from the business, in fact business is the vehicle they use to gain advantage over each other in the gang.' I cannot improve on that. He also says that these are the behaviours that he finds to some extent in most large corporations and, sadly, I would have to say that that has also been my experience.

To summarize, the key difficulties in making real change happen were *people* difficulties. *Vast* people difficulties. This case study is an excellent illustration of the management consultancy mantra, repeated on entry to every client, 'There's always a problem and it's always a people problem.' I could be (uncharacteristically) uncharitable and simply say that pretty much everyone acted rather stupidly (if sometimes with well-intentioned stupidity). But these were not stupid people. What they were actually 'guilty' of was displaying uncommercial acumen and complying with the dominant corporate culture by toeing the line, not making waves, keeping their heads below the parapet, protecting their backsides, looking after No. 1 and going through the motions. Well, hello, this is not exactly unique behaviour in large corporations. In fact, large corporations often *reward* people who display these 'good corporate citizen' behaviours with promotion! So please note that I am not suggesting for a moment that there were any real villains in this piece. I'm sure the key players did not go home and kick the cat and rough up their wives. These were nice people. I'm sure they went home each night sincerely believing that they had put in a good day's work and done what was expected of them. They generally did what they thought to be 'best'. Unfortunately it was not remotely commercially 'best' for the company.

You have got to have the right people with the right skills and the right behaviours making the right practice changes and you have got to carry the hearts and minds of the people who must change to accommodate your changed practices. And even then a wise change programme manager will treat the motives of all the participants with a robust but kindly cynicism. In this case study we essentially see an easily resistible force meeting an almost totally immovable object. The exasperated CIO compared his role to being the captain of a vast supertanker, where even small rudder changes took miles of travel before there was any discernible change in direction (incidentally, quite independently, the CIO of *another* major British retailer described *his* IT function to me as 'a supertanker sailing in corporate treacle'). The root cause for the immense difficulty of making successful changes was that the organization had not addressed the underlying (huge) cultural and behavioural barriers to change. There is nothing more difficult to pin down or more difficult to change than an organization's culture, but this was unquestionably at the root of the problem. The IT transformation programme was in itself trying to institute practices that would drive behavioural transformation but was scuppered by the very culture it was trying to change. In summary:

- There was no clear change leadership (actually, there was no leadership, full stop). The IT senior management team generally did not 'walk the talk' but instead cynically attempted to give the *impression* of supporting the initiatives; knowingly, or unknowingly, they were actually sending clear messages to staff that it would all go away in time.
- Key stakeholders, particularly in the user community, were not remotely supportive and, understandably, saw the changes as being *counter*productive to their parochial interests.
- There was no clear accountability for success and no apparent penalty for failure.
- Solutions developed were poorly co-ordinated and generally 'academic' and commercially unpragmatic.
- There *was* a compelling need for change but the culture of complacency was so strong that this was not recognized by the management and staff until 'too late'.

Incidentally, you may be interested to know how the senior IT management team responded to the points raised above. Our presentation of our findings was certainly not as robustly worded as I have set it out above (we were taking a lot of money out of the company and fully intended to continue doing so) but was still hard-hitting. Their response was salutary. Were they shocked and horrified? Did they immediately take radical action? Well, no. Basically they smiled ruefully and said, 'Yes, that's pretty much the way all big programmes go around here.' And then life went on as before (until they were outsourced).

A final, and very important, point I want to emphasize about this case study is that the company concerned was not at all naive about the need for behavioural change management. This transformation programme began with a considerable weight of change management techniques behind it (including the identification of change sponsors, change leaders, stakeholders, communications strategy etc.). But, once again, they were basically 'going through the motions' – it was 'change management by numbers'. What they needed (minimally) was senior management, project management and change leaders who cared *passionately* about making a *real* difference and actually *realizing value*, not people who were just doing their jobs, however 'professionally'. If they are not losing sleep over it then they are not the right people for the job. And so they *still* hit all these problems, basically because they radically underestimated the vast inertia of their own culture. And before you judge, look *honestly* at your own company and ask yourself how much different it would really be if your organization tackled a similarly ambitious programme of change.

Perhaps now you can see why I am so cynical about programmes to 'transform IT' and why I urge you to set yourself the much more modest (but still hugely challenging) target of transforming IT *value*. Perhaps you can also see why I have become increasingly disillusioned with change programmes that focus on the traditional panacea of implementing 'best practices'. The company in our case study had made enormous strides in improving its 'best practice' capabilities. But it was not achieving improved, value-adding business outcomes.

3.20 CFFs and CSFs for effectiveness improvement programmes

What are the key things that most often go wrong in IT effectiveness improvement programmes? You may well say that that list was probably exemplified in the 'Murphy's law' case study above! But what, *generally*, are the critical *failure* factors (CFFs)? In no particular order:

- Poor calibre people responsible for designing, making or deploying changes. ('I should do what *they* tell me.')

- Lack of stakeholder buy-in. ('These practices are going to make my commercial failures much more visible – *but only if the programme succeeds!*')
- Lack of a really compelling need for change, or, more typically, there *is* a compelling need for change but it is largely *unrecognized or poorly articulated*. ('It'll all go away in time and I can get back to doing things the old way.')
- Lack of senior management sponsorship. ('I'm 100 per cent behind this IT transformation initiative – just so long as it doesn't actually take up any of my time.')
- Lack of business management buy-in. ('I'm 100 per cent behind this IT transformation initiative – just so long as it doesn't make my life any more difficult.')
- Allowing too much special pleading. ('I'm 100 per cent behind this IT transformation initiative but the changes proposed clearly aren't appropriate in *my* cost centre.')
- Taking too long. ('By the time this IT transformation initiative is over the world will have moved on so much no one will be able to say whether we've delivered the benefits or not.')
- Allowing too much smoke and too many mirrors. ('I don't have to *actually* change how I do business, just be seen to go through the motions.')
- Creating unrealistic expectations of the speed of benefits delivery. ('Where are all those quick wins you promised me?')
- Implementing practices that are generally 'academic' and commercially unpragmatic. ('This stuff looks great. Pity it won't work.')
- Being overambitious and failing to focus on the practices that will really add value, i.e. 'best practices', rather than 'best value practices'. ('Well, that should certainly solve world poverty.')
- A conservative, complacent, stonewalling corporate culture. ('Not in my back yard, buddy.')
- A corporate culture that rewards successful political game playing more than actually adding value to the business. ('OK, so the organization lost. But, hey, I won!')

Rather more positively I set out below my 'Top 20' CSFs for an IT effectiveness improvement programme. I appreciate that you may understandably say that you cannot possibly have *20* success factors all of which are 'critical'. All I can say to that is that there is no substitute for experience and I invite you to ignore any of these CSFs at your peril. They are summarized in Figure 3.10.

	20 CSFs for an IT effectiveness improvement programme
1	Ensure that there is absolute clarity on the objectives of the programme
2	Ensure that the programme sponsor clearly articulates the objectives, the benefits and *the compelling need for change* to the whole business
3	Ensure that senior IT managers *demonstrably* commit the time and energy necessary to make a success of the changes to be implemented
4	Critically assess the openness to change of the existing IT management team
5	Put your *best* programme manager and project leaders on the programme
6	Staff the project teams with your *best* people
7	Confront disagreements immediately and actively manage down resistance
8	Conduct a 'change readiness assessment'
9	Identify 'process champions' or 'change leaders' across the IT function and make them *accountable* for the success of specific process changes
10	Identify the various project stakeholders and make them genuinely *accountable* for the realization of the benefits of the programme
11	Don't run change projects 'in silos'
12	Define clear deliverable and benefit milestones for each project
13	Don't try to 'solve world poverty'
14	Be realistic about the level of change that people can accommodate in any given time period
15	Ensure that new working practices established are *pragmatic*
16	Test the acceptability and workability of proposed changes in working practices at the earliest opportunity
17	Don't try to 'reinvent the wheel'; use existing 'off-the-shelf' solutions
18	Ensure that there is extensive 'hand-holding' available to IT staff
19	Ensure that there is extensive QA of compliance with the new processes
20	Monitor and report the success of the programme

Figure 3.10

1 *Do* ensure that there is absolute clarity on the objectives (i.e. desired outcomes – not *what* you are going to deliver but *why* you are bothering) of the programme, whether it be improving the alignment between the IT function and the business, improving systems delivery time to market, improving the reliability of projects delivery to budget and schedule, improving the realization of project benefits, improving service levels, or whatever.

2 *Do* ensure that the programme sponsor (typically the CIO or his immediate superior) clearly articulates the objectives, the benefits and *the compelling need for change* to the whole business (not just the IT function) so they buy in and actively

support the programme. If there is no *truly* compelling need for change it will be *extremely* difficult to make real change happen.

3 *Do* ensure that senior IT managers *demonstrably* commit the time and energy necessary to make a success of the changes to be implemented (it will be substantial, even if it is 'just' about implementing a subset of the best value practices) and *demonstrably* 'walk the talk'. Never underestimate the ability of even the most junior of IT staff to spot humbug, cynicism and hypocrisy in their superiors and then go on to emulate it (because that's the way to get ahead here). Note that in a recent independent survey of 444 organizations, 93 per cent stated that high calibre change leadership was a prerequisite of successful change.

4 *Do* take a long, hard look at the IT senior management team and ask some robust questions about their openness to change. A close-minded, parochial, or defensive group, who may not function together effectively as a true leadership team, is pretty much *guaranteed* to sink any IT change programme.

5 *Do* put your *best* programme manager and project leaders on the job, people with extensive experience of managing complex programmes of work – and do not burden them with strictly unnecessary bureaucracy. Establish reward mechanisms that make it clear that the principal objective is to deliver work products that actually work and realize value, not just to 'mechanically' follow the original plan.

6 *Do* staff the project teams with your *best* people, including subject matter experts in each of the change areas. The teams must include your most capable and experienced staff, not 'special projects' R&D staff who may be out of touch with the mainstream realities of systems and service delivery, and whose recommendations for change may not be respected by colleagues. Establish performance review and reward mechanisms that ensure that, even if the teams are only constructed on a temporary secondment basis, their loyalty and commitment will be to the success of the change programme.

7 When the change programme hits disagreements (and it certainly will, particularly from senior end users who may want no part of your 'brave new world'), *do* confront them immediately and actively manage down resistance – never assume 'it will all sort itself out' – it won't, it will just get worse.

8 *Do* conduct a 'change readiness assessment' to understand whether you are actually capable of the level of change

proposed. Then prepare comprehensive communications plans, stakeholder management plans and training plans and deploy them assiduously. Everyone (including the key user stakeholders) must understand exactly *why* these changes are being made and, through compulsory education/training, have no excuse for not deploying and supporting them.

9 *Do* identify 'process champions' or 'change leaders' across the IT function and make them *accountable* for the success of specific process changes (and incentivize them appropriately).

10 *Do* identify the various project stakeholders and make them genuinely *accountable* for the realization of the benefits of the programme; there must be *consequences*.

11 *Don't* run change projects 'in silos'; there will almost inevitably be many influences, dependencies and synergies and these must be programme managed effectively.

12 *Do* define clear deliverable and benefit milestones for each project (e.g. 'When all IT staff have completed training') that unequivocally either have or have not been reached. Manage the programme by these project milestones *proactively* – missed and moved milestones must have *consequences.*

13 *Don't* try to 'solve world poverty'. Focus on the best value practices in the first instance. If ever a programme required rigorous scope control, it is an IT change programme. Resist the temptation to expand the agenda to address every known ill. For example, a project that starts with the work objective of improving estimating techniques can easily turn into one that is attempting to revolutionize the entire approach to project management.

14 *Do* be realistic about the level of change that people can accommodate in any given time period; true 'transformation' is typically going to take *years*, not months. Therefore introduce changes in phases, first establishing basic disciplines. For example, if one of your change projects is to introduce business transfer charging for IT services, then you may want to start with the establishment of staff timesheet completion. Getting this alone working honestly and accurately is typically going to be a challenge. Only once this is an established discipline might you consider moving on to preparing 'virtual' bills and finally to actually billing users.

15 *Do* ensure that new working practices established are *pragmatic*; a simple process that actually works is far preferable to a highly engineered 'sophisticated' process that is unworkable.

16 *Do* test the acceptability and workability of proposed changes in working practices at the earliest opportunity; don't let the team 'sit in a corner' for months and then spring their fully formed monster on an unsuspecting public.

17 *Don't* try to 'reinvent the wheel'; use existing 'off-the-shelf' solutions that are well proven. In particular, consider mitigating the 'bootstrap problem' (of having inadequate programme/project control of change projects designed to *improve* programme/project control) by 'seeding' the change programme with consultants/contractors who bring propri-etary (or public domain) programme/project management skills and tools with them.

18 *Do* ensure that there is extensive 'hand-holding' available to IT staff attempting to adjust to the new practices (remember, they do have a 'day job'); if possible, take experienced practitioners and 'seed' them into other areas.

19 *Do* ensure that there is extensive QA of compliance with the new processes, but compliance with the *spirit*, not just the letter. The QA programme must be seen as a facilitator of excellence, not a 'gotcha' programme. Similarly, ensure that there are clear compliance incentives ('carrots') and equally clear non-compliance sanctions ('sticks').

20 *Do* monitor and report the success of the programme and publicize success stories widely. It is not enough for good to be done – it must be *seen* to be done.

I don't underestimate the difficulty of complying with these 20 CSFs. But the benefits of making real change happen are surely worth it. When senior management do not *really* believe that their IT function is actually able to 'change its spots' or simply that it would take unacceptably long to do so, the obvious answer is to 'give' the IT function to an ESP and let them get on with it. This is essentially what happened in our case study above. Incidentally, in my opinion, this is actually one of the (unspoken) key reasons why IT functions are outsourced – not 'focusing on our core business', 'moving to a more variable cost base' or 'reducing our cost', but actually just the exhaustion of senior management patience.

So, not wishing to pre-empt your views on becoming employees of CSC, EDS or Accenture, it might be preferable to 'heal thyself' rather than submit yourself to the more aggressive change strategies that ESPs may adopt under commercial duress. Indeed, you may have to look no further to identify your 'burning platform' for change.

In the next chapter I will examine the 'other part' of the supply-side value equation, the cost-efficiency of an IT function.

3.21 Summary

Transfer charging for IT products and services between an IT function and the business it serves is fraught with difficulties but is nevertheless a prerequisite to many value-adding and effectiveness improvement initiatives.

The six key value-adding CSFs are:

- **Optimizing IT function alignment:** optimizing the strategic alignment of the IT function with the business it serves (so they share common commercial goals).
- **Optimizing competitive advantage:** optimizing the identification of IT opportunities that will yield the highest competitive advantage for the business.
- **Optimizing portfolio alignment:** optimizing the alignment between the *products* of the IT function and the business units that they support (so they facilitate the business unit achieving *its* commercial goals).
- **Optimizing projects value:** prioritizing IT work so that the highest value (alignment/cost/benefit/risk) work takes priority.
- **Optimizing value delivery:** *sustaining* the value-adding imperative throughout the development process.
- **Optimizing benefits realization:** optimizing the realization of promised benefits.

Key prerequisites to the success of best value practices deployed to address these CSFs are:

- Effective IT governance structures and procedures.
- The agreement of SMART objectives and KPIs.
- The mapping of business objectives to IT function objectives and the cascading of associated objectives, measures and targets down through the IT function hierarchy.
- *Genuine* accountability by the IT function's management and staff for achieving targets agreed.
- Full total cost of ownership costings for all IT products and services.
- *Genuine* financial accountability by users for both the costs of IT products and services consumed and the benefits realized from them.

- Rigorous definition and quantification of the benefits and the definition of benefit delivery plans.
- *Genuine* project/programme manager accountability for managing business case variations throughout the development process.
- Ongoing cost and benefit monitoring post-implementation.
- End-to-end service level management processes.
- *Genuine* commitment to behavioural change management addressing both the IT function and business user communities.

4

Optimizing cost-efficiency

Everyone is always in favour of general economy
and particular expenditure.

Anthony Eden

The previous chapter focused on the adoption of best value
practices in the effectiveness quadrant of the supply side of the
'value compass' in order to achieve the principal outcome of
improved value-added to the business (as assessed in the value-
added, demand-side, quadrant). This chapter focuses on examining the issue of 'general economy' and how to optimize the
cost-efficiency, supply-side, quadrant, the 'flip side' of adding
value to the business.

I use the quote above from Mr Eden (we should listen to words
of wisdom from the British Prime Minister who gave us the Suez
Crisis in 1956?) to illustrate the fact that while each IT cost centre
manager will doubtless agree that the IT function *as a whole* must
be run economically, *their* particular cost centre is, of course, an
exception and uniquely requires specific investments . . . Beware
the spectre of special pleading.

The cost-efficiency of IT product and service supply can rarely
be ignored, and in times of global, national or company
recession can come startlingly, and rapidly, to the top of the
business agenda. However, if IT cost-efficiency optimization is
simply not on your company's agenda (what a sweet, trusting
CFO you have) then it is perfectly possible to simply skip this
chapter and go straight on to Chapter 5. The book has been
written in such a way as to segregate as far as is practicable the
'cost-efficiency' and 'value-adding' issues so that each chapter
can largely 'stand alone'. However, simply ignoring the cost-
efficiency of the supplier (the internal IT function) is to

potentially walk away from major value improving opportunities. If, in terms of the SAM model set out in Chapter 2, your IT function is operating as a profit centre or service centre, or even more so as a cost centre, then cost-efficiency will be key to IT value. So please think twice before skipping forward!

4.1 Defining the cost-efficiency improvement goal

'Optimizing cost-efficiency' may sound like a long 'weasel words" phrase for 'cost reduction' but I use it very deliberately to help emphasize the fact that our goal is to achieve the *right* IT cost base, not necessarily the *lowest* cost.

Improvements in cost-efficiency (on the supply side) will improve quality (on the demand side) because the 'quality' of which we speak is *commercial* quality (i.e. necessary and sufficient quality *for the price*). It will also improve value-added (on the demand side) because value is a matter of *net* benefits (i.e. the cost of product and service delivery is the 'flip side' of the benefits of the products and services supplied). The cost-efficiency improvement goal is to optimize the economic and efficient delivery of IT products and services.

'Economy' is about the business establishing a commercially appropriate level of spend with the IT function and it in turn managing *its* spend economically. 'Efficiency' is primarily about optimizing the IT function's utilization of assets and productivity of staff. The 'economy' and 'efficiency' aspects interact and are concerned with minimizing (at acceptable risk, and without unacceptably compromising effectiveness) the entire cost base of IT supply.

Basically we want to optimize the price, performance and utilization of 'IT assets', whether these are assets which are 'fixed' (e.g. technology, infrastructure, buildings) or assets that can 'walk' (like 'people'). For example, for a server *of necessary and sufficient quality* we (generally) want to select and buy one as cheaply as possible, with the highest (price-)performance possible and then utilize it as highly as possible. For a person *of necessary and sufficient quality* we want to pay that person as little as possible, ensure that they are as productive as possible and utilize their time (i.e. *productive* time) as highly as possible (while, obviously, fully respecting their work-life balance!). As a general rule, the more 'commercial' the culture of an organization, the more visible (and measured) are these factors.

4.2 Creating a commercial culture

As an example of a highly commercial culture, let's return to our old 'friends' the management consultancy firms. Some years ago I was working in one of the 'Big 5' consultancy firms when it was one of the 'Big 6' – we were merging with our key competitor. When the merger was announced the question that most journalists asked was, apparently, 'where will the merged firm be headquartered?' The lead partner replied that the question was meaningless because, thanks to cellphones, mobile computing and the hotdesking approach applied by both merging firms, the very concept of 'headquarters' had become meaningless. The merged 'firm' would simply be an electronic affiliation of expertise, its 'headquarters' essentially 'virtual'. While this certainly does have more than a whiff of PR rhetoric about it, it is nonetheless essentially true. Most consultants spend most of their time out on client sites, often 'borrowing' the desk of someone who is off on vacation, training or sick leave. In fact, if I could be permitted just a moment of mild cynicism, in many large corporations, where vacation entitlement increases with length of service, there is a 'mandated' 10 days minimum training a year, people are encouraged to attend industry conferences and people with mild hangovers (or world cup soccer games to watch) feel it is appropriate to 'take a sickie', I have found that it is often quite difficult to find people *at* their desks. Anyway, it is true to say that most consultants working for the big consultancy firms effectively 'carry head office around with them', courtesy of their laptop and dial-up connection. And if they are not borrowing a client's desk they are usually on a train downloading emails onto their laptop via their cellphone, working in an airport lounge, in their hotel room or at home. Management consultants have no fixed abode, no daily place to lay their hats and no 'nick-knacks' to place on their desks, because they don't have desks (let alone a corporate head office to which they commute every day). In a very real sense they don't actually work for an 'organization', they work for themselves, under a brand name that increases their value as a result of the customers' trust in that brand. Basically, the entire infrastructure of a management consultancy firm is geared towards maximizing cost-efficiency (principally minimizing or displacing fixed costs), just as its means of service provision is geared towards maximizing value-added (I am referring to value added to the consultancy firm here, rather than value added to the firm's clients).

In the (traditional, advisory) management consultancy business almost all assets (at least of the value-adding kind) are people, the consultants. Consultants are generally near-permanently out of the 'line of sight' of their line manager because the chances of both the manager and the consultant working at the same time on the same project on the same client site on the same day are negligible. In my many years as a consultant in the big consultancy firms I probably saw my line manager at best two to three times a year, typically by accident (and my manager changed on average annually anyway). So how does the manager assess the performance of the consultant? Answer: by *outcomes* (allied to very high levels of trust and empowerment in the individual consultant). And the key outcome is how much value (money) he or she is adding to the consultancy business. The primary measure of a consultant is his or her utilization (i.e. the percentage of available hours booked to client billable activities). Each of those chargeable hours is priced based on three key factors, namely:

- what the consultant is paid;
- how valuable the services being provided by the consultant are likely to be to the client; and
- what the market will bear.

Therefore senior, higher paid consultants performing high value-adding work for a client who is relatively un-price sensitive (principally the financial services sector) will be priced highly, while junior, lower paid consultants performing 'commodity' (typically 'body shopping') work for a client who is relatively price sensitive (principally the public services sector) will be lower priced.

Every consultant knows (generally to one decimal point) what his or her cumulative utilization is, week by week. Every consultant knows exactly what utilization target has been set for him or her. A consultant wanting a pay rise or promotion can quickly work out exactly how much money he or she made for the firm (and whether or not the utilization – i.e. sales – target has been hit) and so go into the salary negotiation knowing their financial worth. And if they get that pay rise their chargeable rate will go up. Which means they will then have to be that much more productive to get through the same amount of work in a given time (i.e. for a given assignment budget). Additionally it becomes that much more difficult to achieve the assigned utilization target because they now cost more, so consultancy managers are less inclined to select them for their consultancy assignments. So they will have to work much harder selling themselves both internally and externally to justify their increased cost. I have known many consultants who actively shunned promotion because they did not believe they could sustain their utilization targets or increase their productivity enough to live up to the increased chargeout rate that would be associated with that promotion. And they knew that as a result of *that* they would quickly become targets for an 'involuntary career event' (i.e. redundancy), quite aside from the misery of knowing they were failing despite working longer and harder. I observed many rounds of redundancies in my time at the big management consultancies and the first to go were almost invariably the people who had not been able to live up to their increased chargeout rates. This is hard – but it is commercial reality.

Additionally, if consultants end up on commodity work for poor paying clients this hits their prospects and their pockets. Tough. That's also commercial reality. It is their job to engineer themselves onto the high profile, high revenue, high margin jobs (through a combination of training, 'networking' with the right people, internal salesmanship and, let's face it, occasional brown-nosing). *And* if they go on training (or attend internal meetings or fall sick or take long lunch breaks) then their utilization will suffer correspondingly. All this focuses the mind wonderfully on whether you really *need* that training, *need* to attend that meeting (or, indeed, can afford to take a day off sick). That is also commercial reality. And if you think *that's* tough, then try being a *self-employed* management consultant where you are not paid at all when you are sick, attending training or 'chasing ambulances' to find work. Then add to all this the fact that management consultancy firms do not employ salesmen – even junior consultants are expected to be out with the client seeking sales opportunities and making sales. No one is going to 'give' you work.

The reason I am labouring this a bit is because the management consultancy industry (like all professional services businesses) is generally an excellent role model for inculcating commercial behaviours (i.e. creating a 'commercial culture'). The key drivers of these behaviours are the business performance measures chosen (and their direct impact on staff at all levels). There is a direct, very visible and measured 'connect' between the cost of staff, the utilization of staff, the productivity of staff and the value they add to the business (note again that I mean the *consultancy* business, not necessarily the *client's* business!). And this is clearly understood by *all* consultants, from the most junior to the most senior (although the most senior will tend to justify *their* pay rises and promotions on their ability to sell work to clients in the first place). And, of course, clients don't just agree to a proposition of, 'We'll put three consultants on this job and the price will be £X.' They want to know whether they are going to get three graduate trainees who will learn on their time and money or three grey-haired consultants who have seen it all before. Furthermore, most consultancy jobs are sold on a fixed price basis (in effect, even if they are contractually on a 'time and materials' basis, because it is typically unacceptable to bill above the quote for advisory work) or on a contingent fee basis (i.e. shared risk/reward). In the latter case, the fees paid are directly related to the benefits achieved. In the former case, if the work has been underestimated, it is the consultancy firm who have to pick up the extra cost, not the client. This concentrates the mind of the project manager who has to estimate the job and deliver it to budget and schedule. It also concentrates the mind of any consultant working on the job because once the individual has booked all the time allocated in the budget there is huge commercial pressure to stop booking time, even if long hours are being worked (because it typically cannot be billed and will simply show as a loss on the job, branding it as a failure). This means that the individual who (either as a result of the work being underestimated or as a result of simply over-running) exceeds the allocated budget is working 'unutilized', i.e. without being able to claim billable hours. Which means the utilization targets (and the next pay rise) are harder to hit. In the 'Big 6/5/4' consultancies in which I worked there simply was no code on the timesheet for 'working flat out for a client but unable to book it to the client code because the job was ridiculously underbudgeted in order to win the work'. Instead you had no option but to book that time to a code bleakly called 'Unproductive', pushing down your utilization and making it look as though your were idling the day away, not working yourself into a state of exhaustion! In other words there are huge management and staff *individual* pressures (personal, psycho-logical and financial incentives) to estimate the job accurately and not over-run on budget or schedule. All this seems very unfair – well, tough, that's also commercial reality.

In a management consultancy organization, hard work, long hours and high competence (not to mention 'permanent' excellent mental and physical health and not allowing any personal problems to affect your work performance) are the 'givens'. These are the *starting point* for achievement which will earn you a 'C' ('adequate performance') rating in the annual performance appraisal. You don't expect to get a pay rise for this – it is simply what you are being paid for. The pay rise has to be justified by *exceeding* your business performance targets.

Translate this highly commercial environment and culture to a 'typical' internal IT function where:

- people 'expect' a pay rise just because they have been competent and hard working (i.e. done their job), irrespective of whether or not their work has demonstrably increased company profitability;
- people are not so much 'paid by results' as paid 'attendance fees' for turning up at their place of work each day ('presenteeism');
- neither individuals nor their management know how productively their time is being spent (utilization);
- individuals have (by implication) no utilization target and certainly no 'sales' target – they are simply 'given' work to do, they don't have to sell the work;
- projects are charged to the business (if at all) on the basis of 'heads' assigned to the project (even if some of the team are trainees on £25 000 per annum and some are contractors on £125 000 per annum);
- the cost of the project (indeed typically the entire cost of IT supply) is carried as a corporate overhead so the project team is not under any *real* budgetary pressure from the business project sponsor;
- the cost of project over-runs are picked up at a corporate level;
- pay rises do not result in any requirement for the individual to be proportionately more productive;
- pay rises do not depress the ability of a member of staff to be selected to work on a project;
- pay rises are not related to the *business* value of the work performed;
- once recruited, staff do not generally have to sell themselves either internally (within the IT function) or externally (within the business) to get work;
- going on training courses, attending internal meetings or going off sick have little or no personal ramifications (and certainly no personal financial ramifications);
- underestimated project work has no personal ramifications for project members (in fact they might even get overtime or a bonus for working late to compensate).

In fact most internal IT functions do not charge *at all* for project costs. They are generally simply 'called off' annually agreed 'slices of the available IT budget cake'. There is therefore only the most indirect, virtually invisible and typically unmeasured 'connect' between the cost of staff, the utilization of staff, the productivity of staff and the value they add to the business. And when was the last time you heard of a business project sponsor vetting the project team proposed? And what about 'shared risk/reward'? When was the last time you heard of an IT function having its budgets reduced (or its management team taking a pay cut) because they failed to deliver an important project on schedule? And when a project is underestimated and has to have resources thrown at it to achieve the deadline, these incur real costs, not Monopoly money. The additional work/ money is being 'stolen' from someone else's budget and ultimately finds its way back to the total cost of IT service provision. But this is so indirect that no real 'connect' exists to (financially) motivate the project manager or staff member. Indeed, if (as a result of underestimation or staff over-run) resources (i.e. *money*) have to be thrown at a project in order to bring it in on schedule, this is typically *rewarded*. The bottom line here is 'consequences'. In a truly commercial organization there are serious *personal* consequences of both success and failure. If work goes over budget or over schedule or fails to delight the customer then *you personally* will suffer. And if you are financially rewarded for success, you personally will have to work harder and be more productive in future to be able to support that reward. Basically, I'm sure I could come up with a scheme better designed to inculcate *un*commercial culture and behaviours than that in place in the typical internal IT function but it does not immediately come to mind.

In a way the above is my fundamental indictment of 'corporate culture'. In fact, I almost regard the word 'corporate' as an antonym of 'entrepreneurial'. This book is an attempt to engender, as far as is practicable, entrepreneurial (or, at least, commercial) behaviours in the IT functions that sit within large organizations. Some of you reading this will, I am sure, take the view that life as a management consultant sounds pretty ghastly, at least compared with the relatively easy ride of working in a typical IT function and that, actually, you rather like working under the cosy blanket of corporate culture. Well, life as a management consultant *is* much tougher. But it is also *much* more rewarding (and I don't just mean financially) to feel at the cutting edge of commerce – it is a highly insecure, highly demanding, 'war time' job that pushes people to work to the limits of their abilities. A great many people have no wish to work in such a culture. What I call 'exciting' they call 'stressful' (but remember that stress is not an inherent property of an activity – stress occurs on *maladaptation* to an activity). If someone is daft enough to keep paying them for riding the gravy train then they are only too happy to 'simply turn in a day's work' and not worry themselves about the commercial realities. Fine. But that is not the basis on which commercially successful businesses are built. Growing a business is about embracing change and risk, not embracing stability and security. Remember what I said in Chapter 2 about confusing busyness with business? In the 1980s IBM itself, that epitome of corporate culture, was almost brought to its knees by entrepreneurial upstarts like Microsoft who did not confuse busyness with business and who did not have a culture in which 'giving good presentation' and successfully playing the internal political game was the way up.

There is another related, and important, point to be taken from the above discussion and that point is the importance of metrics. I tried to illustrate above how just one measure of staff performance, 'utilization', had dramatic ramifications in terms of motivating staff to increase their productivity, sell more work and deliver that work to budget and schedule. It also informed views of personal (financial) worth and drove decisions about the benefits and risks of seeking pay rises and promotions. It even made staff think very carefully indeed about whether or not they could (personally) afford to attend a training course or take a day off sick. Basically, it was key in creating a culture in which each individual member of staff tended to behave like a one man entrepreneurial business, quite the opposite of 'corporate culture'. However, I don't want to suggest that the situation is 'black and white'. If there is a 'perfect' metric I have yet to see it. Even the 'utilization' metric has its behavioural downside, the most obvious of which is the 'protectionism' culture it can easily engender as individuals and groups in the consultancy business fight to make their utilization targets, taking on work that other individuals and groups might well be more effective in performing. Routing work to the expert team when *your* team is not making its targets is certainly the 'right' commercial behaviour (for both the consultancy firm *and* the client) but not behaviour that the utilization metric engenders. In my 16 years within the 'Big 6/5/4' management consultancy firms I saw many attempts to create complementary incentives that would help to balance this key downside of the utilization metric (such as measuring the amount of work 'cross-sold') but it was always like taking a medicine to counteract the side-effects of the main medicine you were taking – it just seemed to create more unwelcome side-effects that in turn needed more medicines. 'Utilization' was just too powerful a metric. I take up the issues and opportunities of metrics in detail in the next chapter.

In the previous chapter I proposed an approach to increasing commercial accountability in IT functions by implementing transfer charging in particular and implementing best value practices in general. In this chapter I am not assuming that these improvements have been effected. However, an organization that *has* implemented transfer charging and best value practices will find that many of the cost-efficiency improvements advocated in this chapter will be easier to implement. It will also find that there will be increasing pressure to implement such cost-efficiency improvements because the 'connect' between the quantity of service taken, the service level provided and the *cost* of that service and service level will be much stronger in the business mind.

4.3 The bottom line – tariffs

Optimizing the cost-efficiency of IT product and service supply is about minimizing the 'tariffs' for all products and services provided by the IT function because these are the 'prices' you 'charge' the business. If you have implemented transfer pricing then these tariffs will be very visible indeed. Even if you have not established a tariff structure and don't transfer charge directly you will still need this information if you are going to be able to build credible project business cases that include full total cost of ownership (TCO) lifetime costs. You may also want to know the total cost of ownership of the products and services being 'sold' in order to manage them effectively (and be able to make informed sourcing decisions).

It is essential (if we are to realize best value) that the tariffs are basically 'honest', i.e. that they include all direct and indirect costs and that any service cross-subsidies that exist are fully accounted for. It is also essential that all tariffs be readily understood (at least at a high level) by customers. This requires that the services tariffed are defined and packaged in such a way as to be immediately recognizable to the business (e.g. a 'desktop' service, including all hardware, software, maintenance and support is 'good', a 'client' service, 'LAN' service, 'WAN' service, 'helpdesk' service etc. is not so good). Only in this way can we present a meaningful 'cost vs service level' proposition to the business that they will truly understand and will help incentivize commercially appropriate (best value) behaviours.

4.4 Why bother?

You may well say, 'I thought this book was about increasing value, not cutting cost'. But cost is a key aspect of value. You ignore it at your peril. Gartner recently reported that the average company wastes approximately 20 per cent of its IT budget on misguided projects and inefficient spending (amounting to about $500bn of corporate IT investment globally). In my experience that 20 per cent figure is a woeful underestimate – however, irrespective of whether the 'accurate' figure is 20 per cent, 30 per cent or more, you have to ask whether CIOs (and CFOs) can afford to ignore it. And while the 'e-business revolution/evolution' may indeed be gradually increasing the perception by senior management of the value-adding role of their IT functions, the fact remains that even today most IT functions are still run as cost centres and are perceived by senior management as business overhead groups. In short, they will not be immune from cost cutting pressures, especially when times get tough. Therefore CIOs should be *seen* to be proactive and innovative in demonstrating the ability to optimize supply-side cost-efficiency and minimize tariffs. If business senior management perceive IT to be essentially incapable of 'changing its spots' their typical instinctive reaction will be to outsource IT as a whole, in the (perhaps touchingly naive) belief that the ESP will deliver the savings to them (I will deal with *why* I say this is naive later in this chapter). The decision by one of my clients to outsource almost their entire IT function (involving over 2000 IT staff) had all the appearance of a classic example of this. They doubtless had other goals, such as moving to a more variable cost base in uncertain revenue times and getting some cash in the door. But this company *could* have pursued the internal cost-efficiency improvement route; instead they chose to largely give the problem to the outsourcer and let *them* sort it out. Of course they *still* had a requirement to identify and size the cost-efficiency improvement opportunities in order to be able to broker the best commercial deal with the outsourcer (basically saying in the negotiations, 'We *know* you can easily take X *per cent* out of the IT supply cost base – so let's talk about your tariffs on that basis').

4.5 Why not just sack staff?

Simplistically, cost-efficiency improvement can be achieved by cost reduction or efficiency improvement (or both). Given the choice, I suspect most CIOs would prefer the latter. But they often don't have the choice (when the dictate comes from above). How do business cost cutting pressures typically manifest themselves? The traditional 'knee-jerk' reaction of most organizations when confronted with a need to reduce costs is to reduce staffing levels. This typically results in the issue of a dictum from on high that *X per cent* of staff will be offered voluntary severance, or, worse, compulsory redundancy. This is a management 'no brainer'.

This 'philosophy' was adopted by the company I worked for back in the early 1980s. I was managing a team of 80 staff in their IT function. One Monday morning I was called in (as were all the other IT managers) and told that I had three days to come up with a list of 10 per cent of my staff who would be made redundant the following Monday. The selection had to be made purely on merit and I was not allowed to confer with anyone on the matter. This resulted in some appallingly difficult decisions since, even where poorly performing staff could be clearly identified, it could not, in all conscience, be so simple a process as to select solely on merit. For example, I knew that certain poor performers had large families and had recently taken on huge mortgages. Other better performers were young, unmarried and in rented accommodation. It was humanely impossible to just ignore these points. Anyway, the deed was done and, despite predictions of the doom and destruction that would ensue as 10 per cent of the work force disappeared, there was, tellingly, *no* discernable drop in service levels subsequently. A year later (after I had left to become a consultant) a virtually identical process was conducted, but this time the effect was felt rather more keenly. This 'philosophy' for cost reduction is known colloquially as 'squeezing till the pips squeak'. I quote it for three reasons, namely:

1 It is a perfectly valid approach to reducing IT costs, which is considerably easier, simpler and more guaranteed to deliver results than the approaches I set out below. It is also, by the way, the approach almost invariably used by management consultancies when *they* perform internal cost reduction exercises. Note, however, that the cost bases of management consultancy firms are dominated by people costs, which is not the case in the typical IT function.

2 If the people who are removed are carefully targeted external contractors or internal management and staff who are, or have become (perhaps as a result of the 'Peter Principle'), non-value-adding then the benefits, never mind the cost reduction, can be substantial. As I said in Chapter 2 in my 'hierarchy of value', a commercially successful organization will *truly* recognize that 'people are their biggest asset' but will *also* recognize that *certain* people should be their most expendable assets.

3 It helps to illustrate why there is a case for pursuing approaches that place capital asset cost reduction (things) above revenue asset cost reduction (people). This is the approach set out below.

So let's switch our management brains (and consciences) on for a moment (and please don't even suggest that your senior management team don't have either!). Making staff redundant is an almost inevitable consequence of optimizing (minimizing) IT service costs. But surely every other avenue for improving matters in the cost-efficiency quadrant should be explored *first* and only then, if it is still necessary to lose staff, ensure that this is achieved as equitably as possible and with minimal impact on business service levels. This is faint consolation for those who lose their jobs, but at least demonstrates that the company is doing all in its power to both minimize job losses and the impact on the business.

4.6 Identifying cost-efficiency improvement opportunities

So, *assuming* that cost-efficiency is a key goal (which, recalling the SAM model set out in Chapter 2, will be very much the case where the IT function operates as a cost centre, less the case where it operates as a profit centre or service centre, and least the case where it operates as an investment centre), *generally* what are the things we most critically need to do most effectively in our IT function in order to optimize supply-side cost-efficiency?

The cost-efficiency quadrant is, in a sense, more difficult to optimize than the effectiveness quadrant, because it is not just about processes. It is also about 'tin, wire and bricks', i.e. it is about the entire IT cost base and how it might be minimized at acceptable risk and without unacceptable compromising our quality improvement and value-adding objectives. This 'push-pull' issue has to be recognized. For example, a key way to reduce the IT cost base is to move from being an 'early adopter' of 'leading edge' technology to being a 'late adopter' of 'lagging edge' technology. But at what price in terms of lost competitive advantage? Therefore below I only set out opportunities that do not compromise the ability of IT to add value (and which do not create unacceptable levels of business risk).

In 'costs' we include all direct and indirect costs associated with a process (in the IT function and the business as a whole). This will include people costs (permanent, temporary, contractors and consultants), infrastructure costs (e.g. equipment, plant, office space, heating, security) and supplier costs. In 'benefits' we include all direct and indirect benefits associated with a process (in the IT function and the business as a whole). These will include reducing existing production system costs, reducing business overhead costs, reducing business investment, increasing business revenue, avoiding revenue reductions, avoiding cost increases and improving business competitiveness. Remember that the IT function is itself a business overhead. So improving the IT function's cost-efficiency will also improve the value-added to the business.

So where should we look for key opportunities to optimize IT function supply-side cost-efficiency? The first, and most obvious, point is that although IT staff costs are, on average, typically about half of total IT spend (and are therefore an obvious target for cost reduction), substantial opportunities for cost reduction may well exist in the other half of the total IT spend, principally hardware, software and other external spend. And when you rationalize *these* things you are hit with neither a substantial redundancy/severance charge nor a recalcitrant union. So the identification of cost reduction opportunities should clearly be across *all* categories of IT spend, not just staff spend.

There are many ways of categorizing IT spend. The most typical breakdowns are based on the direct and indirect costs of services, cost centres and activities. As we will see, different categorizations will serve different purposes when actually identifying cost-efficiency improvement opportunities and modelling the (financial) results. For example, the cost centre breakdown is likely to be most useful when modelling changes to the total IT budget; the activity-based breakdown is going to be essential for activity analysis work; and the service-based breakdown will be most useful in modelling the cost and (if appropriate) profitability of IT products and services. Where cost-efficiency improvement (and, more particularly, cost reduction) analysis is performed (in an IT function or otherwise), it is typically founded on 'activity-based costing' (ABC) and 'priority-based budgeting' (PBB) approaches that essentially build these various cost models and then focus analysis on 'who is spending most' (and is therefore a *de facto* 'prime suspect'). However, for the purposes of specifically identifying *IT* cost-efficiency improvement opportunities, I suggest it is best to structure work around certain key IT 'domains' and *then* focus on cost intensive aspects within those domains. This is principally because the key competencies necessary to effectively diagnose *IT* cost-efficiency improvement opportunities lie not so much in accounting or finance skills but rather more in very specific IT skills; and it makes sense to structure the work around the differing skills that will be required and the differing nature of opportunities that will arise.

I have divided all IT spend into four domains, corresponding to supplied services and products, 'physical' assets, 'human' assets and spend associated with the activities and services of the IT function.

I am contending that improving IT function cost-efficiency to optimize the value to the business can typically best be achieved by:

- **Optimizing sourcing and purchasing cost-efficiency:** optimizing the sourcing of IT services and optimizing purchasing efficiency, the supplier mix and contractual terms.
- **Optimizing technology and infrastructure cost-efficiency:** optimizing the utilization and efficient use of hardware, software and office space/facilities.
- **Optimizing organization and people cost-efficiency:** optimizing the staff resourcing of projects and teams.
- **Optimizing activities and services cost-efficiency:** rationalizing, and improving the efficiency of, IT activities and services.

These are much less specific than our 'value-adding CSFs' (essentially specifying the key 'domains' in which to look for opportunities to improve IT function cost-efficiency). But this is necessary because every organization will have different specific cost-efficiency weaknesses. Here I will set out the 'usual suspects' which are typically the 'big payoff' opportunities. But that is as far as I can sensibly generalize. The 'beauty' of the six 'value-adding CSFs' is that they are very specific and they will,

I believe, be applicable to virtually all IT functions. Since they are also focused on the 'name of the game' (namely, adding optimum business value) and since the improvements in business value achieved by improving IT function cost-efficiency should typically pale into insignificance when compared with the potential to improve demand-side value, I contend that, while both are required for a full picture of 'value', value optimization by tackling the value-adding CSFs is where most organizations will want to focus their energies (especially if the IT function operates as an investment centre, as described in the SAM model in Chapter 2).

As set out above, there are four key IT 'cost domains', each requiring differing skill sets and differing approaches to optimizing the cost-efficiency quadrant. It's not realistically possible here to set out the various methods, techniques and tools available to help diagnose opportunities in each of these domains. A theoretical 'how to' treatise on activity-based costing alone would require a book of its own and would (trust me on this) be less than a page-turning read. Besides which, experience has shown me that while performing such work 'by the book' is certainly the most comprehensive and rigorous way of working (it is 'best practice'), it will almost certainly prove to be unacceptably time-consuming (and expensive) and still fail to deliver optimal savings (i.e. it is not best *value* practice). Furthermore, it is no substitute for practical experience, good technical knowledge of the 'IT domain' being investigated and an enquiring mind. Therefore I will now focus on how to get the biggest bang (the lowest service/product tariff/price) for your cost-efficiency improvement buck. And the way to get the biggest bang for your buck is arguably to 'buy, not build'. By this I mean that before I describe in more detail the processes for identifying cost-efficiency improvement opportunities 'from scratch' I will first set out an 'off-the-shelf' set of IT cost-efficiency improvement opportunities (similar to our six value-adding CSFs in Chapter 3) that may tolerably match your needs. You may well say that this sounds ridiculous. Every company and IT function is unique. It needs a 'clean sheet' analysis that starts with no assumptions. Well, no actually. Although opportunity *instances* are unique, the same *types* of opportunities come up repeatedly in IT cost-efficiency improvement work.

Therefore I believe that what I can best share with you is the top *types* of opportunities that I've seen identified in my IT cost-efficiency improvement work with major organizations over the years. Note that many of these opportunities will not *immediately* reduce IT costs, but will produce a net reduction in IT budgets with time as a result of cash inflow, or deferred or avoided IT spend. This will in turn reduce tariffs, assuming, of course, that cost savings are passed on to the customer. Note also that around 80 per cent of these opportunity types can deliver significant savings without reducing staffing levels. Even those that do have a component of staffing level reduction can be treated as releasing value by freeing staff time. In this way staff recruitment/replacement can be deferred or (expensive) contractors can potentially be replaced by permanent staff. Either way, IT budgets are contained or reduced over time and the need for staff redundancies becomes a matter of last resort.

4.7 Optimizing sourcing and purchasing cost-efficiency

1 *Outsource inefficient non-core services:* typical targets for this are PC/laptop maintenance, WAN management/provision, helpdesk and disaster recovery. Where external benchmarking and/or market testing clearly shows that an ESP can do it cheaper (and quite possibly better), bite the bullet. Note, however, the inefficient services will have to be *extremely* inefficient if significant cost reduction is to be achieved (I will explore this issue later in this chapter under the heading 'Does outsourcing save money?'). The corollary to this opportunity is to re-insource services that are core and/or can be performed more cost-efficiently in-house.

2 *Outsource legacy platforms:* an ESP may be able to maintain your legacy systems at reduced cost until they can be phased out. At the least you should benefit from the resultant skill set rationalization and freeing of management time to focus more on strategic platform development.

3 *Outsource (or sell on) peak computer resources:* computer resources (e.g. CPU, printing) that are only required to accommodate temporary peaks of use could have the excess capacity that is normally unused sold on in the market, or outsourced and bought back to address the peak load times.

4 *Rationalize suppliers:* substantial savings can often be achieved by rationalizing suppliers of similar IT services and products, so improving purchasing leverage and getting better deals. The typical IT function ends up accruing *hundreds* of suppliers with time.

5 *Consolidate contracts and improve contractual terms:* for example, consider consolidating all your network service spend-

ing (voice, data, mobile etc.) into one contract. You may have multiple contracts with the same ESP for the same service, with each contract having a relatively low discount. By aggregating the contracts, the ESP should grant you a higher discount.

6 *Renegotiate contracts with framework suppliers:* this should remove any specified minimum commitment and then drive the usage based on commercially justifiable need (i.e. remove the incentive to simply 'call off' the contract because of the need to take at least the minimum).

7 *Renegotiate maintenance contracts:* companies on tier-based pricing should consider a move to user-based pricing. Companies often contract for 24×7 support, but they should consider actual requirements based on historical trends and, if appropriate, negotiate for lower levels of support (e.g. 8×5) that actually still meet commercial service level requirements. Companies that use little support may consider contracting for support on a per-call basis.

8 *Clamp down on purchasing 'leakage':* 'local deals' are often struck with suppliers by (often well-intentioned) managers who choose to bypass purchasing guidelines because 'they can buy better than the guys in corporate'. Although these deals may look good in isolation, they compromise the size of discounts that can be negotiated in corporate deals when *all* purchasing needs are consolidated. The local managers appear to win their local battles but in so doing lose the war for the company as a whole.

9 *Improve the rigour of purchasing and competitive tendering:* major suppliers will invariably send in the 'prince of darkness' to negotiate the deal. There is no place for IT functions to confront them with 'amateur' purchasers. Skilled, professional negotiators who clearly understand the market and the vendors' agenda will inevitably deliver far more cost-effective deals.

10 *Sell equipment:* where equipment is purchased, consider selling it and leasing it back.

11 *Sell office space:* where office or data centre space is owned, consider selling it and leasing it back.

4.8 Optimizing technology and infrastructure cost-efficiency

12 *Rationalize servers:* many organizations have a history of purchasing new servers for virtually every new application implemented. This often results in a plethora of small servers

whose workload could potentially be consolidated onto superservers. This is typically *far* more cost-efficient from a price-performance point of view. Note that Gartner clients have reported typical 10 per cent to 20 per cent reductions in operational costs through server rationalization. Gartner also state that in the right circumstances, a cost reduction of from 30 per cent to 40 per cent can be achieved over three years.

13 *Improve server utilization:* improve the utilization of servers and/or the load balancing of work across servers. In these days of relatively low hardware costs, the utilization of individual servers may seem unimportant; but when this unutilized capacity is multiplied up across all the servers installed, the wasted spend can be substantial.

14 *Rationalize storage:* Gartner report that consolidation efforts in the storage area have produced a 5 per cent decrease in the number of employees devoted to disk storage and a 22 per cent decrease in unit costs.

15 *Improve network utilization:* critically review the ability of the backbone network to meet service level targets while being driven harder. Also critically review the need for the level of network resilience provided.

16 *Replace old equipment:* for example, a financial services company fell into the trap of believing that they were being optimally economic by continuing to run disk strings that had long since been fully depreciated and so were 'free'. Well, they were 'free' apart from the huge maintenance payments they were making annually. In fact it is often the case that it would quickly be more economic to actually *throw out* old equipment and replace it with new, higher price-performance equipment with long warranties (and no maintenance costs).

17 *Rationalize software products:* for example, IT functions tend to accumulate application development productivity improvement tools (for each of which they continue to pay licence costs), many of which play virtually identical roles or have few (or no) users.

18 *Reduce licence costs:* review licence costs that are based on concurrent user numbers against the actual numbers of users. The numbers originally anticipated may well not have materialized.

19 *Reduce PC upgrade costs:* avoid PC upgrades by deploying thin client applications and/or extending the refresh cycle of PCs by, say, six months.

20 *Reduce PC support costs:* standardize PC configurations and use electronic software distribution (e.g. SMS) to radically

reduce both 'hands-on' software maintenance and the travel time and costs associated with this. Refine PC configurations to include only technologies specifically required by end users to perform their jobs. Local CD-ROM drives, for instance, are included in almost every PC being deployed today, yet very few end users actually require this technology to perform their job. Although they are bundled 'free', local CD-ROMs can increase the total cost of ownership as a result of their being used to install unauthorized software (and the resultant impact this can have on user productivity and helpdesk calls to resolve problems caused by these non-standard images).

21 *Delay software rollouts:* for example, do you actually *need* Windows XP (or even Windows 2000) now?

22 *Rationalize platforms:* obviously a longer-term opportunity to reduce costs, but an excellent one nonetheless. At best, a range of incompatible products and standards will increase the complexity and cost of supporting the infrastructure. At worst, it may cause technical problems and block IT initiatives.

23 *Adopt technologies later:* look critically at the commercial *need* for early adoption of technologies; late adopters can buy at a lower point in the cost cycle. Obviously this is a longer-term 'strategic' opportunity.

24 *Consolidate/rationalize data centres:* many organizations have failed to predict the speed with which equipment foot-prints have fallen and, as a result, can be left with significant amounts of unused (and highly expensive) controlled office environment. Additionally, many have failed to predict the falling use of equipment that accompanied falling business volumes. Rationalizing data centres can, of course, be complex, principally for reasons of the complexity of communications and the 'mutual backup' role they often play. But potential infrastructure savings can be sufficiently high to warrant this option.

25 *Consolidate/rationalize office space:* for example, the IT function of a public utility was distributed across a dozen sites, its two main sites being over 200 miles apart. This resulted in huge travel and subsistence costs, quite aside for the cost of the time spent travelling. Some IT managers claimed to be spending over 30 per cent of their time 'on the road'. Rationalization of office space is obviously unlikely to be a quick or easy palliative but can deliver high savings.

4.9 Optimizing organization and people cost-efficiency

26 *Reduce the use of contractors:* contractors can cost double the total remuneration of permanent staff. Look especially at contractors working in areas towards the end of the systems development life-cycle (e.g. testing) where there can be little technical or commercial justification for their presence.

27 *Increase management spans of control:* the appropriate span of control (i.e. the number of staff reporting to a given manager/supervisor) obviously varies with the nature of work being performed but on average might be expected to be about six to eight staff to one manager/supervisor. Often it will be found to be far below this, particularly in public sector (or recently privatized) organizations where promotions may have taken place more in order to get staff into management positions with grade pay scales that allow them to be retained rather than because of their managerial or leadership skills.

28 *Improve staff workload balancing:* many, if not most, IT functions manage their staff resources 'in silos', typically aligned with the business unit supported, but often even within specific development teams. When there is a delay or a work trough, team managers will often 'find something for staff to do' rather than 'export' them temporarily to another team (if only for fear of not getting them back!). By optimizing staff utilization right across the IT function, significant savings can often be made.

29 *Don't staff up for the peak workloads:* address temporary work peaks with temporary staff.

30 *Relocate support groups:* if a support group does not actually *have* to be co-located with those they support (e.g. helpdesk), consider relocation to lower cost locations.

4.10 Optimizing activities and services cost-efficiency

31 *Reduce customization levels of code, packages and services:* there are obviously times when bespoke code will be required, principally when no package can be found that tolerably meets key business needs or when the service to be developed could yield significant competitive advantage if tailored appropriately. The key point, however, is that *every* significant development must have an explicit management checkpoint where alternative business cases are prepared

for alternative delivery vehicles, whether they be internal bespoke, external bespoke or package purchase. A commercial decision can then be taken on the most cost-beneficial route to follow thereafter. Note that assessing the market for the possibility of appropriate packages is *not* unacceptably expensive or expensive. Various research organizations exist (e.g. OTR, AMR) who will scan the market (typically at low cost and in few days) and provide enough information to let you take an informed decision on whether or not a full request for information and potential subsequent package selection exercise is commercially warranted.

32 *Rationalize and standardize services:* internal IT functions can offer a range of services that in the world of commerce would not be viable. Often these services arise simply because someone somewhere asked for them, even though the ongoing 'market' for the service is too narrow to make commercial sense. Substantial savings can also be achieved by standardizing existing services so that, for example, there is a standardized 'portal' service, a standardized 'web' service and so on. The total cost of ownership for each standard service can be determined and used as input to project business cases consistently. Variations from a standard can also be separately (punitively) priced to help optimize the 'service level vs cost equation'.

33 *Cease non-profitable external business:* if the IT function sells any of its services externally, look critically at its profitability and cease non-profitable business. Even where the service *appears* to be profitable, look critically at whether or not this apparent profitability is essentially only achieved as a result of 'hidden' cross-subsidies.

34 *Improve the automation of activities:* there are particular opportunities here in data centre operations. For example, Gartner report that LAN management tools can reduce annual helpdesk labour costs by as much as 15 per cent.

35 *Terminate (or suspend) discretionary activities:* at a time of fiscal pressure, is it *necessary* to continue general research work? Is it *necessary* to gain BS7799 accreditation? Is it *necessary* to conduct routine external benchmarking? Is it *necessary* to attend external conferences? Note that since staff training is clearly discretionary, is typically a high expense and can be 'switched off' almost immediately, it is very tempting to clamp down here. But the impact of this on staff morale and retention may make this otherwise attractive option inadvisable.

36 *Reduce the frequency of activities:* for example, if the quarterly capacity planning report were only produced annually, would the IT function really collapse? If system software updates were only applied to address known or anticipated problems, would this really cause major operational problems? If application releases were batched weekly, would this actually have an adverse impact on the business? The key answer to alert you here is, 'But we've always done it that way.'

37 *Rationalize product/service tariffs:* if transfer charging is in place, rationalize product/service tariffs to ensure that they give a true reflection of the total service cost and so generate commercially appropriate customer behaviours. For example, the IT function at a financial services company priced a Mb of mass storage higher than a Mb of DASD, despite the total cost of ownership of mass storage being significantly below that of DASD. This effectively incentivized users to *increase* IT costs.

38 *Merge groups with similar activities, services or skills:* for example, many organizations maintain technical support groups (for performance monitoring, capacity planning, software maintenance etc.) aligned with each platform (so, for example, there is a mainframe support group, a Unix support group, an NT support group etc.). Although there will obviously be some need for technology specific skills, many of the activities of these groups are common and could be merged with potentially significant economies of scale. Similarly, many organizations run multiple helpdesks that might achieve significant economies of scale and reduce infrastructure, software and support costs by being merged.

39 *Transfer out support activities:* consider the opportunities to achieve economies of scale by 'outsourcing' internal IT support groups (e.g. IT personnel group, IT finance group) to the equivalent groups in the business.

40 *Rationalize activities:* it is almost an endemic problem (particularly in large IT functions) that every new activity is translated into a job, rather than a role. Significant savings may be made by largely disbanding 'niche' groups (e.g. staff recruitment, internal communications, resource management) and distributing their roles out into the field. So, for example, a project manager might take on an internal communications role, if only on a temporary basis, before passing it on to a colleague after performing the role for, say, 12 months.

40 candidate opportunity areas for cost-efficiency improvement – the usual suspects	
Sourcing and purchasing	
1	Outsource inefficient non-core services
2	Outsource legacy platforms
3	Outsource (or sell on) peak computer resources
4	Rationalize suppliers
5	Consolidate contracts and improve contractual terms
6	Renegotiate contracts with framework suppliers
7	Renegotiate maintenance contracts
8	Clamp down on purchasing leakage
9	Improve the rigour of purchasing and competitive tendering
10	Sell (and lease back) equipment
11	Sell (and lease back) office space
Technology and infrastructure	
12	Rationalize servers
13	Improve server utilization
14	Rationalize storage
15	Improve network utilization
16	Replace old equipment
17	Rationalize software products
18	Reduce licences costs
19	Reduce PC upgrade costs
20	Reduce PC support costs
21	Delay software rollouts
22	Rationalize platforms
23	Adopt technologies later
24	Consolidate/rationalize data centres
25	Consolidate/rationalize office space
Organization and people	
26	Reduce the use of contractors
27	Increase management spans of control
28	Improve staff workload balancing
29	Don't staff up for peak workloads
30	Relocate support groups
Activities and services	
31	Reduce customization levels of code, packages and services
32	Rationalize and standardize services
33	Cease non-profitable external business
34	Improve the automation of activities
35	Terminate (or suspend) discretionary activities
36	Reduce the frequency of activities
37	Rationalize product/service tariffs
38	Merge groups with similar activities, services or skills
39	Transfer out support activities
40	Rationalize activities

Figure 4.1

Note that in all these 40 opportunity areas (summarized in Figure 4.1) there has been no mention of customer service level reduction. If your users are prepared to accept lowered service levels (e.g. longer helpdesk call wait times, longer transaction response times) for lowered cost then further significant savings can be made. For example, disaster recovery equipment costs (or disaster recovery contract costs) may be lowered substantially by reducing contingency service levels to those indicated by the inherent risks the business faces (i.e. providing necessary and *sufficient* disaster recovery). This obviously requires an understanding of the IT services which are actually key to business continuity and the commercial impact with time of IT service loss. For example, local contingency arrangements may well mean that the business impact would be minimal for 48 hours and then soar, so immediate 100 per cent fallback may be an unnecessarily risk-averse approach.

Note also that the list of opportunities does not include 'Reduce IT staff remuneration to market norms'. This is simply because many organizations will already be struggling to retain key staff as a result of existing remuneration levels. However, if you are in the fortunate position of having a highly rewarded work force, this controversial opportunity may have to be explored.

So with your 40 opportunity *types* you should have a good idea of where to start looking for opportunities and, with luck, even a 'default' list of opportunities that apply directly to your organization. Some of them may even fall into the hallowed category of 'quick wins'.

In Figure 4.2 I set out the main tasks to be performed to help identify a portfolio of cost-efficiency improvement opportunities. I propose three parallel streams of work: one to analyse opportunities, one to develop the cost models and one to conduct external benchmarking.

Analyse opportunities: this central stream is typically divided into substreams associated with the four different 'domains' in which opportunities are typically found. A key reason for this is the fact that each substream typically requires a quite different mix of experience and skills. The 'underlying' substream is the pursuit of quick wins, based on opportunities typically 'brainstormed' early in the project. I have found that using the 'Top 40' opportunity types (set out above) can be a very useful prompt for such brainstorming sessions. Each opportunity should be valued and prioritized based on the '80/20' rule of looking for the big win opportunities that can be implemented at least cost

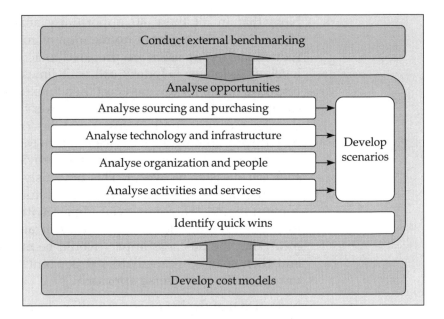

Figure 4.2

and risk. Opportunity analysis will typically complete with the development of various scenarios, based on logical groupings of opportunities, various levels of risk and various levels of ambition in the scale of the savings to be realized. Workshops are then conducted with the key stakeholders to agree the optimal scenario and its portfolio of candidate cost-efficiency improvement opportunities. Each opportunity definition would typically set out a description of the opportunity and different ranges of potential cost (and/or headcount) reduction and implementation cost depending on the aggressiveness of implementation (and risk).

A variety of skills are needed to effectively perform the four work substreams. The sourcing and purchasing substream needs people highly experienced in purchasing and contract management, who will profile purchasing demand levels, map spend to suppliers, assess whether purchasing leverage is being optimized and challenge SLAs and contracts (for both product purchases and services purchases). The technology and infrastructure substream will require a high level of technology proficiency in the platforms being reviewed in order to be able to credibly challenge the technical 'status quo'. The organization and people and activities and services substreams principally need people with strong skills in 'activity-based costing' (ABC), 'priority-based budgeting' (PBB), 'cost driver analysis' (CDA) and, if service level reductions are permissible, service level analysis.

ABC/PBB analysis is principally about examining each activity in the IT activity model (see 'Develop cost models' below) for its total cost, its proportion of total IT costs (obviously looking for the cost intensive activities) and the potential ability to reduce costs and/or improve efficiency by performing that activity in a better (best value) way. It is also necessary to look at which IT practices, if performed in a better (best value) way, might most contribute to reducing IT costs. So you are looking at reducing the *cost* of the activity and its potential for *reducing* IT costs.

CDA is simply about looking at each (significantly expensive) IT activity and asking what causes it to be as high as it is. It is then about robustly challenging why these drivers of cost levels cannot be reduced. This is actually much more difficult than it sounds. I can virtually guarantee that the most common reply you will receive from an IT group manager to the question, 'What is your key cost driver and how could we reduce it?' is, 'Business demand is my key cost driver and this is outside my control so I cannot reduce costs' (either that or they will dryly tell you that their main cost driver is the time they spend being interviewed!). It is at this point that the interviewer either buckles in the face of the conviction of the interviewee or, rising to the challenge, starts asking robust, but polite, questions about how demand is actually challenged, how changes are justified, how frequently activities are performed etc. Furthermore, the fact that the interviewee has not got the remit or authority to make changes that would reduce costs is no reason to ignore the opportunity. You are not so much challenging *him* as challenging the established 'system'. So, for example, when the capacity planning manager says that he has no control over demand, push back with questions like:

- 'Have you tried to remove little used but resource intensive transactions?'
- 'Have you tried moving "background" jobs outside prime shift?'
- 'Have you tried offering your customers reduced service levels at reduced cost?'
- 'Have you tried changing computer resource tariffs to penalize computer resource usage peaks and so incentivize users to balance their work throughout the day?'

You have to remember that most IT managers within an IT function (and even more so in an ESP!) just want to keep their customers off their backs, and the easiest way to do this is give them the services they ask for and the highest service levels that can reasonably be delivered. They simply do not typically think in terms of managing demand to minimize cost.

Develop cost models: this stream typically builds the various IT cost models (generally by activity, by cost centre and by product/service). The process adopted is typically first to build and agree an IT activity model that encompasses all activities performed by the IT function (a granularity of about 100 activities usually suffices). ABC champions are then trained to go out and get the IT function cost centre managers to populate the cost spreadsheets with direct and indirect costs, noting whether staff are contract, permanent or part-time and noting the grade of staff employed. This stream feeds the opportunity analysis stream with accurate costing data so that opportunities can be financially sized. It, in turn, maps the effect of the opportunities identified onto the cost models, so indicating their effect on, for example, cost centre budgets, total IT budgets, and IT service prices. Only those who are true masters of spread-sheets should apply for this role because the cost models can become immensely complex.

Conduct external benchmarking: while the opportunities are being identified, the external benchmarking stream is feeding in significant gaps in cost-efficiency relative to peer organizations, and so potentially generating new opportunities. Conversely, the opportunity analysis stream is feeding *its* opportunities to the external benchmarking stream to help confirm and size the opportunities. Key metrics typically produced are the cost of services/products, an analysis of staff costs per workload driver and an overall spend distribution analysis.

A variety of niche IT benchmarking organizations exist (e.g. Compass, Gartner). A benchmarking partner would typically be selected on the basis of the strength of their database (in terms of comparability with your organization) and, of course, their price. The cost modelling team need to work very closely with the benchmarker to ensure that the various cost models are normalized as far as is practicable (so that external comparisons of cost and price are as fair as possible and stand up to critical scrutiny). As I will set out in some detail in the next chapter, this is actually extremely difficult to do credibly.

Once the opportunity set (defining the full set of signed-off opportunities and the agreed savings targets) is agreed, a programme to actually *implement* them would then have to be established.

The high level process diagram set out above could give the impression of a conventional project structure. But it is critically important to keep in mind that this is first and foremost not so much a *project* as an *investigation*. It would be idiotic to expect the investigating officer of a crime to tell you at the start of his investigation how many suspects he was going to find, how much evidence he would accrue and when he was going to obtain a conviction. Similarly, when we start a cost-efficiency improvement programme we don't know how many opportunities we will find, how much evidence we will accrue to support those opportunities and whether or not we will succeed in getting these opportunities accepted. Therefore run the 'project' in such a way as to keep your 'detectives' continually focused on the 'prime suspects'. This requires a very dynamic and 'hands-on' approach to project management and a very mature and flexible project team that can accept (and possibly even enjoy!) the fact that the shape and direction of their work is continually evolving. If they are suddenly taken off working on 'opportunity A' (that is looking increasingly unlikely to get accepted) to work on 'opportunity B' (that looks increasingly likely to deliver a large acceptable 'prize'), they have to have the resilience to appreciate that this is no direct criticism of their work, it is just the 'nature of the beast'.

A corollary to this project management challenge is that cost-efficiency improvement projects are inherently risky since:

- the project is obviously typically perceived as a threat by IT function management and staff (who see their jobs at risk and may well seek to actively, if covertly, subvert the project);
- it needs an extremely technically competent team, able to actively and credibly challenge IT staff who may have, for example, specialized in some arcane IT discipline or software product for the last 15 years; and
- project success (and, dare I say it, failure) is *very* tangible (you either do or you don't hit the set cost reduction target).

4.11 Implementing cost-efficiency improvements

The basic steps of implementing identified cost-efficiency improvements are set out in Figure 4.3.

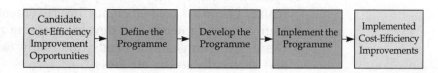

Figure 4.3

4.11.1 Defining the programme

Define the programme

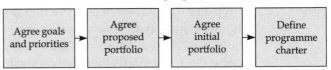

Figure 4.4

- Agree the goals of the programme (e.g. primarily to drive up delivered IT value? Primarily to drive internal IT cost-efficiencies? Primarily about fending off IT outsourcing? Primarily about positioning the IT cost base in preparation for outsourcing?).
- Agree the immediate priorities for cost reduction, as informed by the opportunity identification process (e.g. staffing levels? technology? purchasing?).
- On the basis of the goals and priorities, choose or define the 'proposed portfolio', i.e. those cost reduction initiatives that you believe need to be implemented/improved in the foreseeable future (e.g. two to three years?).
- Agree the proposed portfolio with key stakeholders in the business.
- Choose a subset of the proposed portfolio for an initial implementation – the initial portfolio (generally the 'highest value', 'least cost to implement' set that requires least change in existing IT processes and disciplines to be effected).
- Define the programme charter setting out the programme objectives, scope, sponsor, stakeholders, change leaders, deliverables, milestones, dependencies, business case, risks, assumptions, organization, roles and responsibilities, controls and plans.

4.11.2 Developing the programme

- Design and develop necessary enhancements and/or changes in procedures, practices and disciplines necessary to realize proposed cost-efficiency improvements.
- Specify, select/design/develop automation tools necessary to realize proposed cost-efficiency improvements.
- Define training needs and develop training materials.
- Define communications needs (internally to the IT function and externally to the business).

Develop the programme

Develop new/enhanced procedures
Develop automation tools
Develop training and communications
Develop roles and responsibilities

Figure 4.5

- Define and allocate roles and responsibilities for supporting the changes inherent in implementing the programme (e.g. programme management office roles).

4.11.3 Implementing the programme

- Implement the initial portfolio of changes.
- Conduct training and communication.
- Determine and implement incentives for staff to support the programme and act on its outcomes (and penalties for non-compliance).
- Establish quality assurance of the delivery of the changes.
- Assess and refine the initial changes implemented, applying lessons learnt.
- Implement the full (proposed) cost reduction portfolio.
- Measure and report the cost reduction realized (see Chapter 5).

Implement the programme

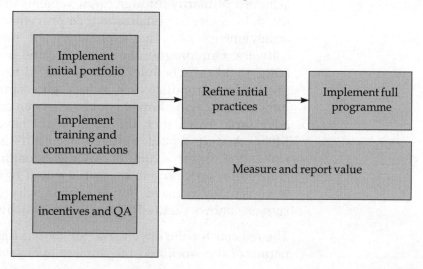

Figure 4.6

4.12 Case study – identifying cost-efficiency improvements

So that is the theory (conventional 'best practice') for both identifying cost-efficiency improvements and then implementing them. But does it work? To put it another way, is it guaranteed to result in optimized value to the business? The simple answer is, of course, no. I can probably best illustrate why with a case study. My client was one of Britain's major clearing banks. The bank had reached a point where it was forced to examine its cost base carefully and reduce overhead costs dramatically. This was a result of a number of factors, but mainly a combination of:

- 'dubious' third world lending decisions;
- the shock of *genuine* competition from telephone 'direct' and internet banks without the huge physical infrastructure costs associated with the traditional bank branch network; and
- what could only be described as a deeply risk averse, conservative, hierarchical, patriarchal, nepotistic, sexist, bureaucratic culture beset by management cronyism (they spoke highly of me, too).

Our team was brought in to run the 'IT part' of an 'enterprise-wide cost reduction' programme. This was structured and run essentially along the 'best practice' lines set out above. The study was driven by the techniques of activity-based costing, cost driver analysis, service level analysis and cost-efficiency benchmarking and identified over £20m ($30m) of annual savings on the total IT function cost base. This was to be achieved primarily through improvements in IT staff productivity, data centre rationalization, improvements in contingency arrangements and the exploitation of new hardware and software. Our programme of work came in almost exactly to budget and on schedule. So, a successful result? Well, had the project been conducted in a less adversarial way (and it is difficult to imagine how it could have been conducted in a *more* adversarial way), then the £20m might have been as high as £40m. And it would only be a 'result' in terms of value realization if the £20m of savings identified were actually realized. In fact, no one *knows* the extent to which the savings were actually realized (I will explain why in a moment) but *everyone* knows that only a fraction was delivered.

The reasons for the adversarial (or should I just say 'war like'?) nature of the work and the dubiety over savings delivered are manifold and interesting: in no particular order, I have set them out below:

- There was no real senior management sponsorship. Although the programme was ostensibly sponsored by the CEO himself, he acted solely as a figurehead and other than circulating periodic 'ritual' memos stating his support for its goals, played little active part. This, for example, led to the situation where during the first five weeks of the 12 week phase of 'opportunity identification' work, the consultants were blocked from access to the IT function by the CIO's attempts to duck out of the exercise. This was crucial to the IT stream of work because it was not 'just' a matter of starting later and so ending later. First, a team of eight IT consultants, together costing around £18 000 ($27 000) a day, were reduced to performing 'background research', as they waited to be granted access. Second, the IT stream was just one of many (including, for example, the properties team, the head office team, and so on). We all had to finish at the same time. Therefore the IT team ended up attempting to perform 12 weeks of work in seven. This severely constrained our ability to collate evidence to build sound business cases to support proposed cost reduction initiatives (as was well understood by, and exploited by, the CIO). It was only when the issue of lack of access became critical (actually, way past 'critical') that the CEO *ordered* the CIO to give our team access.
- The CIO's key justification for why his IT function should be exempt from the study was that he sold IT products and services successfully in the open market. Therefore he was, *de facto*, commercially cost-efficient. The problem with this wonderfully plausible ploy (quite aside from the fact that only around 3 per cent of his income was externally generated) was that the only reason he was able to secure external business was by cross-subsidizing it by charging more to the bank! This was 'obvious' but virtually impossible to 'prove' because of the incredibly arcane tariff algorithms in place.
- Once we had gained access, every possible obstacle was put in our way while, at the same time, everyone *avowed* commitment to the study. This largely took the form of the near impossibility of gaining access to diaries. We were not allowed to interview staff until we had interviewed their managers. But the key managers generally offered us dates from three to six weeks off! The surreal nature of this was epitomized by our discovery that many of the key managers we urgently needed to see were unavailable because they

were running 'recruitment fairs'. In other words we were unable to interview them to discuss potential staff reductions because they were recruiting more staff! At one point, in deep frustration, I asked a stonewalling senior IT manager (whose diary I had eventually cracked) if, strictly within those four walls, he had been asked to covertly obstruct our study. He smiled sardonically and said, 'Frankly, yes.' The adversarial nature of the work was epitomized by one extraordinary (and entirely true) story. The manager of a particular IT function cost centre took me aback by actually *agreeing* that her group was overstaffed and that a saving was easily possible. This was duly documented as a cost reduction opportunity and I subsequently stood up to present it to the group of senior IT managers who were the final sign-off for opportunities. They refused to accept the opportunity, stating that such a reduction was simply impossible. It was at this point that the uncharitable word, 'gotcha!' (and a few others) came to mind and I took quiet pleasure (oh, all right, sadistic glee) in pointing out that this was not just my opinion, it was the opinion of the manager of the cost centre herself. For a few moments they conferred among themselves before stating that it was *still* not possible. I swallowed hard and asked if they could kindly explain why. They coolly replied that the cost centre manager concerned was pregnant, highly hormonal, and not currently a reliable decision maker. I sat down.

- Every cost reduction opportunity found was vehemently challenged by IT management who demanded 'proof' that proposed savings could actually be realized. But other than saying 'it's bloody obvious' how do you 'prove' that, for example, merging two 10 man groups both performing virtually identical tasks can achieve a 10 per cent economy in scale? The IT management team demanded external benchmarks to support the case that such cost-efficiencies could be achieved, knowing full well that since they were one of the biggest IT functions in Europe (not to say the world), it would be virtually impossible to produce credible comparisons.

- Many of the cost reduction opportunities depended on making (typically marginal) IT service level reductions to the business for significant reductions in cost, i.e. many of the products and services were radically 'overengineered'. However, the business stakeholders would not sign off these opportunities. Why? Because the IT costs, although being fully billed, were simply 'billed upstairs'. As far as the business departmental managers were concerned, IT was still 'free' so they virtually always asked for the highest service levels they could get (and the supplying IT function was delighted to comply because this meant higher revenues). Basically, they were just acting like a 'good ESP'.

- One of the key savings opportunities required that the five main data centres be rationalized down to four. The bulk of the savings came from the sale (or rental) of the freed data centre. But the relevant cost centre managers refused to sign this off because there would be no *guarantee* that the site could in fact be sold or let.

- Another of the key savings opportunities required the termination of a system that helped bank branch staff make lending decisions. The value of the application to the business was predicated upon interest rates being over 15 per cent (which they were when the application was implemented!). Now it was costing about £1.5m ($2.3m) a year to continue to run and support the application *and* it had but a handful of (low profile) users left. But the cost centre managers concerned refused to sign off the opportunity because it 'might antagonize customers' (and reduce the IT function's revenue).

- Another key opportunity required the termination of external business that was *actually* (once the cross-subsidies from the business had been removed) unprofitable. The CIO was never going to agree to that because this was the very cornerstone of his 'we are really a competitive ESP' edifice.

- Another key opportunity related to printing. The credit card part of the bank owned an army of 'industrial quality' laser printers whose almost sole role was to print off statements over the same two to three days each month. On the remaining days the printers were virtually idle. We recommended that statement printing be spread across the month, so dramatically reducing the capacity requirements. The client refused on the grounds that 'their customers expected their statements at the beginning of each month'. End of story.

- Every opportunity found had to be signed off by all IT managers whose cost centres would be affected by the savings. This resulted in what could only be described as an 'opportunities approval industry'. At the completion of the analysis it took *13 months* (I am not exaggerating here) of tense, highly adversarial and often deeply unpleasant, negotiation to get opportunities signed off by the cost centre managers, as they started from a position of 'it is completely unachievable, whatever it is', moved on to 'it can only be partly achieved and not in the timescales you say', to an eventual deeply compromised agreement. As I have shown above, many entirely feasible opportunities were simply written off because there was no real will to make any changes. The *board* desperately wanted and needed the reductions in cost. But their IT function (who were a wholly owned subsidiary of the bank and who were, with the board's blessing, acting as an ESP) wanted exactly the opposite. The importance of the long delay (in signing off opportunities) to the IT function was that while this was happening, major reorganizations were happening in the bank as a whole and within the IT function itself. Cost centre structures were also subject to a major revamp. So various (in fact, most) IT groups who would be affected by the proposed cuts had transferred or regrouped or in some other subtle way had slipped between the fingers of the proposals. Furthermore, during this time the plummeting cost of hardware coupled with wildly changing demand meant that it became virtually impossible to relate the proposed cost reduction initiatives to the world as it then existed. Basically, we had been played brilliantly. Note that the *reason* we were given for the obduracy of the cost centre managers in signing off proposals was that, because we, the consultants, were being (partially) paid on a con-tingent fees basis (i.e. our fees were tied to the level of savings we eventually got signed off), they were quite properly trying to save the bank's money by minimizing the fees paid! The CIO told us this with an entirely straight face.

I could go on but it would be too depressing. It was certainly the 'cost-efficiency improvement programme from hell' and not (entirely) typical. But it is important to plan assuming the worst. To this end I will now generalize the inherent difficulties of performing an IT cost-efficiency improvement programme and set out how to make a *success* of such a programme. Above all else we want to avoid such a programme being run as an adversarial 'campaign', the outcome of which is little more than a budgetary 'smoke and mirrors' game in which no one, a year down the road, can either prove or disprove that savings have actually been realized. Instead we want a co-operative venture that delivers real, demonstrable savings.

4.13 CFFs and CSFs for cost-efficiency improvement programmes

What are the key things that most often go wrong in cost-efficiency improvement programmes? In other words, what are the critical *failure* factors (CFFs)? In no particular order:

- Adversarially attempting to take costs out of an IT function that is being run 'as an ESP', because their costs are also their profit/revenue when they bill it to the business. ('I'm going to have lower costs which means I'm going to have lower revenue which means I'm going to get a lower bonus – *but only if the programme succeeds!*')
- Lack of stakeholder buy-in. ('I'm going to have fewer staff, a smaller budget and a tougher life after this exercise – *but only if the programme succeeds!*')
- Lack of a really compelling need for change, or, more typically, there *is* a compelling need for change but it is largely *unrecognized or poorly articulated.* ('It'll all go away in time and I can get back to doing things the old way.')
- Lack of senior management sponsorship. ('I'm 100 per cent behind this IT cost reduction initiative – just so long as it doesn't actually take any of my time.')
- Lack of business management buy-in. ('I'm 100 per cent behind this IT cost reduction programme – just so long as it doesn't make my life any more difficult.')
- Allowing too much special pleading. ('I'm 100 per cent behind this IT cost reduction initiative but the cuts proposed clearly aren't appropriate in *my* cost centre.')
- Taking too long. ('By the time this cost reduction exercise is over the world will have moved on so much no one will be able to say whether we've delivered the savings or not.')
- Allowing too much smoke and too many mirrors. ('I don't have to *actually* lose this cost, just quietly displace it.')
- Unrealistic expectations of the speed of cost reduction delivery. ('Where are all those quick wins you promised me?')
- Allowing bun fights over who identified particular savings ('Oh no you didn't – oh yes we did – *oh* no you didn't etc.') and therefore which savings are attributable to the programme.
- Setting an unrealistic burden of proof on the project team. ('Show me five other directly comparable companies who have achieved this level of cost reduction and *then* I'll believe you.')
- A conservative, complacent, stonewalling corporate culture. ('Not in my back yard, buddy.')
- A corporate culture that rewards successful political game playing more than actually adding value to the business. ('OK, so the organization lost. But, hey, I won!')

Rather more positively I set out below my 'Top 20' CSFs for an IT cost-efficiency improvement programme, based on my (often extremely painful) experiences with several major British organizations. The CSFs are summarized in Figure 4.7.

	20 CSFs for an IT cost-efficiency improvement programme
1	Get explicit, *demonstrable* sponsorship for the programme at the highest level possible
2	Get absolute clarity on the budget baseline from which savings will be estimated
3	Make it the responsibility of *the IT management team* to identify and deliver the savings
4	Put your *best* people on the programme team
5	Keep the team *continually* focused on the opportunities that appear to be offering the highest payback
6	Define and implement a clear communications plan, stakeholder management plan and risk management plan
7	Use external benchmarks
8	*Don't* start with a 'blank sheet of paper', identifying opportunities from first principles
9	Gain stakeholder 'buy-in' to developing opportunities as you go along
10	Don't get hung up on 'ownership' of an opportunity
11	Agree and get documented the definition of a 'quick win'
12	Get clarity on whether or not avoided or deferred spend can be counted towards the cost saving target
13	Get agreement on the assumptions that are to be made on trend issues
14	Get explicit agreement at the outset on the period over which savings will be averaged
15	Get explicit agreement at the outset on the format and content of the deliverables of the programme
16	Apply the 'principle of materiality' to the work
17	Be prepared to 'make deals'
18	Establish clear, independent responsibility for the measurement of savings actually realized
19	Think carefully before you try to strike a 'contingent-based fee' deal with any consultants brought in to assist
20	Remember that 'turkeys don't vote for Christmas' and conduct the cost reduction programme correspondingly

Figure 4.7

1 *Do* get explicit, *demonstrable* sponsorship for the programme at the highest level possible. Note that this does *not* just mean a memo from the finance director stating he is 'right behind you' (probably a very long way behind you indeed). It means active, ongoing visible support for the exercise, lobbying key stakeholders, resolving conflicts, opening up the diaries of busy people and generally ensuring that the team has full co-operation and access.
2 *Do* get absolute clarity on the budget baseline from which savings will be estimated right at the start of the project and then stick with it. Is it next financial year's planned budget? Is it this year's actual budget? Does it take account of staff

vacancies? Basically, when you say, 'This cost reduction opportunity will save 5 per cent in cost centre C326', there must be no debate whatsoever about the value of that 5 per cent, because the budget baseline was agreed and signed off.

3 *Do* agree on a minimum total savings target at the start of the exercise and make it the responsibility of *the IT management team* to identify (and sign up to) the opportunities to meet or exceed this target. The crucial point here is that it is most emphatically *not* the responsibility of the cost-efficiency improvement team to deliver the opportunities, let alone deliver the actual savings from the opportunities being implemented. Their role is to facilitate the opportunity identification process. They are there to ensure that the targets are met with least pain, and so they are the 'friends' of the IT management team, not the enemy. And, paradoxical as it may sound, if possible, strongly financially incentivize IT managers to find the biggest opportunities and meet or exceed the savings targets.

4 *Do* put your *best* people on the team. In particular, you are going to need people from finance who are 'spreadsheet kings' to man the cost models (which can get *extremely* complex). Also consider complementing the skills and internal perspective of your internal staff with external consultants who have *demonstrable* experience of similar exercises. A crucial point, however, is to ensure that any external help you bring in has extensive *IT* cost reduction experience and a *genuine* track record of success. The typical approach adopted by the 'Big 6/5/4' consultancies to any cost improvement proposal is to use activity-based costing (ABC) and priority-based budgeting (PBB) techniques to find cost reduction opportunities. After all, those techniques did the job well enough in other, non-IT, departments. What is so special about IT? The problem is that IT *is* special. Conventional ABC/PBB approaches to cost reduction that have proved effective in reducing revenue (mainly staff) costs in large groups of staff performing largely homogeneous tasks can be wholly inadequate to the job of effectively reducing revenue *and* (typically substantial) capital costs in multiple small, specialized groups of staff performing largely heterogeneous tasks (namely, an IT function generally, and a data centre in particular). These conventional ABC/PBB 'best practice' approaches are also relatively ineffectual in the one area of an IT function that typically *does* have a large group of staff performing largely homogeneous tasks (namely,

systems development) since the key cost reduction issue here is the continuing cost justification and scope of the *project*, not the activities performed to deliver the project. My point is not to knock ABC/PBB. To attempt serious cost reduction in an IT function without a comprehensive understanding of how money is being spent by activity, by cost centre and by service/product is to virtually doom the exercise from the start because you will be building cost reduction opportunities 'on sand'. My point is that ABC/PBB *alone* is not nearly enough.

5 *Do* keep the team *continually* focused on the opportunities that appear to be offering the highest payback and/or the greatest ease of implementation. If the closer they get to an opportunity, the more the implementation costs rise, and the more the savings bleed away, then *stop* work on the opportunity and set the team after opportunities that *are* looking like winners. Basically, don't pursue an opportunity just because it is in the plan. At the simplest level, opportunities that can be realized by a decision (e.g. 'stop doing this') or which only involve capital expenditure (e.g. 'stop buying this') will tend to be the easiest to realize. Opportunities that require processes to change within IT are harder, and harder still if they need business process change too. The very hardest are those that will require behavioural change, in particular changing an uncommercial culture throughout the business into a commercial one.

6 *Do* define and implement a clear communications plan, stakeholder management plan and risk management plan. IT management and staff generally, understandably, perceive cost-efficiency improvement work as highly threatening. No matter how much spin you put on the 'efficiency improvement' angle, all they will hear is the 'cost reduction' angle. So tell them all you can and should tell them, but without scaremongering about issues you must look at (such as outsourcing) but which may not come to fruition. This is particularly critical in organizations with a high level of unionization. A corollary to this is the need to keep rigid version and issue control on all documents leaving the 'project space', such that you know exactly *who* has been issued with *what* version of *what* documents. In a major cost reduction assignment with which I was involved some years ago a critical document 'accidentally' (and untraceably) found its way into the hands of the unions (with predictable results).

7 *Do* use external benchmarks, both to help identify further cost saving opportunities and to help confirm and size opportunities found by other means. But do ensure that any such benchmarks cover the *entire* cost base so that *all* service/product direct and indirect costs are accounted for. Also take great pains to ensure that the peer groups chosen by the benchmarker are *genuinely* comparable. And do ensure that the benchmarker's service model (i.e. how it defines and scopes a 'product', such as the helpdesk or portal) is closely normalized to your service/product model, as is their activity model. The importance of all this is the value and credibility of the comparisons. External benchmark comparisons cost money – but if they are not readily credible and will not be accepted by the IT management team then this will simply be a *waste* of money. I will go into considerably more detail about the difficulties of externally benchmarking IT service/product cost-efficiency in the next chapter. After reading my concerns you may well take the view that best practice for IT cost reduction is to *avoid at all cost* external benchmarking! That is why I give you the 'alternative' CSF 7: *Do not* set any expectation that the size of every cost reduction opportunity will be corroborated by an independent benchmark. If the response to every proposal is 'prove to me that five other similar organizations to mine can run this function with that few staff' then you will have to budget up front for extensive benchmarking costs. Far better, of course, is to agree up front that this sort of challenge (which will often be actually impossible to prove or disprove – as the challenger well knows) is disallowed, and get an independent arbitrator to decide on the reasonableness of proposals.

8 *Do not* start with a 'blank sheet of paper', identifying opportunities from first principles. You will almost inevitably end up with some subset of, or variation upon, the 'usual suspects' (my 'Top 40' opportunities set out above). Therefore, while conventional 'best practice' may tell you to rigorously and formally deploy the activity-based costing, cost driver analysis and service level analysis techniques, 'best value practice' (with its '80/20' mandate) tells you to pursue the likely outcomes first.

9 *Do* gain stakeholder 'buy-in' to developing opportunities as you go along – there should be no 'surprises'. This can be achieved by various techniques, ranging from 'coffee machine' chats to 'formal' working party meetings. Note, however, that the latter can consume an extraordinary

amount of team time in preparation and delivery, time much better spent actually developing opportunities. And do establish at the outset a clearly defined process for signing off savings identified. Beware of the 'obvious' solution to this of getting each cost centre manager to sign off the savings opportunities that will affect his or her cost centre (see my case study experience above if you need convincing). Instead I would strongly recommend the approach adopted at my last major cost-efficiency improvement assignment where an 'independent arbitrator' was brought in to assess the reasonableness of the cost reduction proposal and, if then accepted, simply *tell* the cost centre manager to deliver against it.

10 *Do* get it explicitly agreed at the outset that 'an opportunity is an opportunity' irrespective of who claims to have identified it. It is not a competition between the opportunity identification team and the IT management team. So long as the savings and costs associated with an opportunity have not *already* been built into the budget baseline then it is a valid opportunity.

11 *Do* agree and get documented the definition of a 'quick win'. Business senior management always demand them and you will probably have no option but to try to deliver them. So what is the importance of documenting the definition? We all know what a 'quick win' means, don't we? It sounds trite but I have seen extraordinary tension arise over this issue. If you do not agree and define this *precisely* and right at the start of the work, the resultant mismanagement of expectations will result in your paying, and paying hard, later. For example, it may well be the case that the programme team regard a quick win as something that can *begin* to be realized by the end of the financial year. And I can almost guarantee that business senior management will picture a quick win as something that is *fully* realized within three months! Remember that any opportunity that requires staff redundancies will almost inevitably cost more (in severance payments alone) in year 1 than it will save. If you can pull it off, see if you can get senior business management to accept 'sustainable wins' rather than 'quick wins' because otherwise the danger is that you are pushed into finding opportunities that look good briefly but are actually not cost-efficient in the longer term.

12 *Do* get clarity on whether or not avoided or deferred spend can be counted towards the cost saving target. For example, improving mainframe utilization does not actually save any

money today, it 'just' delays your next upgrade. But in the longer term that is still definitely saving money.

13 *Do* get agreement on the assumptions that are to be made on such trend issues as the price/performance of equipment, staff salaries, the cost of money etc. so that these assumptions can be plugged into the spreadsheets predicting the future savings. On one IT study with which I was involved, these numbers were not debated until close to the end of the project and then appeared to change on a daily basis, requiring seemingly endless reworking of cost spreadsheets.

14 *Do* get explicit agreement at the outset on the period over which savings will be averaged and how these savings are to be expressed (e.g. minimum, stretch target, expected). For example, an opportunity may exist to consolidate two HR support groups and so achieve staffing economies of scale. The team may take the view that a 30 per cent staff reduction is possible if the opportunity is implemented aggressively (the stretch target), that 20 per cent reduction would probably be achieved in practice (the expected target) and that it is impossible to believe that less than 5 per cent reduction could be achieved, no matter how badly implemented (the minimum target). Similarly, do get explicit agreement at the outset on how implementation costs (especially redundancy/severance costs) will be accounted for, and over what time scale. Some savings and implementation costs may have to be 'taken' immediately, while others, like building/premises savings and costs, may be averaged over periods of up to 10 years. Also take great care to distinguish between one-time savings and repeatable savings and be realistic about the speed at which savings can actually be realized. For example, savings that depend on outsourcing a service or function will almost certainly deliver no savings at all for at least a year.

15 *Do* get explicit agreement at the outset on the format and content of the deliverables of the programme so that the team can develop those deliverables incrementally and iteratively as they go along, not in a sudden panic in the last week. Essentially, the only 'report writing' task in the plan should be producing the management summary. Note that there is a world of difference between producing a one page opportunity statement for each of your (probably 50 to 100) cost-efficiency improvement opportunities and producing a 50 page detailed business case and project objectives document for each. If the team's expectation is the former and

senior management's expectation is the latter, then you are going to be in serious trouble.

16 *Do* apply the 'principle of materiality' to the work. If there are 100 cost centres in the IT function then sort them in descending spend sequence. You will almost inevitably find that something like 80 per cent of the total spend is in something like 20 per cent of the cost centres. Therefore don't try to 'solve world poverty'; focus your analysis on the big cost centres and accept the fact that it is better to 'get it right' with the big numbers than cover the ground entirely. Having said that, do not just *ignore* smaller cost centres. A rapid assessment may show that there are material savings to be had cumulatively. For example, it might be the case that by standardizing on PC configurations/images and implementing automated software distribution tools, many (below the cost centre size threshold) regional support groups could be disbanded, with potentially huge savings in both staff costs and travel and subsistence costs. Be realistic, however, when identifying small, incremental opportunities. You cannot save a third of an FTE (full time equivalent) – which third would you remove? The arms? The legs? And you cannot end up with a situation where, for example, the remaining staff would have no holiday cover or would be required to work ridiculous shifts.

17 *Do* be prepared to 'make deals'. I appreciate that this is a controversial CSF, but at the end of the day it is better to agree a major cost reduction opportunity with a cost centre manager 'in exchange for' dropping a relatively minor cost reduction proposal that would kill his 'pet project'.

18 *Do* establish clear, independent responsibility for the measurement of savings actually realized. This would typically be by an established Programme Management Office. Be realistic, however, about how long it is meaningful to maintain such tracking. As I point out in my final CSF, the real world has a way of overtaking the longer-term cost reduction plans.

19 *Do* think carefully before you try to strike a 'contingent-based fee' deal with any consultants you may bring in (i.e. relating a proportion of their fees to the scale of savings achieved). This may sound like a bizarre CSF, since surely it is best to incentivize the consultants to deliver the highest savings possible? The problem is that (as occurred in my case study above) you immediately create a contradictory and adversarial position in which IT management potentially seek to *minimize* savings defined in order to minimize the fees of the consultants. Anyway, it is extremely unlikely any

consultancy firm will be prepared to predicate its fees on your management team actually following its cost reduction recommendations and then wait for the savings to be realized. Note that in some cases savings may take years to be fully realized and, because of such things as reorganizations, mergers, acquisitions, outsourcing or any other number of external events, the full realization of certain savings may actually be unprovable. Furthermore, incentivizing consultants in this way will cause them to push for the agreement of 'stretch targets' which maximize savings (and therefore their fees) but may do so with unacceptable pain and risk for your company.

20 *Do* remember that 'turkeys don't vote for Christmas' and conduct the cost reduction programme correspondingly. It is generally the case that IT managers' remuneration and status is directly or indirectly tied to the number of staff they manage and the size of the budget they manage. A cost reduction exercise directly attacks both these areas. So the team must be sensitive to this but, at the same time, must be highly challenging and have sufficient technical knowledge to respond intelligently to the 'it just cannot be done' litany. This is where 'cost driver analysis' comes into its own, if performed robustly.

To help illustrate the importance of these CSFs, let me give you an example from a few years ago when I was called into a corporate cost reduction programme at a large British insurance company (two weeks *after* the programme had started) to give the IT part of the programme the 'once-over'. The first thing I did was run through my CSF list (I think I had 'only' 15 CSFs at the time) with the project manager responsible for IT cost reduction. His response to almost every one of my CSF questions was either:

- 'Oh, we'll get around to that stuff later, after we've documented the opportunities'; or
- 'Oh, it's too late for that'; or
- 'Why on earth would I want to do that?'

For example, the team was going to agree the budget baseline 'later'. And, no, it wasn't the IT management team but 'of course' the cost reduction team who were responsible for delivering the savings. And why on earth should he be bothered about documenting the definition of a 'quick win'. Everyone knew what a quick win was, didn't they?

Basically, he just didn't 'get it'. I knew immediately the programme was doomed (which, indeed, it proved to be). And no, I did not go back later and say, 'I told you so', if only because it was so obvious *after* the event.

In conclusion, IT cost-efficiency improvement is both difficult and risky. But as I said at the start of this chapter, if you do not do it to yourself, it will very probably be done to you, by senior management 'inflicting' consultants on you or by their outsourcing the IT function to an ESP – and rest assured that the ESP will do it to you with all the ruthlessness inherent in the need to move quickly into profit and reward the ESP's shareholders.

This then leaves one key issue unexplored, that of outsourcing. Is it the universal panacea to cost-efficiency improvement? Should we forget all about the hassle of running a cost-efficiency improvement programme and just give the job to an ESP?

4.14 Does outsourcing save money?

The Outsourcing Institute reports that more than 80 per cent of Fortune 500 companies have now outsourced either part or all of their information processes. And Gartner are predicting an 18 per cent growth rate in IT outsourcing across Europe. They add that the *global* IT outsourcing market will be worth $188bn by 2003. So IT outsourcing is clearly, to say the least, in vogue. *However*, a recent survey reported that 60 per cent of organizations that had outsourcing contracts in place were dissatisfied and 40 per cent were trying to end them. Another study reported that 70 per cent of total outsourcing contracts were 'unsuccessful' (without, admittedly, explaining what 'unsuccessful' meant). A further study showed that 26 per cent of the organizations surveyed that had outsourced services were trying to bring those services back in-house (and only 5 per cent were achieving really substantial benefits).

It is dangerous to read too much into surveys, but on face value these results tend to suggest that outsourcers are promising the kind of benefits that organizations increasingly seek, but that they are often not adequately living up to those promises once the deal is done. This is all (not) very well, but does not tell us *which* benefits are being sought, *why* these benefits are not being adequately delivered and whether the problem lies with the outsourcer, the customer or both parties.

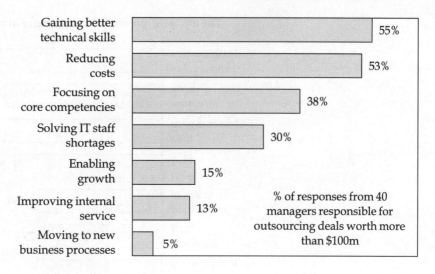

Gaining better technical skills	55%
Reducing costs	53%
Focusing on core competencies	38%
Solving IT staff shortages	30%
Enabling growth	15%
Improving internal service	13%
Moving to new business processes	5%

% of responses from 40 managers responsible for outsourcing deals worth more than $100m

Figure 4.8   *Source*: Forrester

First, what are these sought-after but elusive benefits? Well, there are many business drivers for pursuing outsourcing (e.g. focusing on your core business, moving to a more variable cost base, getting a cash injection, access to wider skills base), but cost reduction is still typically one of *the* key drivers (see Figure 4.8).

However, as organizations increasingly outsource *business* processes and/or divest themselves of non-core business groups, so demand on IT services can fluctuate wildly and rapidly. The typical IT function with its high fixed cost base is very poorly positioned to respond to this and so I believe that increasingly the benefits of moving to a more variable cost base will overtake cost reduction as a key benefit of outsourcing in time.

So, given how key cost reduction currently appears to be, *are* organizations *actually* failing to realize promised savings from outsourcing? Given the dramatic improvements in the price/performance of equipment with time, in the area of infrastructure service outsourcing alone you might certainly expect substantial reduction in costs throughout the contract life. Economies of scale potentially available to the large-scale ESP also lie in the areas of accommodation, software fees and maintenance, hardware capital costs and leases, hardware maintenance charges, network charges and staff costs. The resultant cost savings *should* be reflected in lower service charges than are generated in-house. But surveys tend to indicate that

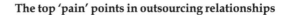

The top 'pain' points in outsourcing relationships

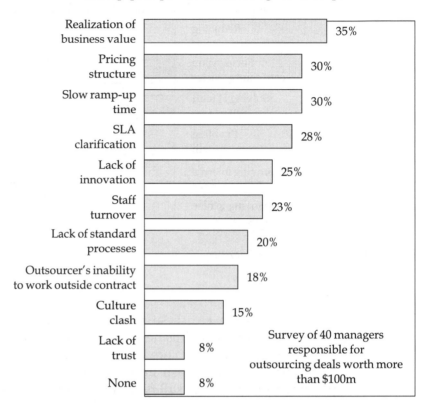

Realization of business value	35%
Pricing structure	30%
Slow ramp-up time	30%
SLA clarification	28%
Lack of innovation	25%
Staff turnover	23%
Lack of standard processes	20%
Outsourcer's inability to work outside contract	18%
Culture clash	15%
Lack of trust	8%
None	8%

Survey of 40 managers responsible for outsourcing deals worth more than $100m

Figure 4.9   *Source*: Forrester

the value improvements sought are difficult to extract (see Figure 4.9).

Realization of business value from the arrangement is the number one grouse. So why is it apparently so difficult to realize the promised cost savings on which outsourcing deals are almost invariably struck? And why is the typical failure to deliver such a key benefit not more widely reported? Why, in short, do people persist in associating outsourcing with cost reduction?

My own suspicion is that a certain tacit conspiracy exists here. The ESPs obviously don't want their inability to deliver promised cost savings made any more visible than necessary, while the CIOs are a tad embarrassed by their failure to extract the savings from the ESPs (coupled with having signed contracts that don't financially penalize the ESPs for that failure). Added to this is the fact that it is often extremely difficult to track requirements and systems changes sufficiently rigorously to be able to establish whether the savings originally expected from outsourcing *have* actually been maintained in the longer term.

What level of savings are we talking about? Well on a major IT outsourcing deal with which I was recently associated, the six favoured suppliers were all 'promising' application development savings of around 30 per cent per annum and infrastructure delivery and support savings of around 15 per cent per annum. Note that the savings promised used to be more like 40 per cent, but the increasing focus of IT functions on their costs and the trend towards shorter contracts have forced ESPs to be a little more conservative in their hype. But even at 15 per cent to 30 per cent we are not talking about insignificant sums. The failure of an ESP to deliver this level of promised saving is obviously going to be a cause of dissatisfaction, to say the least.

I believe that there are two root causes of the often deeply unsatisfactory nature of the 'post-deal' relationship problems generally, and delivery of cost savings, specifically. First, there is the failure of customers, when negotiating an outsourcing deal, to really face up to the fact that their agenda is typically *radically* different from that of the potential supplier. Second, there is the failure of customers to really face up to the fact that it is typically *immensely* difficult for the supplier to actually deliver cost savings, especially in the shorter term. I believe that both of the problems are rooted in the prevalent commercial naivety of the 'corporate' men in the company who come up with the idea of outsourcing and then try to negotiate a deal, like 'real businessmen'.

Taking the agendas issue first, here are the key things that you, as the customer, want from the deal:

- transfer of the risks of IT service provision from you to the supplier;
- guaranteed cost savings increasing over the life of the contract;
- cost reductions from improvements in equipment price/ performance passed on to you;
- cost reductions from supplier efficiency improvements passed on to you;
- a short contract;
- high flexibility in the contract (should your circumstances change);

- open book accounting with caps on permissible supplier margins;
- frequent price reviews;
- simple to understand pricing structures;
- regular external price benchmarking (requiring the supplier to maintain presence in the upper decile of performance);
- improved service levels (and contractual penalties on failure to meet the improved service level targets);
- services customized to your specific requirements;
- no guarantees of the level of business you will give the supplier;
- control over the supplier's technology architecture;
- access to the latest technology and the corresponding skills;
- supplier commitment to refresh the technology regularly;
- guarantees on staff retention and staff training;
- key IT staff dedicated to your account (i.e. not attempting to service multiple customers);
- formal and spot customer satisfaction surveys with guarantees of increasing satisfaction (and financial penalties on falling satisfaction);
- 'ring fenced' service provision that will not incur 'service creep' from supplier salespeople directly approaching your end users and selling on further services (unless, of course, they are clearly external to the existing contract and paid for directly by the user);
- non-exclusive rights for the supplier bidding for additional services;
- retention of all intellectual property rights resulting from services provided;
- exclusivity and confidentiality commitments enshrined in the contract where services that provide competitive advantage for your company are being outsourced; this is to help ensure that there is no loss of competitive advantage from the supplier offering the same or similar outsourced services to other customers;
- the maintenance of competition (by not outsourcing everything to one supplier) so you do not become 'locked in' to one supplier;
- as much money up front for your assets as possible;
- non-disruptive exit provisions (so if it all goes wrong you can get out with minimal hassle);
- contract exit provisions that give you the credibility and leverage to 'threaten' the supplier with taking your business elsewhere;
- the ability to terminate the contract quickly and easily, with or without cause.

Of course, paradoxically, you *also* want the supplier to make a profit, because if he doesn't, at the least your service levels will suffer and, at the worst, the supplier will go under. Yes, the supplier would also like to make a profit on the deal but this is about as far as your common interests lie. In fact the supplier wants *exactly the opposite* of the above list and can be relied upon to send in the 'prince of darkness' negotiator to ensure that this is achieved. In particular, they want the biggest contract they can sell and they want to lock you into that contract for as long as possible so as to be able to spread their sales and transition costs over a long period and exploit the price/performance improvements in technology to help enhance their profits.

I am contending that a deal struck based on a mature and realistic understanding of where the supplier is *really* coming from will stand a far higher chance of success than one that makes essentially naive assumptions about the common goals of the supplier and customer 'working in partnership'. I mean, *please*. The deal that is likely to succeed is the one that delivers a sensible balance of what *both* parties are seeking from the relationship.

Now I want to examine the second root cause, the great difficulties faced by ESPs in actually delivering cost savings and set out 10 CSFs that should at least ensure that you strike an outsourcing deal that does optimize the level of savings actually achievable.

Before the contract is signed both you and the supplier will apparently enjoy focusing on cost reduction – you, because you want the savings, and the supplier because salesmen love to sell a proposition that they claim will not only not cost anything, it will actually *save* you money. So suppliers will always *promise* cost reduction – but once that contract is signed, you and the supplier have opposite financial objectives. So when the supplier talks (as they all do) of the superb 'partnership' you will have, take this with a barrel load of salt and ensure that you get *your* homegrown 'prince of darkness' to negotiate the deal. The 'partnership' may just be a trap in which the supplier moves up the value chain and increasingly influences the nature of services supplied. That is the name of the game for any external service provider (including management consultants).

I think the difficulty of actually reducing total IT costs as a result of outsourcing is illustrated well by Figure 4.10.

Basically, at the time of transfer of your costs to the ESP, the total cost of service provision is going to *soar*, not reduce. Quite aside

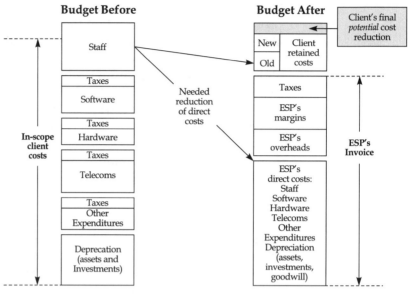

Figure 4.10   *Source*: Gartner

from taxes generally (and, in Europe, value added tax – VAT – in particular), overheads and supplier profit, you must add the (often seriously underestimated) retained costs of, for example, managing the supplier relationship, managing demand, developing strategy etc. Stated simply, the ESP must be able to make *dramatic* cost reductions in your cost base over time if he is going to be able to send you bills that, when added to your retained and new costs, actually reduce the IT budget after outsourcing. And to this you need to add the typically substantial costs of managing the transition (typically over a 9 to 12 month period). Additionally, remember that the supplier is incurring high costs bidding for your business – ultimately you are not only going to have to pay for this but also for the failed sales costs of all those contracts the supplier *didn't* win.

Note that after the supplier has taken on your people, infrastructure and technology assets (assuming these assets were transferred and paid for by the supplier), he will inevitably initially be making a loss. It is only by subsequently reducing the direct costs of service provision that he will get to the 'break-even' point and start to make a profit, which will typically be anything between one and three years after the contract is let. So the crucial thing for the supplier is to get those direct costs down as fast as possible. The outsourcing market is highly competitive and suppliers will invariably 'low ball' the initial contract price on the understanding that they will be able to ramp up the revenue once the contract is signed.

ESPs (particularly the major players, like EDS and IBM) typically have very high overheads *and* have to meet shareholders' profit expectations. This leads to a situation in which the supplier's direct costs generally cannot exceed 65 per cent to 70 per cent of revenue. So if the supplier is really going to reduce your total IT budget, then your budget before outsourcing is going to have to be around 50 per cent higher than the supplier's equivalent direct costs. Ask yourself the question, therefore, 'Could my organization take a one third reduction in its IT budget and still manage to provide the same services at the same service levels?' And if the answer to that question is 'No way', then how do you expect the supplier to do it? What magic wand do they possess that you do not? OK, the supplier may be able to share indirect costs with other contracts and may get higher leverage with *their* suppliers. But that alone is not going to deliver the sort of savings required. Precisely because ESPs have increasingly been 'forced' to benchmark their cost-efficiency against the market, their results have been building up in benchmarking databases. And increasingly the conclusion seems to be *that a good ESP is no more cost-efficient than a good internal IT function*.

4.15 CSFs for realizing cost reduction with ESPs

So, given the typically fundamentally opposed agendas of the customer and the supplier and the typically immense difficulty of the supplier to realize promised cost savings, what can be done to maximize the chance of both delivering a successful deal and such savings as are realistically achievable? To this end, here are my 'Top 10' CSFs (summarized in Figure 4.11):

1 Negotiate from a position of strength, in which you clearly understand the supplier's commercial agenda. Probe and understand the supplier's expectations of revenue, cost, margin, risks, market development and sell-on opportunities – basically, never cease to see the deal from his point of view. Note Gartner's Strategic Planning Assumption: 'Through 2003, ESPs will outnegotiate enterprises through superior skills so that ESPs will enjoy more favourable terms in 90 percent of deals (0.7 probability).' No matter what the supplier says, you are *not* about to enter into a partnership –

10 CSFs for realizing cost reduction with ESPs	
1	Negotiate from a position of strength, in which you clearly understand the supplier's commercial agenda
2	Ensure that you have a team of first class specialists with a proven track record in successful IT outsourcing
3	Understand the scale of opportunities for cost reduction available to the supplier if he wins the contract
4	Tell the suppliers bidding for the contract anything they want to know *except* your current costs
5	Ensure that you have a clear understanding of how you would expect your IT cost base to change over the life of the contract if you did *not* outsource
6	Understand *exactly* what is in and out of scope of the services to be provided
7	Critically review the supplier's standard contracts and SLAs to ensure that proper provision is made for monitoring the costs of service provision against the service levels provided
8	Separate out transition costs and 'recharges'
9	Consider a joint venture approach to help retain some control over the outsourced service
10	Don't be bulldozed into signing the contract until all the key service levels and the detailed responsibilities matrix are completed and signed off

Figure 4.11

instead you are probably about to enter into a war, or, perhaps a better analogy, a marriage! Once the deal is consummated, there are going to be rows, disappointments, disillusionment and occasional bouts of despair. So get the prenuptial agreement rock solid so that you both articulate what you want from the relationship (and when you want a divorce, you don't end up being fleeced).

2 Ensure that you have a team of first class specialists with a proven track record in successful IT outsourcing. This should include:

- accountants (principally for detailed asset valuation and construction of budgetary models);
- taxation specialists (to address such issues as VAT/tax and customs duties optimization, corporation tax optimization, PAYE optimization for transferred staff etc.);
- lawyers (to address such issues as restrictions on existing supply contracts, TUPE and OJEC requirements, maturity status of share schemes or pension plans, trade union representation, confidentiality, IPR, non-disclosure agreements, warranties, acceptance criteria, penalties, liabilities etc.); and

- consultants (to bring an understanding of the outsourcing market and key ESP players for the services you are considering for outsourcing, to perform due diligence on the preferred supplier and to help manage the outsourcing process and its attendant risks, such as the loss of key staff, loss of control, industrial action, impact on key projects etc.).

Basically, outsourcing is not a job for amateurs. In particular, ensure that you have a first class negotiator on your side, even if it means recruiting him or her from an ESP. The guy in your purchasing department who got a great deal on the supply of pencils will be taken to the cleaners by the ESP negotiators.

3 Understand the scale of opportunities for cost reduction available to the supplier if he wins the contract (by conducting a diagnosis of opportunities and/or performing external price benchmarking – but remember that benchmarking is *backward* looking; costs may fall significantly by the time your deal is actually completed). Note that meaningful price benchmarking may require the supplier to unbundle his service prices so that a 'true' comparison is possible. Not also that it implies that your existing services are well defined and fully costed and that existing service levels are well understood. Remember that although the ESP's salespeople love to offer cost reduction as an 'it will more than pay for itself' incentive to buy, ESPs also *hate* cost reduction as a key driver because of all the reasons for outsourcing it is the single most measurable one, and therefore their failure here will be most visible. Therefore they will naturally try to fudge the issue, or at least delay getting into detail until *after* the contract is signed (see CSF 10).

4 Tell the suppliers bidding for the contract pretty much anything they want to know *except* your current costs. If you tell them your current costs and *then* ask them if they can achieve a significant reduction on these costs (no matter *how* low they currently are) what do you *expect* them to say? Of *course* they will promise savings, *before* there is any clear understanding of the exact services, scope and service levels to be provided. By keeping them in the dark about your costs, but being explicit about your services, they have to demonstrate the price at which they can provide comparable services while only being able to guess your existing baseline for cost reduction. Accept the fact that they will hate you for

this! Only once they have made their initial bid should you reveal your costs. Then, assuming their predicted price is below your predicted internal cost over the duration of the contract, interrogate the supplier to understand how *exactly* they are going to realize the cost savings they say they can achieve – and don't just accept the 'economies of scale' line. If your hardware and software costs are already well leveraged (as they typically are these days) then the supplier is going to have to focus on service level reduction and/or staff level reduction. Ask how many staff they think will have to be made redundant. Ask how they will reduce costs while making high severance payments to those staff. Ask whether disaster recovery service level will be affected. Ask whether service levels *will* be compromised. Ask about what service standardization they intend to apply. Even if your hardware and software purchasing left much to be desired, existing lease or contractual obligations may make rational-ization and consolidation unrealistic, at least in the short term. So, again, exactly *how* are these savings going to be achieved? Note, by the way, that if a supplier *cannot* actually demonstrate to you convincingly that the hoped for cost reductions are actually feasible then they will change their bidding focus to other areas, such as the size of the cash input they will provide on asset transfer (and for which you will pay – through the nose – later in the life of the contract). Basically, remember that these charming, smiling young men and women the ESP sends in to discuss its services don't have to like you and you don't have to like them. You just want mutual respect based on mutual exploitation. Mutually beneficial exploitation is at the very heart of successful commercial relationships.

5 Ensure that you have a clear understanding of how you would expect your IT cost base to change over the life of the contract if you did *not* outsource. It is this predicted cost of services over the *life* of the contract that is important. Without this it will be extremely difficult to assess the extent to which the charges you are incurring plus your new and retained costs are actually delivering cost reduction. Armed with this information you will be much better placed to negotiate with the supplier. But do not underestimate how difficult it will be to construct such a long-term cost model! You are going to have to make many very difficult assumptions about the future of your business, the future of the market in which it operates, the level of demand for services etc. Remember that if these assumptions turn out to

be wrong, it will be extremely difficult to determine whether or not the ESP has actually delivered the promised cost savings – a point that ESPs depend on!

6 Understand *exactly* what is in and out of scope of the services to be provided. For example, a deal struck to 'outsource the provision of portal services' is meaningless unless both parties agree *exactly* what the scope of 'portal' is. Does it include only PCs that are LAN connected? What about ISDN connected devices? Does it include Applemacs? What about LAN/WAN cabling? What about UPS? What about client software? Where does the responsibility lie for the LAN shared devices, such as file servers? Also avoid shocks from finding out about the extensive activities (and costs) that you must retain *after* the contract is signed. Similarly work out the real cost of retained (and potentially new) activities, like contract management, supplier management and demand management. And on that last point, remember that there is no better way of reducing IT costs than managing down your demand levels! I will have a lot more to say about the retained activities in the next chapter.

7 Critically review the supplier's standard contracts and SLAs to ensure that proper provision is made for monitoring the costs of service provision against the service levels provided.

8 Separate out transition costs and 'recharges' associated with asset transfers from the costs associated with ongoing service provision (i.e. understand the *real* supplier price of service provision).

9 Consider a joint venture approach to help retain some control over the outsourced service and potentially avoid Europe's value added tax (VAT) costs. Note that unless you have special VAT status, moving from paying VAT primarily only on purchased hardware and software to paying VAT on *all* costs can make a substantial difference to the cost of service provision. Reducing the VAT burden will obviously make it easier to achieve the desired reduction in total IT costs.

10 Don't be bulldozed (either by the supplier or by your exasperation with the negotiation process) into signing the contract until all the key service levels (including targets and penalties) and the detailed responsibilities matrix are completed and signed off. The 'standard' supplier contract will invariably state that all these tiresome minor details will be addressed during the many months of transition after the contract is signed. Of course these things are tiresome,

because this is where the detail resides on the service levels you want at the price you want. A corollary of this CSF is that you have to understand and accept that a properly structured deal will almost certainly take 9 to 12 months to broker.

And if I am to be allowed a covert 11th CSF, it would be, 'Do ensure that, despite the previous 10 CSFs, the supplier makes a profit!' It won't be just him that suffers if he makes a loss.

To conclude, let me quote a few more apposite Gartner Strategic Planning Assumptions:

- In 75 per cent of outsourcing deals involving wide-ranging asset transitions up to 2002, significant cost reductions to clients are either vendor hype or a client misunderstanding, and promised savings will not materialize (0.7 probability).
- In 50 per cent of outsourcing deals started before 2001 to obtain cost reduction, the projected three-year cost reduction will be approximately the same as the evaluation margin of error (0.6 probability).
- Through 2005, outsourcing will not provide real savings unless the enterprise's internal costs are at least 50 per cent larger than the vendor's direct cost (0.9 probability). In 60 per cent of these deals, the enterprise will lose potential savings due to poor skills in negotiating and relationship management (0.7 probability).

Basically what Gartner is saying is that if you are truly *grossly* inefficient then the outsourcing supplier might just be able to get savings, but you probably won't be able to credibly measure it even then; and, anyway, the supplier is not likely to pass those savings on to you. Am I being cynical or just plain realistic?

So, my bottom line answer to the question, 'Does outsourcing save money?' has to be, 'It is not actually impossible'. But if ever the phrase *caveat emptor* applied, this is it. Saving money may be the single most cited reason for outsourcing but, in my view, it is also the single *worst* reason for outsourcing, and is almost certainly going to cause disappointment and dissatisfaction. But if you *must* cling to it, make sure you follow my 10 CSFs above. As Terry White puts it in *Reinventing the IT Department*, 'The choice about outsourcing is a company one and there is no reason why an in-house IT function cannot provide the same value added services at cost competitive rates as most outsourcers. The emphasis should be on value added rather than cost though.'

The Institute of Value Management states that a root principle of value management is 'a continuous awareness of value for the organization, establishing measures or estimates of value, monitoring and controlling them'. In the next chapter I will address this issue of how to *measure* IT value in order to understand current value realization levels, identify where to focus limited management time, energy and cost in value transformation initiatives, and then track and report improvements in value realized. In particular, this should help you measure your success at implementing value transformation programmes. I hope to also show how important measures are to influencing behaviours, in particular engendering more commercial behaviours.

4.16 Summary

Cost-efficiency is an important aspect of the value of IT to the business, especially where the IT function operates as a cost centre (in SAM model terms). Cost-efficiency improvement is concerned with minimizing (at acceptable risk, and without unacceptably compromising supply-side effectiveness or demand-side quality or value-added) the entire cost base of IT supply. Key to the optimization of cost-efficiency is the creation of a commercial culture. It is generally the case that IT functions (particularly of large organizations) display strongly 'corporate', 'uncommercial' behaviours. The selection and effective implementation of appropriate metrics can have a pivotal role to play in engendering commercial behaviours.

Optimizing the cost-efficiency of IT product and service supply is about minimizing the 'tariffs' for all products and services provided by the IT function. Tariffs must be based on the total cost of ownership of products and services supplied. These products and services should be packaged in such a way as to be directly comprehensible to the business user. Key approaches to optimizing cost-efficiency are:

- optimizing the sourcing of IT services;
- optimizing purchasing processes, the supplier mix and contractual terms;
- optimizing the utilization and efficient use of hardware and software;
- optimizing the utilization and efficient use of buildings;
- optimizing the staff resourcing of projects and teams;
- rationalizing, and improving the efficiency of, IT activities and services.

Outsourcing IT to an ESP is a valid option in the pursuit of cost reduction but extensive evidence suggests that real savings are immensely elusive. Added to this is the great difficulty of striking a deal with the ESP that meets the conflicting agendas of customer and supplier and the great difficulty for the ESP to actually deliver the savings promised (in terms of the total IT budget, including retained costs) *unless* the internal IT function is *inordinately* inefficient.

5

Measuring success

[Feeling patient's pulse] 'Either he's dead,
or my watch has stopped.'

Groucho Marx in *A Day at the Races*

If you are going to take the pulse of your IT function then you had better be confident that the tools you use are credible and up to the job. It could just be that the tools are sicker than the patient. Their prognosis of the imminent death of your IT function may be premature! So this chapter is focused on building credible tools for measuring an organization's degree of success at transforming the business value of IT. But before that I want to briefly explore why we should bother to measure at all.

5.1 Why bother?

Gartner report that about $1.5bn is spent annually on IT performance measurement. They add that this is apparently 'only' about 2 per cent of total IT expenditure (presumably in order to imply that $1.5bn is not *serious* money – or perhaps to imply that far more should be spent, provided it is spent with, say, GartnerMeasurement). But I think that most of us would regard this sum as still being rather more than 'loose change' and we would like to believe that this money was being spent to good effect, in terms of giving the business an accurate and objective understanding of the performance of its IT function and the value it extracts from its IT investment. Despite all this money being spent on measurement, the Meta group report, 'The Business of IT Portfolio Management: Balancing Risk, Innovation and ROI', reveals a startling survey result – '89% of companies are flying blind, with virtually no metrics in place except for finance (akin to flying a plane by monitoring the fuel burn rate)'. Even if we treat both these metrics with a touch of scepticism we still appear to be spending a lot of money to achieve very little.

So just how important is measurement? Jac Fitz-Enz (Benchmarking Staff Performance 1996) has this (reasonably typical) thing to say: 'Measurement of any work process or practice is more than possible. It is imperative. Without metrics, managers are only caretakers. They are administrators of processes.' This is very much in the spirit of the 'you can't manage what you can't measure' message. It is such transparent nonsense it is incredible that people keep saying it. Some of the finest managers (both 'staff' and 'project') I have known performed their role with little or no metrics to support them and they were most emphatically neither 'caretakers' nor mere 'administrators'. They succeeded through their leadership skills, through caring passionately about results, through superb attention to detail, through having a keen eye for what was important and what was relatively unimportant, through having a keen nose for bullshit and through having a keen insight into who to trust (and could be relied upon to deliver the goods) and who not to trust (and so required a watchful and sceptical eye). Metrics would not have hurt, but that was the least of their problems. So let's not get *too* hung up on the 'metrics imperative'.

Remember that metrics don't directly add value. They can, however, be immensely powerful in *indirectly* adding value through their ability, *if wisely chosen and implemented*, to shape value-adding behaviours in staff (and so helping to inculcate a more 'commercial culture'). In Chapter 3 I made the point that one of the key drivers of the endemically strong commercial culture in management consultancy firms was the metrics set chosen to measure the staff. In particular, one simple measure, 'utilization'. *This* is why metrics are actually key, *if* they are chosen and implemented with immense care. The fundamental problem with many (in fact, most) measurement programmes I have seen is that they are not thought through rigorously – in particular, the behavioural implications are typically *very* poorly considered. There is no place for woolly thinking in metrics programmes. This is why I set out below nine key criteria for selecting metrics. The wrong metrics can have an extremely adverse effect on individual behaviours (and easily inculcate *un*commercial behaviours); the right metrics can be absolutely key in inculcating commercial behaviours. As with just about every initiative I advocate in this book, a carefully thought through and well-executed implementation should have a major positive impact on the business value of IT – but an ill-thought through and poorly executed implementation may well do more harm than good. So, once again, my message is that you should only implement a metrics programme if you are really serious about it.

Having said all that, given limited time, energy and money, it is far preferable to invest in implementing practices and initiatives that are aimed at hitting the effectiveness and cost-efficiency goals than investing in implementing an IT performance measurement system. Having said *that*, we would obviously like to be able at least to indicate (if not conclusively *prove*) that we are adding more value to the business with time and, ideally, that no one else out there (whether they be competitors or ESPs) could add significantly more value (so, CEO/CFO, please get off our case). At the very least, we would like to be able to indicate that implementing improved best value practices has, indeed, raised IT value. I have a particularly vested interest in that specific indicator!

Well, this leads my thoughts to the renowned physicist Werner Heisenberg who, in the late 1920s, developed various theories that came to be known collectively as the 'Uncertainty Principle'. There are two essential aspects of this principle. First, it is *impossible* to measure all aspects of a system accurately. You have to be selective, you will never be entirely accurate and the more you try to measure (and improve) one particular area (such as cost-efficiency) the more you will tend to compromise measurements in another area (such as effectiveness). Second, there is no such thing as an 'objective' observer (measurer) whose presence has no bearing on that which is measured. What the management observer chooses to measure will typically have a substantial effect on what is measured. This can be a good thing if you select and construct your measures with great care so as to incentivize commercially positive effects or a bad thing if you are sloppy. Before any smart-ass particle physicists start writing to me care of the publisher, please note that I *do* know that I am abusing the Uncertainty Principle here. It is just an *analogy*.

The difficulty of measuring 'IT performance' and, in particular, doing so in business meaningful terms, came home to me when I met with the CFO of a large privatized utility. His company was in the process of acquiring other smaller utilities and vertically integrating them into the company's business portfolio. But he had a problem. Increasingly he was finding that whatever the intrinsic merits of the businesses acquired, there seemed invariably to be major issues around IT generally, and about integrating the acquired IT function specifically.

'At the macro level I can assess the target company we are thinking of acquiring by a few key metrics', he said, 'like return on capital, profitability, price/earnings ratio, etc. so *surely* there must be a few key metrics I can use to warn me if I'm about to buy an "IT turkey".' What he wanted was a 'quick and dirty' IT due diligence test that could be applied to the IT function of the business being considered for acquisition based on readily available data that would require little or no access to the IT function or its financial 'books'.

Put that way, I had to admit that it didn't sound unreasonable. But when I replied, 'Well, of course, it's not that easy', he all but rolled his eyes in cynical disbelief. It just *couldn't* be that hard. 'What', he insisted, 'were the KPIs of an IT function?' 'Well, it depends', I replied. It was at this point that I got the 'just another IT consultant trying to make something simple sound complex to justify his overblown fees' look. So I asked him what sort of metrics he was looking for. Not surprisingly, he turned this one round and asked me what the typical metrics *were* for measuring the performance of IT functions (or, indeed, ESPs complementing the internal IT function). I talked to him about the need to measure cost-efficiency and effectiveness as set out in earlier chapters. Unfortunately I then had to dampen his ardour by pointing out that he probably stood more chance of winning the national lottery two weeks running than finding an IT function that actually maintained such metrics, at least of the breadth and depth I was suggesting. Which is odd, considering that 'balanced scorecards' are hardly an innovation. In fact the measurement of cost-efficiency and effectiveness is very similar to the original 'balanced scorecard' approach set out by Kaplan and Norton in 1993, illustrated in Figure 5.1.

The Kaplan and Norton approach is so established that it has effectively become a *de facto* standard for measuring IT performance (for those few who actually do try to measure it). It is based on the assumption that the business objectives and measures will be used to drive the IT function's objectives and measures and it is 'balanced' in as much as it does not just measure IT from the 'traditional' economic perspective (e.g. IT spend as a percentage of revenue) but includes a broader range of indicators of the performance of the IT function. My cost-efficiency measures correspond (approximately) to the financial

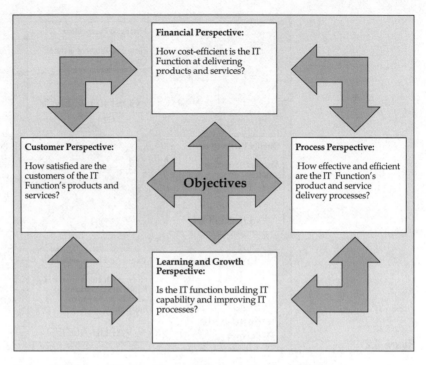

Figure 5.1

Source: Kaplan and Norton; Harvard Business Review 1992

perspective. My effectiveness measures correspond (approx-imately) to the process perspective (once the efficiency of processes has been 'moved up' into the financial perspective). The customer perspective is clearly key to any assessment of the quality of services and products provided and is included on the demand side of my 'value compass'. Learning and growth measures I explicitly omit, not because they are irrelevant but because, pragmatically, they are extremely difficult to measure in any meaningful way and, more importantly, I believe they pale into insignificance against the other measures (especially when your focus is business value-based). The crucial differ-ence, however, is my broadening of the picture of 'IT perform-ance' to encapsulate the *value-added* and deliverables' *quality* measures. In short, my problem with the traditional Kaplan and Norton balanced scorecard approach is its excessive focus on measuring the performance on the supply side. Surely to be truly 'balanced' it should be focused 'equally' on commercial outcomes (the demand side of the equation)? Value is a product of both the 'supply-side' view (is the IT function run economic-ally, efficiently and effectively?) and the 'demand-side' view (does the IT function deliver quality products and services that

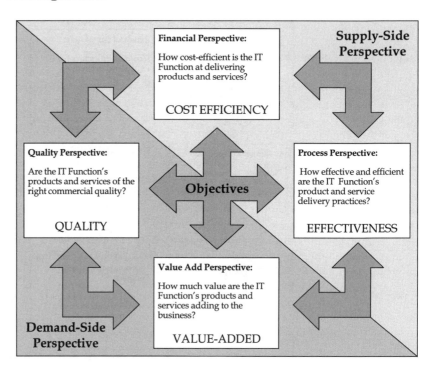

Figure 5.2

add value to my business and result in satisfied customers?). My revised picture is set out in Figure 5.2.

Note that the 'objectives' in the middle of the figure may be derived principally from the business or the IT function itself and the focus (or weighting) on each of the four segments will depend principally on the SAM alignment of the IT function (whether it be cost centre, investment centre, profit centre or service centre). Note also that the four dimensions are *generic* characteristics of value. In practice a 'balanced scorecard' set up for a specific IT function would also be expected to reflect its success against its delivery commitments (in terms of *specific* projects to be completed, e.g. replace the stock replenishment system, build a second data centre, outsource the helpdesk).

I think that my despairing CFO would have been quite happy with these four measures because he would have been able to relate them to the basic assessment he would make of a business as a whole, namely:

- Were its costs/overheads under control (he is a bean counter, remember)? – economy in cost-efficiency.
- Was it productive enough to compete commercially? – efficiency in cost-efficiency.

- Were its processes geared to produce quality products and services? – best practices in effectiveness.
- Were its processes geared to produce products and services which would attract high margins? – best value practices in effectiveness.
- Did it actually *deliver* quality products and services? – quality.
- Did it actually *deliver* profitable products and services? – value-added.

On the final point, note, however, that in this *internal* IT context we are talking about 'profitable' as the extent to which the IT function's 'business' contributes to the profitability of the business served, *not* the 'profitability' of the IT function. As examined in Chapter 2, in a very real sense we don't want our IT function to be 'profitable' because that essentially would mean that they were making money at the business's expense. This is a key way in which the IT function should *not* be managed 'like an ESP', a point I will emphasize in the next chapter. What we *do* want is our internal IT function to be highly *commercial*, quite a different matter.

Note also that when the business uses measures of the IT function to help it decide if it wants to 'invest' with its internal IT function or an IT ESP, the 'supply-side' focused measures (cost-efficiency and effectiveness) are not really what you should worry about. What you should be worried about is whether or not these guys actually deliver high quality, value-added solutions and have happy customers. After all, if you were to contract with an ESP to 'replace' your IT function (or just outsource your IT function to them) you would not really care *how* they did what they do (once you had negotiated the contract). What you would be doing is contracting with them to deliver a product or service for a price. How they set about delivering for that price is *their* worry (so long, of course, that the service they deliver is of acceptable quality). So, again, I would argue that our 'demand-side' measures are 'of higher value' than the other, more traditional, measures.

About now I see the IT auditors who are reading this book (and moving their lips, obviously) start to jump up and down and cry out, 'What about risk!' And of course they are right, at least in theory. For example, a CIO who achieves spectacular cost-efficiency with such techniques as, say, outsourcing all systems development offshore (to Taliban Technology in Afghanistan), replacing his management team with new graduates or Accenture consultants (only kidding!), running his mainframes at 100 per cent utilization or providing no disaster recovery is hardly going to be said to be a success (at least not for long!) But I am going to assume that, whatever their commercial credentials, the IT managers are not technically stupid and that therefore these are truly *theoretical* risks and, for simplicity, exclude them from my argument.

Our four measures are targeted on measuring the value of the IT function, from all aspects of its expenditure on behalf of the business. We want our measures to encompass all the key Kaplan and Norton measures, but with increasing focus on the outcome oriented 'demand-side' measures. My point, once again, is to emphasize the importance of the 'demand-side' measures of the IT function compared with the traditional 'supply-side' measures.

Our measures are not so much going to be key performance indicators (KPIs) as key *value* indicators (KVIs). The need for metrics to support these KVI areas (and the relative importance of these KVI areas) will depend largely on the strategic role of IT in support of the business (i.e. its SAM positioning, as set out in Chapter 2). So, for example, we might want to highly populate (and weight highly) the cost-efficiency KVI areas if the IT function operates largely as a cost centre. The relative import-ance will also tend to vary with time as management priorities shift between cost containment/reduction and growing the business.

5.2 Selecting metrics

The next challenge is obviously to 'populate' the four quadrants of our 'value compass' (see Figure 5.3) with specific KVIs. What we need now is a filtering mechanism to tell us how to differentiate a 'good' value indicator from a 'bad' indicator so we can find the smallest possible subset that could reasonably be called 'key'. In a sense, what we are seeking is 'high value' value indicators. We would certainly like our full metric set to address all the key services of the IT function. But we want some help in selecting the highest value ones. Ideally they must *tolerably* satisfy *all* of the nine criteria set out below:

1 Be accurate (±5 per cent? e.g. a 5 per cent improvement in performance ±5 per cent isn't going to impress anyone).
2 Be objective (i.e. it's not just a matter of opinion).
3 Be consistent (i.e. everyone reporting this measure does it exactly the same way).

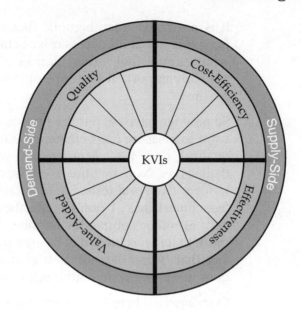

Figure 5.3

4 Be 'unfudgeable' (i.e. not susceptible to cynical manipulation by vested interests).

5 Be unambiguous (i.e. there must not be multiple interpretations – high/low numbers are always good/bad and changes in the value are almost certainly attributable to changes in the thing being measured rather than some other factor).

6 Be externally 'benchmarkable' (i.e. tell us how we compare with, say, our competitors or ESPs).

7 Be important (i.e. measure things that say something important about the value of IT to the business. Ultimately it should be related to the company's financial results. This is the 'so what' test).

8 Be readily understood by non-IT managers (in particular, the board).

And we would also like them to be:

9 Quick, easy and inexpensive to obtain.

For example, let us take the metric 'number of man-days spent in training per person per year' (presumably one of Kaplan and Nortons' learning and growth metrics). It would not be at all difficult for this to meet our criteria of being accurate, objective, consistent, unfudgeable, quick and easy to obtain and readily understood by non-IT managers. It is even reasonably benchmarkable (10 days a year seems to be the 'going rate'). However, it is not really unambiguous (because more days training per person is not at all necessarily 'better', in terms of value) and I would argue that, other than in a *very* indirect way, it is not remotely important (in terms of indicating the value of IT to the business).

So now we have set out the four *characteristics* of IT delivery we want to measure (cost-efficiency, effectiveness, value-added and quality) and the *characteristics* we require of the metrics themselves. Note that these 'metric characteristics' are not going to form *theoretical* tests. So, for example, when I say a metric is 'benchmarkable', I don't mean that you *could* benchmark it if only all other companies happened to maintain that metric. I mean that *in practice* today it is not tolerably benchmarkable. The fact that 'some day, all metrics may be maintained this way' does not concern me (although that would be nice!).

Our objective here is to move away from the question typically first asked in setting up measurement programmes, 'what *can* we measure?' towards asking the question, 'what *should* we measure?' Here, before even asking what specifically we *should* be measuring, we sought to define the characteristics of any 'metrics set' that would be credible and sufficient for our purposes. Now we need to populate our measurement model with candidate metrics that meet our 'acceptance criteria'.

5.3 Measuring cost-efficiency

Let's start with cost-efficiency and seek measures that satisfy our nine criteria.

I contend that the measurement of cost-efficiency has four key components:

1 Supply economy – characterized by how economically the business can 'buy' IT products and services supplied by its IT function, i.e. what the IT function 'charges' the business it serves.
2 Buy economy – characterized by how economically the IT function (or, indeed, the business) can buy IT products and services from third party suppliers, i.e. what the suppliers charge you, their customer.
3 Asset utilization – characterized by how well you 'sweat' your IT assets (be they people, technology or office space).
4 Staff productivity – characterized by how much IT 'output' is produced per unit 'input'. In an IT context, those outputs

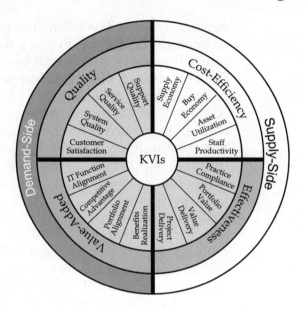

Figure 5.4

might be the quantity of business systems functionality delivered per unit time/resource/cost (on the 'systems development' side of the 'IT factory') or the quantity of services delivered (e.g. functionality supported, portal, mainframe, network) per unit time/resource/cost (on the 'service delivery' side of the 'IT factory').

Let's start with **supply economy** metrics. As a representative metric for the economics of supply I will take 'IT spend as a percentage of revenue'. This must be the IT industry's best known metric, economic or otherwise.

What about being accurate, objective and consistent? I was working at a major UK food retailer a few years ago and, in a workshop that included the CIO and the CFO, I asked the 'simple' question, 'How much do you spend annually on IT?' At precisely the same time, the CIO replied '£60m' and the CFO replied '£120m'. There was a moment's silence as they looked at each other in some bewilderment and then a *long* and entirely inconclusive discussion ensued. Subsequent investigation (which, incidentally, took several skilled people several *weeks* to complete) revealed that the £60m was, as expected, the CIO's budget, but the £120m (or was it £130m? or even £150m?) included IT spend outside the IT function's budget (in particular, EPOS equipment, PCs, LANs etc. etc.).

So when a company receives its survey questionnaire to collect its 'IT spend as a percentage of revenue', which IT spend number is reported? And are they going to put a team of skilled accountants on the job to get a tolerably accurate figure? Of course they aren't. And even if we 'assume' that it is only the IT function's budget that we are supposed to be reporting, are they taking account of what parts of the business's revenue are actually being supported by the IT function? For example, in a review I performed of an energy supplier's IT function, I found that there were no less than four other (admittedly smaller) IT functions supporting specific parts of the business and other parts of the business received IT support from other specialist third party suppliers. The bottom line question is, 'What confidence can we have in the accuracy (±100 per cent!) of the IT spend figure that has probably been jotted down hastily, probably (but not necessarily) reflects only the IT function's budget (and which will treat depreciation in different ways and include or exclude different expenditure) and what confidence can we have in its correlation to the business revenue figure, probably plucked from the company's annual report?' Basically, we have to conclude that we can have little confidence in the accuracy, objectivity or consistency (criteria 1, 2 and 3) of this metric. Additionally, depending on what we choose to include/exclude in the 'IT spend' figure we can easily manipulate this metric value. So it is clearly not 'unfudgeable' (criterion 4).

What about ambiguity? At the simplest level the IT function exists to build applications and then run them on behalf of the business. What does this metric tell us about the performance of these services? If we break the IT spend between these two service areas and the 'build applications' spend looks high compared with 'market norms' then they are overspending on applications development, right? Or are they underspending on technology? Or do they simply make great purchasing deals on technology? Or are they very efficient in systems operation? And even if we still conclude that development spend is excessive, is it because their developers are overpaid? Or are they overstaffed? Or are they making disproportionate use of expensive contractors? So this 'simple' metric may indeed cover all the key services of the IT function, but it seems to raise more questions than useful answers.

And *anyway* we have a numerator and a denominator here. Maybe the business has had a good year which *temporarily* enhanced revenue, so decreasing the 'IT spend as a percentage of revenue' figure. Maybe the IT function is in 'catch-up mode' and has recently had to invest disproportionately in technology, so increasing the metric value. And the metric value will greatly depend on the company's product life-cycle stages, the strategic importance of IT to the business, the extent to which it is a 'leader or lagger' in the use of technology, the scale, distribution and complexity of its IT solutions etc. So our metric certainly does not appear to be unambiguous (criterion 5). A high value may be 'good' or it may be 'bad'.

Which leads me on to the next metric criterion, namely, the extent to which 'IT spend as a percentage of revenue' is externally 'benchmarkable'. In various spend survey reports over the last year I have noted that for the electricity sector, IT spend (or is it IT function spend?) as a percentage of revenue has been given at a variety of figures, ranging from 0.9 per cent to 3.6 per cent. So who do you believe? As Gartner themselves state, 'By itself, IT spending is not a valid metric for comparing the value of IT to the business or differences in IT capabilities among organisations . . . It does not provide valid comparative information than can, or should, be used to assess IT performance.' And Gartner, remember, make a good living from IT cost benchmarking! So there goes 'externally benchmarkable' (criterion 6). And if, as Gartner say, IT spending is not a valid metric (at least in isolation) for comparing the value of IT to the business, IT spending as a percentage of revenue, although intrinsically 'better' (in that it at least recognizes that the spend is relative to some measure of the size of business served) is still unlikely to tell us something important about IT value (criterion 7).

However, the board will understand this metric (or at least they will *think* they do) and it is apparently quick and easy to obtain (criteria 8 and 9).

So, in summary, the most quoted metric in the IT industry as a measure of IT performance fails seven of our nine criteria. Not too impressive, you might say. Anyway, it can be argued that the metric 'IT spend as a percentage of revenue' is fundamentally flawed since it treats the IT function specifically (and IT investment generally) as a business *overhead* whose spend must be rigidly contained, rather than a value-adding part of the business in which investment is rewarded. Which is not too good if you are running your IT function as an investment centre (as defined in the SAM model).

I'm afraid that when I am told that a company's IT spend as a percentage of revenue is below market norms, my typical response is 'so what?', at least in so far as I am seriously expected to draw any conclusions about the performance of the company's IT from this *alone*. It is one small piece of the 'performance jigsaw' and needs to be treated with extreme caution in isolation. Each piece of the jigsaw must be treated as 'circumstantial evidence' and only if the majority of the pieces fit together to paint a mutually reinforcing 'picture' should we feel we have enough evidence to either 'convict' or congratulate our IT function.

Of course, 'IT spend as a percentage of business revenue' is just one economic metric. There are potentially many others, such as 'IT capital spend as a percentage of business revenue', 'IT spend as a percentage of business costs', 'IT spend per employee', 'IT spend per user', 'Percentage of IT spend allocated to support', or 'Percentage of IT spend allocated to infrastructure projects'. But the fundamental problems set out above apply to them too. Then we can have economic metrics that focus on the financial *control* of the IT function, e.g. capital and revenue expenditure budgetary plan vs actual, cost recovery plan vs actual, working capital plan vs actual. Economic metrics of this sort do generally meet all of our nine criteria other than benchmarkability and, I would contend, importance. It is at this point that any financial accountants reading this have a sharp intake of breath (and CFOs have heart attacks). How can I possibly say that rigorous financial control over the (typically) huge sums of money invested in IT is not 'important'. My answer is that it is a very poor indicator of IT *value* and that it only becomes important if there are serious problems with it. And in the vast majority of IT functions financial control of this sort is the least of their worries. So all I am saying is that common sense should be applied. By all means add financial control metrics to your 'key metric set' but perhaps only if it is known to be a problem area for you (or you know it will really turn on your CFO).

So which of these economic metrics am I advocating you to consider? The answer is, 'All of the above!' The reason for my making this apparently bizarre statement having apparently just largely rubbished these metrics is rooted in one word: 'benchmarkable'. Many of the fundamental problems, if not actually 'going away', do at least get ameliorated significantly if you stop trying to pretend that these numbers are some sort of 'IT industry standard'. So long as you use the metrics primarily for internal trend tracking purposes (i.e. trying to answer the question, 'Are we getting better or worse?' rather than trying to answer the question, 'Are we better or worse than the competition?') then you can (potentially) tolerably satisfy many of the criteria. There will still be some degree of ambiguity but this is where the 'jigsaw' analogy comes in. When all the parts are fitted together does a consistent picture emerge? It is the mutually reinforcing (or otherwise) nature of the metric results that helps you draw conclusions.

Basically, you are never going to get a simple 'fuel meter'. You have got to *think*. If, for example, 'IT spend as a percentage of revenue' has risen while business revenue has been stable and the *other* value indicators suggest that this *relative* increase in spend has not been accompanied by a proportionate rise in the 'benefits realization' measure, it is time to worry. So, taken in the context of all other metrics, we can certainly learn something useful about the value of IT *over time*, *assuming* we compile the numbers in an entirely consistent manner. Any attempts to make external comparisons should be *extremely* circumspect. It is only if there appears to be a substantial discrepancy with external figures that you would have to say that *something* is awry. So if, for example, you are a food retailer and your IT spend as a percentage of revenue figure is 2.8 per cent while industry averages reported in various surveys range from 0.6 per cent to 1.2 per cent then *something* is probably wrong (if only the fact that you are being more honest than your competitors!) and further investigation will be warranted.

Please note that although I assert that in the above circum-stances many if not most of the nine criteria can be met satisfactorily, I am being a little disingenuous with one of them. If we want our economic metrics 'quick and easy' we will almost inevitably pay the price of a generally completely unacceptable level of accuracy, objectivity and consistency, the resultant economic metrics perhaps serving little more than internal political purposes. As Sir Alec Douglas-Home once said, 'There are two problems in my life. The political ones are insoluble and the economic ones are incomprehensible.' If you want economic metrics that are comprehensible and valuable (and not just political window-dressing), accept that there is going to be a price to be paid.

But we are not finished with **supply economy** metrics. I've saved the best for last. Our final metrics are concerned with measuring the extent to which we are optimizing (i.e. minimiz-ing) the cost (i.e. price) of all IT products and services that the IT function 'sells' to the business it serves. The purchase costs of hardware have been falling dramatically year after year. Although this has been offset somewhat by rising software costs the net effect should still be to reduce operational costs (per service unit). Similarly, the availability of hardware and software with dramatically higher availability and reliability coupled with the increasing availability of operational automation tools means that operational support costs (per service unit) should also be reducing. And improvements year on year in the rigour of systems development practices should be delivering more robust systems that require less support and maintenance (and, indeed, less enhancement, particularly of the 'failure-driven rework' kind). This should be reducing the overall systems development, support and maintenance costs (per system).

In other words, optimizing service costs is measured by measuring the 'tariffs' for the products and services because these are the 'prices' you charge the business. I am making the (admittedly naive) assumption, by the way, that the tariffs are basically 'honest', i.e. that they include all direct and indirect costs and that any service cross-subsidies that exist are fully accounted for. Even if you have not established a tariff structure you still have to have costs for these things if you are to be able to build credible project business cases that include full total cost of ownership lifetime costs. These 'internal service supply tariffs' measures can, with reasonable effort, be made to be tolerably accurate, objective, consistent and unfudgeable (assuming we establish the appropriate disciplines to prevent, in particular, cross-subsidies), unambiguous (assuming the lower price is not achieved at unacceptable risk), relatively easy to produce and they are important to the business (from a value perspective). *Provided* (and that's a big 'provided') they are expressed in units that the business user can relate to (i.e. 'price of bundled product/service') they may well be understood by the business (the user will be very unlikely to understand a metric about the cost/price of his 'percentage' or measured utilization of a LAN but should understand what a 'portal' is, as a 'package deal'). Tariffs *are theoretically* benchmarkable with the outside world (ESP quoted prices or cost-efficiency benchmarking companies' databases). However, I make a detailed argument below why I am less than convinced (to say the least) that this is meaningfully achievable in practice.

I would actually go further than saying that the *'tariffs'* should be reducing year on year. I would also argue that there is a good case for setting an *absolute* cost reduction target, at least post-production, so that the *total* cost of running systems reduces year on year. This might seem unfair since we are presumably typically adding more and more system functionality to the production environment every year and so surely that will *increase* running costs each year. But my argument is that the cost-efficiencies available in this environment (principally from productivity enhancement tools and equipment price-performance leaps – 'Moore's law') coupled with the fact that redundant (and now no longer value-adding) functionality should be 'dropped off the end' of the life-cycle means that absolute budgets should be decreasing.

In conclusion, therefore, our internal service supply tariff metrics can be made to tolerably satisfy eight of our nine criteria, generally failing only the benchmarkability test. This is the basis by which I will assess all other metrics from now on (unless explicitly stated otherwise). So when I say that a metric is, for example, 'tolerably accurate' I mean that with sufficient disciplines in place it can be *made* tolerably accurate for internal purposes only. If I *also* 'tick' the benchmarkable column, then I am saying that the accuracy should also be adequate for meaningful external benchmarking purposes.

Let's move on to **buy economy** metrics. We spend money on services, things (assets, such as equipment and buildings) and people.

To measure how economically we buy services from ESPs we might measure 'external service supply tariffs'. The arguments set out above for the value of such metrics hold true here too, as do the extent to which they meet our nine criteria. Remember, though, that the external service supplier may feel less constrained than the internal supplier to prepare his tariffs consistently and unfudgeably! Beware also the temptation to directly compare the IT function's internal supply tariffs with those of the ESP (I explain why in some detail below).

We might measure how economically we buy things with a metric called 'physical asset cost' (e.g. price/cost per MIP bought, price/cost per portal bought, price/cost per server bought, price/cost per square foot of office space). These metrics can generally be made sufficiently accurate, objective, consistent, unfudgeable, unambiguous, understandable and relatively quick and easy to obtain. They will provide trend analysis measures but they will be extremely hard to benchmark externally. I will explore the difficulties of benchmarking in some detail below, so let's take a rain check on this point for now. That leaves one criterion: 'importance'. In my experience, most IT functions these days run reasonably well-automated, 'tight ship' data centres and leverage their major purchases well.

Furthermore the ease with which equipment can be incrementally scaled (from PCs right the way through to mainframes or 'enterprise servers') has improved dramatically, so failures of capacity planning have far smaller consequences. In fact I believe that all these 'capital' spend metrics have to be examined carefully on the criterion of 'importance'. Let's remember that independent IT spend surveys typically show IT personnel costs as over 50 per cent of total IT function spend and equipment costs typically at around 10 per cent. Therefore you may well think that there is a good argument for focusing your spend metrics on your spend on people.

Staff are also an asset (although in the case of some you might not think so!). 'Staff asset cost' (i.e. average total remuneration, including all benefits, for staff of a given role/grade/seniority) is a metric that can typically be compiled with acceptable accuracy, objectivity and consistency. It is largely unfudgeable, is readily understood by non-IT managers and is relatively easy to obtain. It is even reasonably externally benchmarkable, since many remuneration benchmarking surveys are available (in Britain the 'Computer Economics' survey is probably the best known), although there can be considerable problems with making direct job title comparisons (one company's 'vice president of systems engineering' may be another company's 'programmer'). The key problem is that it is not at all unambiguous, i.e. paying less is not *at all* necessarily a good thing ('if you pay peanuts you get monkeys') but paying more is not intrinsically 'good' either. Of course, if your metric is a little more sophisticated and focuses on, say, alignment of remuneration with upper quartile market norms, then the ambiguity can be decreased. This leaves the criterion of 'importance'. I would argue that where the focus of your measures is to be on value creation the price you pay for your staff should be the very least of your concerns. As I stated forcibly above (in Chapter 2), there simply is no better way of increasing value than having high calibre management and workforce. A 10 per cent increase in costs here might yield a 100 per cent increase in value yielded to the business. Therefore I believe that this measure is only important if poor rates of pay are inhibiting the recruitment of excellence (and if it is, this becomes a key metric).

Let's move on to **asset utilization** metrics. We utilize both things (physical assets, such as equipment and buildings) and people. As an example let's create a metric called 'physical asset utilization' and, for illustrative purposes, consider just the utilization of computer equipment (since the same principles apply to, say, hotdesk utilization or floor space utilization). Measuring the utilization of equipment is generally *relatively* easy to do and will also probably be acceptably accurate, objective, consistent, unfudgeable, unambiguous and externally benchmarkable (so, seven of the nine criteria down). It might even be understandable to non-IT managers (even though they might not understand why you can't run the mainframe at 100 per cent utilization). But is it important? That is, if you will forgive me, a value judgement for you. An exception to my generalization is certainly the server world, and the recommendation, 'Consolidate and rationalize poorly utilized servers' has almost become 'boilerplate' in IT performance reviews I conduct. But you probably don't need a metric to tell you that you've got a cost-efficiency problem here.

Measuring 'staff asset utilization' is generally *relatively* easy to do (once you have bullied them into completing timesheets), it is readily understood by non-IT managers and it is an unambiguous measure (higher utilization is 'good'). However, the data collected will typically be wildly inaccurate, highly subjective, highly inconsistent, highly fudgeable and extremely difficult to benchmark externally. The reason for this is that unless staff truly understand the importance of this data, some will indeed record time accurately against the correct project and non-project time codes, but most will simply treat the process as an annoying joke, for example block booking time to project codes (despite having spent many hours in internal, non-project, meetings, attending training, going to the dentist, sorting out filing, attending 'awaydays', waiting for management decisions or just plain reading the back pages of the computer press to see if better paid work is around, preferably with an IT function that doesn't expect you to fill in timesheets). To get round these problems you either have to apply enormous discipline and compliance checking to the timesheet completion process and/or you need to be using the timesheet data directly for the raising of bills to the customer (which concentrates the mind wonderfully but is a separate issue – transfer charging – which I dealt with in some detail in Chapter 3). The 'reason' that transfer charging largely removes these issues is that criteria such as accuracy, objectivity and consistency change their nature. You are no longer trying to accurately, objectively and consistently get staff to record how they *actually* spend their time, but how they spend their time for customer billing purposes, which is quite another matter. What counts in this circumstance is recording the hours than can and should be billed. This may well mean, for example, that long hours worked as deadlines approach are simply 'buried' because the customer sees that as 'your problem' and so they cannot be billed or the project manager may simply not want poor estimating or planning to be visible. Whatever the reasons, staff time recording for billing purposes is intrinsically, and deliberately, very fudgeable and may bear little resemblance to the hours *actually* worked.

All professional services firms (e.g. lawyers, accountants, management consultants) *live* by this utilization metric because it (coupled with recovery rates – how much billable time booked actually gets billed and paid) determines their revenue. When you join a firm of consultants (as a member of chargeable staff) the first thing you are given is a utilization target and woe betide you if you fail to hit it. But no one seriously believes that the hours booked to client codes reflect the hours *actually* worked. Therefore in an IT context, hours booked for billing purposes could never, for example, be used as input to a project estimating model. So do you ask staff to fill in *two* timesheets, one for billing purposes and another one (the 'accurate' one) for *real* utilization purposes?

It can be argued that staff utilization is not generally a particularly important measure in internal IT functions because there is typically a seemingly endless 'forward order book' (otherwise known in internal IT functions as the 'backlog') so there is no 'excuse' for being underutilized. This is not to say that it doesn't happen (particularly when staff are waiting for management decisions to authorize the start of the next part of their project or when team managers hang on to unutilized staff that could be productively utilized elsewhere). Therefore the argument is that staff utilization is a *relatively* unimportant metric where there is a captive internal market and high demand levels and where the focus of the metrics is on assessing the value of IT to the business. Clearly it would be an entirely different matter if the IT function were 'genuinely commercial' (i.e. an ESP). Of course, if you have good reason to suspect that poor decision making or poor IT staff resource management are rife in your organization then this might still be an important measure (*provided* you instil and enforce the necessary disciplines). Please note that although the points I raise above do call into question the value of measuring the utilization of internal IT staff, I am definitely not questioning the value of getting them to fill in timesheets – I dealt with this in Chapter 3 (section 3.5) under the heading 'CFFs and CSFs for transfer charging'. Furthermore there is the important point of how much time is spent on *non*-productive activities. I was recently working at a client site and was given a desk for the day in the middle of a team of permanent staff. I couldn't help overhearing what was going on around me because I was listening. The unlucky man who was sitting next to me spent the *entire* morning on the telephone organizing a short holiday in Amsterdam, having a heated debate with his house insurance company about the difference between 'storm damage' and 'an influx of water', having a slightly surreal discussion with the painters working at his home about the precise shade of off-white that was required in his kitchen and booking his car into a garage for a service and then chatting at length with his wife about canals, loss adjusters, paint tints and the fact that garages ran an extortion racket. He then announced that he had to go out for a while because he had a dental appointment. Obviously this was extreme (and not too bright when you have a management consultant sitting next to you). Clearly work was a major irritation getting in the way of his domestic life and I told him this to his face. Well no, I'm lying. I didn't say anything actually. But would he have behaved in this way if he had had to complete a timesheet and account for how productively he had spent his day? My point is that we would certainly like to have measures that help us identify the '*un*productivity' of staff and set targets that incentivize people to minimize non-productive activities (and leave their domestic lives at home).

That leads on neatly to **staff productivity**, i.e. how much they 'produce' per unit of time/cost while they are *not* being unproductive. Let's look first at staff responsible for the development and support/maintenance of applications. There are a variety of measures of 'systems development and support staff productivity'. For example, one of my clients used the number of project milestones reached each month as a key measure of development productivity. This was acceptably accurate (it's easy to count milestones achieved), objective (you've either passed the milestone or you haven't), consistent (all project managers count in decimals, apart from ex-CICS programmers, who, of course, still count in hexadecimal and think that Deep Purple are a really happening band), unambiguous (it is better to pass more milestones than less), reasonably readily understood (although some people do actually have a problem with the very concept of 'milestones'), *apparently* important (faster progress in system delivery is certainly a 'good thing', not only from a cost-efficiency point of view but also from the point of view of delivering product earlier and so potentially realizing benefits earlier) and was certainly quick and easy to obtain. The project managers were happy because they were consistently improving on the number of milestones delivered each month (and these targets were set in their personal development plans). The CIO was happy because his productivity improvement initiative was demonstrably paying off. And the CFO was happy because he had an IT metric that he could actually understand. Great! So what's the problem? The problem is rooted in the 'fudgeability' criterion. Of course, all that was happening was that increasingly trivial milestones were being defined so only *apparently* increasing productivity. Indeed several project managers were making extensive use of a milestone called 'Friday'. That way they were sure to hit at least four milestones each month! Such a metric is also inherently not susceptible to external benchmarking.

It is the basic human nature problem: whenever you set a measure (and particularly if the achievement of a particular target affects staff remuneration) you potentially modify human behaviour. People quickly find ways to spin a metric result that their bosses want to see, *if* that metric is intrinsically fudgeable. This was epitomized for me on an assignment some years ago where the IT function was run as a profit centre, operating as a wholly owned subsidiary of the business it served. The holding company set its subsidiary two key objectives, namely:

1 To minimize the cost of service provision to the customer (i.e. them).
2 To maximize the revenue of the IT function.

But in this context these are essentially contradictory objectives! Cost (plus margin) *was* the revenue. In terms of how IT staff were actually measured it was the second objective that clearly prevailed. They were effectively being incentivized to *increase* the cost of IT to the business. Incidentally, quite aside from the fact that the transfer charging system employed a small army of administration staff and accountants, further pushing up costs, at the end of the year the 'profits' were simply 'given back' to the business as a rebate!

Similarly, in a recent assignment with a client that also ran its IT function as a 'pseudo supplier', I saw a business case for an eminently sensible development productivity improvement project fail. Why? Because the *costs* of implementing the improvements would fall to the IT function but the *benefits* would fall to the business. The 'contribution' of the IT function (effectively its 'profits') would be reduced and *the* key metric by which all IT groups were measured was 'contribution'! So a metric introduced as part of an initiative to 'commercialize' the internal IT supplier incentivized behaviour that was actually commercially *counter*productive for the business as a whole.

So such indirect measures of productivity as 'milestones achieved' are always going to be highly suspect. More credible measures must be more directly related to actual 'quantity of product' delivered, which in our IT context means the 'amount' of functionality delivered and supported per unit of effort/cost. In bygone days, when Bill Gates was playing on a swing and dreaming of future world domination and I was playing on an IBM 029 card punch and dreaming of girls, this was measured by counting lines-of-code as the quantity of product. This was typically acceptably accurate and objective. It could also reasonably easily be made consistent and unfudgeable (by enforcing rules, such as exactly which lines of code to count, how to treat rewrites etc.), was very quick and easy to obtain and was even reasonably understandable to non-IT managers. The fact that different organizations applied different rules did, however, make external benchmarkability a problem. So it looks good, doesn't it? In fact, in the days when 'everyone' in the private sector wrote Cobol code on IBM mainframes and 'everyone' in the public sector wrote Cobol code on ICL mainframes (oh, happy days) this had much to recommend it. The fundamental problem then was that it was ambiguous, in as much as it only told you how much *code* had been delivered, not how much *functionality*. So, for example, an appalling programmer who had to produce twice as many lines of code to achieve one 'unit of functionality' (whatever that is) was apparently twice as productive as his more talented colleague. This code, incidentally, would also then probably be a nightmare to maintain post-implementation, so depressing *support* productivity. Lines-of-code was also useless as a measure when code was bought (a package) rather than bespoke (i.e. custom built). However, the thing that essentially kills lines-of-code as a credible measure *today* is the proliferation of languages and technologies. A hundred lines of code in one technology might achieve much the same as one line of code in another so you are restricted to smaller and smaller valid 'comparison sets'.

So is there a *credible* development productivity metric (covering both systems development and systems support productivity)? Well, how about function point metrics (e.g. function points developed per man-month, function points supported per £/$)? This was the main successor to lines-of-code. I think I would have to start by saying that whenever I have quoted function point metrics to a business executive I have invariably received variations on the reply, 'What in the name of goodness is a function point?', although generally not in exactly those words. Clearly we fall down immediately at one of our nine required metric characteristics, namely, understood by non-IT managers. And it gets worse.

First, few IT functions actually maintain function point metrics (in Europe it is generally estimated at about 10 per cent) and even those who do often do so with questionable rigour. In one of my clients a project function point count of 50 (as supplied by the project manager) turned out to be closer to 400 (as determined in a one hour QA 'spot check' by a function point 'guru'). So the accuracy, objectivity, consistency and fudgeability criteria are challenged. And even those who do maintain function point counts rigorously, rarely have sufficient data for the various sizes of project developed with different techniques on different technologies to be statistically credible. This also means they are not able to be credibly benchmarked against peers (the first nail in the coffin of external benchmarkability). And implementing function point measurement is non-trivial. Indeed, the cost of training staff to count function points, actually do the counting on all non-trivial work and maintaining the models and reporting systems has been cited to me on more than one occasion as a key reason for poor development productivity! So, there goes 'quick and easy to obtain'.

Second, the metric doesn't address (increasingly prevalent) package selection and implementation. It also can produce anomalous results for different *types* of development. For example, let's say that a team of six developers labour for six months producing a corporate database system that maintains a consistent picture of all the key attributes of the company's products. It produces very little functionality (and possibly none that actually directly adds value to the business) because it is primarily concerned with data issues (and system interfaces). Another team of six developers then labour for six months to write a suite of programs that report against this corporate database. They produce a veritable *mountain* of functionality, much of which adds substantial value to the business. So was our first team appallingly unproductive compared with our second team? Almost certainly not, but this is the sort of anomaly that can easily arise (particularly with data/infrastructure-oriented developments). So even *internal* comparisons become difficult (at least with any credibility). In short, while function points are unambiguous in as much as higher is 'better', they are not unambiguous as a true indicator of the level of value delivery (at least in all cases). Furthermore, in a similar manner to lines-of-code, it can also suffer from the 'even worse functionality faster' interpretation of 'higher productivity'.

Third, 'function point counts' are often indirectly computed from a statistical surrogate, with *very* dubious accuracy. Furthermore, there are many 'grey areas', such as counting cancelled or rewritten code, taking account of non-productive time and inclusion of indirect costs. This further undermines the accuracy, objectivity, consistency, fudgeability and benchmarkability of the data. In fact a leading research group estimates that function point metrics have an accuracy of about ±14 per cent. So, imagine an honest CIO (this is just a theoretical illustration, you understand) proudly telling his CEO that his systems development productivity has gone up a full 10 per cent (adding a mumbled 'plus or minus 14 per cent').

Finally, external benchmarking providers vary widely in their average function point productivity figures, not just by a factor of 10 per cent or 20 per cent but by a factor of 10! So if you want to prove how productive you are compared with your peers, choose your benchmarking supplier carefully! Furthermore, this problem is compounded by the widely varying productivity figures for different sizes of project. Figures of 400–500 function points per person year are not uncommon for small developments (in fact, some web-based developers can hit over 1000). But this figure can fall to the 100–200 function point mark for large, complex developments. This need to compare yourself with peers on a project size/complexity basis adds further to the difficulty of making statistically valid comparisons (because, for example, you may never actually develop enough 'large, complex, 3GL-based, non-corporate' projects to get a statistically valid data sample set).

So what *can* we say for function points? Well, although it has clearly failed no less than eight of our nine 'tests' it *is*, perhaps unfortunately, important. As I noted above, staff costs are typically around half of total IT costs and the cost-efficiency of the 'capital element' is *generally* not key to optimizing value. Plus, speed of solution to market is often critical, particularly when the planned solution either offers competitive edge to the business (or helps 'catch up with' a differentiating system implemented by a competitor). For example, the implementation of loyalty cards by Tesco Stores, Britain's largest and most successful food retailer, was *highly* dependent on IT. It was a key milestone in Tesco's crusade to steal market share from Sainsbury's, their arch rival, and was a major success (especially since Sainsbury's CEO had just gone on public record stating dismissively that loyalty cards were nothing more than electronic 'green shield stamps'). The upshot was a frantic scramble by Sainsbury's to develop its own loyalty card system, speed to market here being absolutely key to the business. So much as we might like to dismiss development staff productivity, the fact remains that it is typically a very important value measure. And function point counting is generally the best metric we have to do it. The best advice I can give on this is that you can pursue one of two options:

1 Accept that measuring development staff productivity is simply too hard to do credibly, and focus instead on other value measures; or
2 Implement function point metrics, but do so with such disciplined rigour (coupled with extensive support, infrastructure and quality control) that you are at least tolerably *internally* accurate, objective, consistent and unfudgeable. But you will have to accept that even then the results will not be credibly externally benchmarkable, no one on the board will have the slightest idea what you are talking about and the results will most emphatically not be quick and easy to obtain. In other words, it becomes almost entirely an *internal* productivity trend measure, and not just internal to the company but internal to the IT function. And even *then* you may well find that by the time your 'productivity measurement team' has collated sufficient data on productivity for a particular kind of development (e.g. RAD) on a particular kind of technology (e.g. JAVA) to be statistically useful, the method/technology set will probably have become redundant! You may then take the view that if even with your very best (productivity sapping!) efforts to maintain function point metrics you cannot draw sufficiently reliable conclusions, why bother?

That was 'systems development and support staff productivity'. What about operational 'service delivery and support staff productivity'? There are many potential measures of operational staff productivity. For example, for the helpdesk alone we can compare staffing levels with the number of handled calls, call abandoned rates, first call resolution rates, and so on. For technical support staff we can compare the number of staff supporting a configuration of a given size and complexity, the number of sites supported, the number of network nodes supported, and so on.

These types of metrics can generally be collated *reasonably* easily with acceptable accuracy, objectivity, *internal* consistency and, with care and discipline, unambiguously and unfudgeably. Even if non-IT managers cannot understand what a MIP or a node is, they can at least understand the *concept*. What about 'import-ance'? In the typical 'full service' IT function the area where productivity has by far the biggest impact, in terms both of cost and time to market, is the applications development and support area. It is here that you typically find about half of the staff costs; productivity in *this* area is therefore key since this is effectively the company's 'IT solutions factory'. An IT function that is highly productive will deliver and support its applica-tions at reduced cost per function unit, with increased function-ality per time unit and will be faster to market with solutions (thereby delivering earlier business benefits). So I would contend that while operational service delivery staff productiv-ity is certainly not *unimportant*, it is not *as* important (from the point of view of value delivery) as development productivity. Furthermore, problems come with external consistency (i.e. benchmarkability). The benchmarking issue is rooted in the fundamental difficulty of comparing services and service levels. For example, there is a world of difference between a helpdesk that simply acts as a 'call referral' service and one which is staffed to actually resolve the majority of incoming calls. Once you drop this criterion you have a reasonable chance, however, of passing the other eight 'tests'.

The more observant reader (yes, I mean you) may have noted a theme emerging here, namely, external benchmarking is inord-inately difficult. This is something you probably badly want because without it you have no credible basis for assessing the 'competitiveness' of your IT function other than putting them (or a subset of their services) out to ESP tender. And even then the ESPs who bid may well low-ball their quote to get in the door, get a 'quality' client name on their books or open up a new market for them. So *why* can't we generally successfully externally benchmark IT performance?

The answer is to do with accuracy, objectivity, consistency (and fudgeability) of data maintenance across companies. I can now hear GartnerMeasurement, Compass and other niche bench-marking companies irascibly pleading 'but accuracy, objectivity and consistency are at the very *heart* of our business'. That, I reply, is what I call a 'Mandy Rice-Davies'. (For the benefit of my younger readers (and Americans), Mandy was a 'good time girl' involved in the Profumo political scandal of 1963 that brought down the British government of the day. When confronted in the witness box with a statement from a respected Lord of the Realm to the effect that 'he had not indulged in any inappropriate behaviour with her', she replied with a smirk, 'Well, he would say that, wouldn't he?') To put it another way, 'he who pays the piper calls the tune'.

While certainly not wishing to impugn the integrity of niche benchmarking suppliers, they do, obviously, have a commercial agenda. Key to that agenda is repeat business. A five year contract that incurs only one cost of sale is obviously *much* more lucrative than a 'one off' sale. Therefore biting the hand that feeds you is obviously bad business and that hand is almost invariably the CIO (or direct reports), i.e. the people paying are the people being judged. I certainly don't mean to imply that these companies 'fix' their results to tell their buyer what he wants to hear. Heavens no. Perish the thought. But there are 'ways and means', which I will illustrate in a moment. But first (lest I hear the words 'pot', 'kettle' and 'black') let me say that the issue of 'conflict of interest' is not unique to IT benchmarking companies.

I have worked for several of the big professional services firms whose independence and objectivity are at the heart of their audit (and management consultancy) business. But the fees (often *huge* fees) are being paid by the organization being audited so there is always going to be that quiet incentive not to ask too many difficult questions (and, anyway, audits are not designed to uncover fraud, are they?) and, above all else, not to qualify the accounts (i.e. effectively tell the world that your client's management is incompetent at best and possibly crooked at worst). Additionally, because audit work is won competitively and because it is widely perceived (*very* erroneously) to be a 'commodity service', price tends to be the key predictor of success in winning an audit. To get the costs (i.e. price) down, audit firms generally have to reduce the amount of work they do to assure the integrity of the accounts and/or put more junior, inexperienced staff on the job. Furthermore, the big professional services firms earn more than half their revenue from non-audit services (such as IT consultancy!) sold on the back of the audit – so losing a client can have disastrous financial implications for the audit firm. And what if the client has outsourced, say, its internal accounting department to its auditor (an increasingly prevalent practice)? What if it has outsourced its IT function to the audit firm's management consultancy practice? Can we rely on the policemen to police themselves? My point is that even organizations whose service (and high fee rates) are predicated largely on their independence, objectivity and integrity cannot be regarded as beyond reproach. I am certainly not saying that these are key factors that together conspire and contribute to produce such fiscal disasters as the Polly Peck, Barings, BCCI, Maxwell, Enron, WorldCom or Xerox affairs. Others have reportedly so alleged, however. And, quite frankly, if we cannot entirely trust the big professional services firms (who build in huge margins to reward themselves – well, their partners anyway – for the level of risk they carry), why should we put our trust in relatively tiny, relatively low margin, niche IT benchmarking suppliers?

So what 'ways and means' do benchmarkers use? As a simple example, some years ago I was called upon to review the helpdesk benchmarking reports supplied by a leading niche benchmarking company for the CIO of one of Britain's largest clearing banks. I noticed that in just one year, the productivity (in terms of calls handled per helpdesk staff member) had almost doubled. I was, of course, awed (American edition) and gobsmacked (British edition). How, I asked myself, had such an astonishing improvement been achieved? It took little subsequent investigation to find that while the call levels had remained roughly static, the number of staff included in the 'denominator' had roughly halved. This had been achieved by recategorizing about half the helpdesk staff as a 'business support unit' rather than IT helpdesk. Now, let us be generous (and naive) and assume that no cynical deceit was intended by the IT function and let us also recognize that the benchmarking company's report did indeed note (in an 8-point type footnote) the main reason for the apparent 'improvement'. Nevertheless, this had not stopped the CIO from touting the metric (but not the footnote) to the business as indicative of the prowess of his IT function. Is the benchmarking supplier going to openly challenge the CIO? No, after all, they *did* bring the matter up in the footnotes of their report, so their consciences are clear.

That was a trivial example, but what about this one? I was recently involved in a study to identify IT cost reduction opportunities in a large public utility. The IT function operated as a 'pseudo supplier' to the rest of the organization and 'sold' (albeit in 'wooden euros') a range of products internally. A major product was 'portal' (basically, a desktop PC and its immediate technical infrastructure). In defence of the price charged for this product the IT function produced a report from a highly reputable IT benchmarking supplier which clearly demonstrated that their portal product improved significantly on market norms for price competitiveness. It was clear to me that the IT function had considerable faith in their benchmarking supplier and *sincerely* believed in the evidence.

Since our team had been commissioned to perform our study by the *business*, not the IT function (a rare event this, to say the least), we employed *another* leading IT benchmarking company to independently benchmark the cost of *all* the IT function's products in order to help corroborate (or otherwise) the other benchmarking supplier's results. I'm sure it will come as no surprise when I say that the results of 'our' benchmarks generally differed very materially from the IT function's benchmarker. To try to avoid a 'bun fight' over the numbers, we investigated the reasons for the divergence. In summary, the key differences were as follows:

1 The IT function's benchmarker had been commissioned to conduct a series of independent benchmarks on each product *in isolation*. The crucial point is that significant, very material, 'cross-charges' between products were not being included. However, our study (benchmarking *all* products) addressed these cross-charges and could demonstrate that almost 99 per cent of the total cost base was accounted for.
2 Because of the business 'sensitivity' to the cost of certain products, the IT function had made a commercial decision to cross-subsidize these products. The original benchmarker had not taken account of this.
3 The original benchmarker's reports generally relied on a peer group made up of 'world class peers'. However, quite aside from the fact that there seemed to be no clear basis on which they had determined the organizations in the peer group as 'world class', the 'work load drivers' on which most metrics were based (e.g. number of users, number of calls handled, number of network nodes) were invariably *far* below those of the IT function. Quite simply, the organizations in the peer group were *much* smaller and the significant economies of scale and reduced proportion of fixed cost base that this large IT function could achieve were not being factored in.

A further key point worth making is that, quite aside from the time of the analysts provided by the niche benchmarking company we commissioned, it additionally took about three members of our own team (highly specialized, and highly expensive, financial accountants) to gather credible data to feed the benchmarking cost model and resolve the many complexities that arose. These included:

- the treatment of depreciation;
- the inclusion of VAT/taxes;
- the inclusion of product cross-charges;
- the inclusion of product cross-subsidies;
- the need to pro rata software tools/utilities across products;
- the need to take account of peer organizations who had outsourced part of their IT product cost base;
- the need to factor in helpdesk costs and the factoring in of 'group' IT costs not part of the IT function's budget but part of the cost of products (in terms of setting product strategy, performing product R&D etc.);
- the need to take account of geographic anomalies (in particular, marked differences in networking costs between Europe and the USA).

Another key complexity was the differences between the scope of products as defined by our client and those as defined in the benchmarker's model. For example, differences were found between the benchmarker's definition of 'portal' and the client's definition in no less than 17 areas, including whether or not the PC was LAN connected, ISDN connected, included Eicon Aviva client software etc. Even something as apparently simple as the definition of a helpdesk 'abandoned call' was debated. Normalizing the data to achieve true comparability was actually impossible with anything approaching 'total' accuracy and many assumptions had to be made. As if this was not bad enough, nowhere were we assessing the risk implications. For example, the client delivered an apparently very price competitive mainframe product, but partly through running only one data centre with no contingent fallback site (instead relying on a 'Portakabin' contract that would provide very limited disaster recovery).

In short, achieving 'true' like-for-like comparative benchmarking of IT services is a decidedly non-trivial exercise. It took *months* of work and costs measured in six £ figures to arrive at what we believed to be a credible comparison, and even then the team was of the view that there was *still* scope for ±5 per cent error.

In fairness, the original benchmarker had done a very reasonable job within the limitations of their database and, of course, the limitations imposed by the budget implied by the competitive quote required to win the work. Database limitations aside, to have done the job properly might have required them to quote a price an order of magnitude higher than the one they issued (in which case they would not, of course, have won the work). But the end result was a set of benchmarks which were *highly* circumspect, and certainly not a foundation on which product price competitiveness (or product pricing) should sensibly be based.

I close this examination of cost-efficiency metrics with a favourite quote from ex-superwoman Shirley Conran, namely, 'You have to be efficient if you are going to be lazy.'

5.4 Measuring effectiveness

Let's move on to effectiveness and seek measures that satisfy our nine criteria.

I contend that the measurement of effectiveness has four key components:

1 Practice compliance – characterized by the level of compliance of IT working practices with best practice 'standards'.
2 Portfolio value – characterized by the value of the total portfolio of projects to be undertaken (when originally planned and justified).

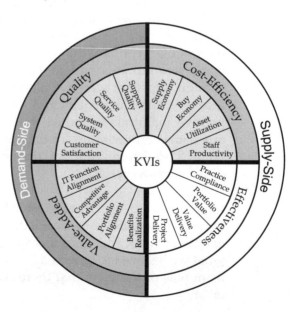

Figure 5.5

236

3 Value delivery – characterized by how well the value promised by the total portfolio of projects is sustained throughout the development process (i.e. how much value is delivered into the production environment).

4 Project delivery – characterized by how 'successfully' projects have been managed.

Let's start with **practice compliance** metrics. 'Practice effectiveness', *as it is 'traditionally' understood*, is primarily about the 'professionalism' of the 'IT products and services delivery factory'. This is primarily about the level of compliance with 'best practices', i.e. the formality, coverage, completeness and consistency of the working practices adopted. The principal objective of deploying best practices is to improve the predictable delivery of a quality product. The need for formality, completeness and consistency in deploying best practices is to 'educate' the (majority?) who are typically less capable in them (and 'up their game'). It is also, however, to do with the *outcomes* of product delivery because such a quality (available, reliable, resilient) product should be capable of:

- realizing more benefits (because it is available to deliver benefits when the user needs to do so and it is available more of the time when it is needed);
- reducing post-implementation systems support and maintenance costs (because it has fewer defects and so fails less frequently and because it is faster and cheaper to correct defects when they do occur);
- reducing operational costs (because a 'quality' design should make optimum use of computer equipment); and
- reducing the level of post-implementation 'enhancement' that replaces poor functionality with the functionality that was actually originally envisaged by the user!

This last point (rooted in the maxim 'there is never time to do it right but always time to do it over again') is a tad contentious but is actually, in my view, the key value-adding outcome of producing 'quality' solutions. IT people describe this work as 'enhancement' because it was not specified in the original 'systems requirement document'. Users describe this work as 'just giving them what they wanted in the first place' (i.e. certainly *not* an 'enhancement' that must be separately justified) because the original requirements specification was flawed, or simply because the users signed off a 100 page document full of IT gobbledegook that they didn't really understand and, anyway, they didn't have the time or inclination to read fully. Such documents constitute yet more 'get out of jail free' cards for IT functions (and ESPs) who smugly (and perhaps cynically) hide behind the largely (user) incomprehensible specification as evidence that 'they fulfilled their part of the bargain, didn't they?' So this work might be *called* 'enhancement' but it is *actually* what cost management specialists call 'failure-driven rework', which falls into an activity category they call 'non-value-adding'.

Best practice deployment is primarily geared towards the improvement of both supply-side effectiveness and demand-side quality (in terms of more predictably delivering IT products and services against the 'agreed specification', whether that be a systems requirements specification or a system SLA). Best *value* practice deployment is primarily geared towards the improvement of both supply-side effectiveness and demand-side value-added (in terms of more predictably delivering IT products and services that add value to the business).

If we take the two key work products of an IT function as the systems it delivers and then, post-implementation, the operation and support service it offers, then the key metrics we need (to assess the extent to which best practices are being deployed) are for the effectiveness of the practices that *produce* systems (systems development practices) and the effectiveness of the practices that *run and support* these systems (generally, the service management practices).

As has been set out in Chapter 2, all the 'Big 6/5/4' consultancies (and others) have proprietary 'best practice' models of IT against which they can assess an IT function (although few will claim to be able to credibly externally benchmark the effectiveness ratings they 'award'). However, there is indeed an internationally recognized, public domain, benchmarkable measure of systems development practices, called the Software Engineering Institute (SEI) Capability Maturity Model (CMM). Unfortunately over 70 per cent of organizations on the SEI database are at Level 1 in the five level model (i.e. all you are likely to prove is that your IT function is pretty much as poor to mediocre as everyone else's) and, anyway, although CMM is reasonably well established in the USA, only a handful of IT functions across Europe actually assess their CMM level. In fact, to find organizations that are routinely at Level 5 you need to go way offshore, to India, where systems development ESPs are increasingly teaching American and European IT functions a thing or two about pukka development practices.

If we assess 'practice effectiveness' metrics of this type against our nine criteria we find that, because they are essentially based on the judgement of individuals, they certainly will not satisfy our accuracy criterion. As a guess I would say that something like ±10 per cent accuracy is the very best you can hope for (although you are not 'measuring' something intrinsically countable so even that is a highly questionable claim). Although they are derived from a 'methodology' (and even when they are derived by 'accredited' practitioners), there is inevitably going to be significant subjectivity and inconsistency, even internally (it would be remarkable if two CMM practitioners produced identical ratings, even if the end result 'sum of the parts' happens to produce the same 'out of 5' rating). There is certainly a strong possibility of fudging the result, because the results depend primarily on interviews with staff who perform the practices being assessed (and who have a self-interest in 'selling' their 'professionalism'). Furthermore, even the most disciplined 'rater' is likely to have some axe to grind based on his or her background and experience. For example, people with a predominantly technical or operational background will tend to be tougher, ask more penetrating and challenging questions (and rate lower) technical and operational processes. People with a project management or systems development background will tend to be tougher, ask more penetrating and challenging questions (and rate lower) project management and systems development processes. Raters with a quality management background (an area from which raters are often taken) will tend to perceive quality management processes as crucial. I, for example, know that when I deploy methods of this sort, it is extremely difficult for me not to bring my 'value' prejudices to bear and be tougher, ask more penetrating and challenging questions (and rate lower) processes that I believe to be key to value delivery.

Metrics of this type are also inherently ambiguous, for the reasons examined in detail in Chapter 2 (essentially, a high rating is not *necessarily* better than a lower rating, because the process may be *over*engineered for the inherent risk or difficulty of the task). The lack of adequate accuracy, objectivity and consistency (coupled with the points I made above about CMM) make external benchmarking particularly problematic. The consultancy firms doing the ratings (and even more so the Software Engineering Institute) would, of course, disagree

Value-Driven IT Management

stating that the sample size of their database is great enough to 'cancel out' the inaccuracy, subjectivity and inconsistency problems. They would also say that hundreds of organizations benchmark their results against their database each year. However, the fact that lots of people sincerely *think* that they are making a rigorously valid comparison does not necessarily mean that the comparison *is* rigorous and valid. Whatever the validity of benchmarks, these types of metrics are generally relatively quick and easy to obtain (although not always inexpensive, as I explain below), are generally understood by non-IT managers (they may not really understand what the process being assessed actually *does* but they understand the concept of 'how well you do a thing') and, I contend, are relatively important from a value perspective (*assuming* the IT function is not entirely populated by outstandingly competent and widely experienced staff with best practices in their bones).

Given the fact that assessing practice effectiveness as suggested above would almost certainly require that you bring in external consultants at significant expense, you may well want to simply focus your assessment on your level of compliance with the *best value practices* I set out in Chapter 3. These were the practices that I contended were key to IT adding the optimal value to the business. In the Appendix I have set out various 'diagnostic profiles' to help an organization understand its current effectiveness in these areas and prioritize targeted practice improvement initiatives. The completion of these profiles is discussed in Chapter 6. Like all the other 'practice effectiveness' measures I discussed above, the end result will suffer from inaccuracy, subjectivity, inconsistency, fudgeability, ambiguity (you can be overengineered in value adding practices too, although I believe the impact and risks of overengineering will generally be less than that for other 'lesser' value-adding practices) and will not be seriously capable of external benchmarking. *But* they are important (obviously, in my view, *very* important!), quick and easy to obtain and will be understood by non-IT managers.

The above metrics were concerned with the 'conventional' measurement of the compliance of practices with 'best practice' (or 'best value practice') definitions. But what about the *outcomes* of such practices? These fall into two categories, namely, supply-side outcomes and demand-side outcomes. The demand-side outcomes are about the value that is *actually* added to the business served and the quality of the products and services delivered and are therefore dealt with under value-added and quality metrics below. In the remainder of this section we will deal with the *supply-side* outcomes of effective practices. Remember our six value-adding CSFs from Chapter 3:

1 Optimizing IT function alignment.
2 Optimizing competitive advantage.
3 Optimizing portfolio alignment.
4 Optimizing portfolio value.
5 Optimizing value delivery.
6 Optimizing benefits realization.

Numbers 1, 2, 3 and 6 all have measurable (demand-side) business outcomes, but numbers 4 and 5 are about how well we *plan* to deliver value and how well we then sustain that promise throughout the development process, i.e. they do not have measurable (demand-side) business outcomes since they do not in themselves add business value – they are about the *promise* to deliver value – but they do have measurable (supply-side) IT function outcomes. The better the IT function is at CSFs 4 and 5, the greater the likelihood there is of maximizing the value actually delivered to the business.

First, we want **portfolio value** metrics which will help tell us if our strategy/planning processes have come up with the best (highest value) overall project portfolio and whether we are focusing our limited IT time and money on developing the (potentially) highest value-adding solutions, i.e. we want measures of the extent to which the agreed project portfolio *potentially* adds value to the business. Assuming that you have used the information economics (or similar) approach to 'valuing' your portfolio (see Chapter 3), this 'planned portfolio value' is simply the sum of the project scores awarded. Even with a disciplined and independently assured approach to arriving at these scores I believe that they will *individually* be inherently inaccurate, subjective, inconsistent and fudgeable (although all of these reduce as the discipline of the scoring process and the sample size, the number of projects, grows). But they are unambiguous, relatively easy to obtain, readily understandable to non-IT managers and the final figure is clearly important (the total size of the bang we *intended* to deliver for the business buck). It is, of course, unbenchmarkable.

Let's move on to examine the potential value sustained during the systems development process and seek project **value delivery** measures that satisfy our nine criteria.

First, we want a measure for the 'planned projects value', i.e. the total *tangible* net benefits (i.e. tangible financial benefits minus costs) over an agreed system life of all *original* project business cases we actually prepared and authorized to proceed. In a perfectly planned and predictable world these would simply be taken from the more detailed and accurate versions of the justifications for all projects in the planned portfolio agreed. Since, however, projects in the originally agreed portfolio may have been dropped or rescoped, and new, unforeseen projects will have been identified, this will almost never be the case. This 'planned projects value' is 'simply' the sum of the net benefits from the detailed business cases prepared for every project actually authorized. Very similar arguments to those set out above for 'planned portfolio value' apply in assessing accuracy, objectivity, consistency and unfudgeability. As I explained in Chapter 3, the accuracy of the ROI in the original business cases is probably somewhere around ±50 per cent, objectivity, partic-ularly in the matter of benefits quantification, is problematic and consistency and unfudgeability would require considerable discipline and independent assurance. But it is probably as good as we can do at the time (and should certainly be *more* accurate, objective, consistent and unfudgeable than the earlier portfolio valuation). It is not externally benchmarkable but is unambig-uous, relatively easy to obtain, readily understandable to non-IT managers and is clearly important (the total size of the bang we *intended* to deliver for the business buck during the year).

If projects whose business case collapsed during systems development were *still* taken through to implementation then they would contribute *negatively* to the *delivered* project's valuation figure. But the whole point of the 'best value practice' of managing the business case effectively is to *stop* non-viable functionality making it all the way to implementation. So we would also like to measure the level of 'development wastage' we have prevented. This is the 'flip side' of the value we have added with best value business case management practices. Through 'systems development wastage' measures here we want to directly incentivize project managers to say 'stop!' more frequently when work being performed is no longer credibly likely to deliver its original promise. We have to be careful here. We don't want to incentivize people to cancel work in progress (e.g. measure: number of subprojects terminated pre-imple-mentation). That would be an easy metric to maximize. You just stop working! What we want is to incentivize people to cancel (what has become) *non-viable* work in progress. So our measure might be the number of *non-viable* (sub)projects terminated pre-implementation. This 'non-viable project terminations' metric should be accurate (you can count projects/subprojects cancelled), objective (you either cancelled it or you didn't), consistent, unfudgeable, unambiguous (you want, of course, to cancel as *few*, projects/subprojects as possible, but you do want to cancel as many *non-viable* projects/subprojects as possible), easy to obtain, readily understood by non-IT managers and important. In fact the one 'test' it fails is, as usual, external benchmarkability.

This measure is still quite crass because it does not tell you how many projects/subprojects were identified as heading in a non-viable direction and were rescoped to remove the high cost, low benefit components and so retain overall viability. That is surely preferable to actually killing the whole project/subproject. However, it may be 'a bridge too far' so far as measurement is concerned!

This measure also does not tell you *how early* you caught the rogue work and stopped it. Clearly, the earlier in the development cycle the better. So you might also want a further 'systems development wastage' measure that indicates the extent to which you have minimized the total amount (in man-days, or, better, cost) of wasted effort. This measure might be the *cost* of subprojects terminated pre-implementation. This measure should be reasonably accurate (even if you don't track the 'exact' man-hour X man-day-rate figure for wasted time you can at least say a team of six worked on it for three months before we killed the project), objective, consistent and unfudgeable (assuming you impose a common discipline for effort/cost counting), unambiguous, easy to obtain, readily understood by non-IT managers and important. And, yes, it is not externally benchmarkable.

These metrics for the measurement of 'project governance success' might appear tough because projects and subprojects don't just 'go bad' (turn non-viable) because of factors within our control (e.g. inept systems development or project management practices). They may well go bad for any number of (often, but not necessarily, completely unpredictable) reasons, such as:

- a change in company strategy (e.g. the project benefits were predicated on reducing warehouse management costs and the board has just decided to outsource warehousing and distribution);

- a change in company organization (e.g. the project benefits were predicated on improving the automation of work performed by the sales demographics group and it has just been decided to disband that group);
- a change in the stance of the unions (e.g. the project benefits were predicated on reducing the head count in business group *XYZ* but the unions have now negotiated a policy of no redundancies).

But this is as it should be. We are trying to assess the level of value, not attribute blame.

We might well also want to try to measure the work performed that 'fell through the net', i.e. the extent to which non-support/ maintenance work (i.e. project work) is justified and approved with an independently validated business case (note that this assumes a clear definition of what is, and is not, 'project work') by, say, measuring the percentage of work that was *actually* project work but was not supported by an independently validated business case. This 'unjustified project work' metric should be reasonably accurate, objective, consistent, unfudge-able and unambiguous (obviously *assuming* that unjustified project work is clearly recognized and logged and the level of effort on such work is monitored). It is not externally bench-markable but it is relatively easy to obtain, readily under-standable to non-IT managers and is clearly important (basically, the amount of work that goes by 'on the nod'). You may say that there should surely *be* no unjustified project work. This is true, but only in the same sense that there should be no poverty in a rich country like America.

Next, we want to know the extent to which the projects that completed during the year actually lived up to their promised business case at the time of implementation (i.e. did we control the business cases effectively?). This is effectively the 'delivered projects value' assessment, i.e. the extent to which projects deliver within X per cent of the original net benefits predicted. Note that this assumes that predicted benefit variances are rigorously determined at the end of the project, at least. This metric should be *reasonably* accurate, objective, consistent and unfudgeable (because we now know a great deal more about the costs and benefits than we did when we started the project and it is harder to get away with massaging numbers that relate to what has actually happened than what is promised). It is not externally benchmarkable but it is unambiguous, relatively easy to obtain, readily understandable to non-IT managers and is clearly important (the total size of the bang we delivered – on solution implementation – for the business buck during the year).

Finally, we want to assess the success of **project delivery**. For this we might measure 'project delivery to budget/schedule', i.e. the extent to which projects deliver to within X per cent of the final approved budget and schedule. Note that this assumes that rigorous processes are in place to produce a comprehensive and independently validated budget and that budget variances are rigorously monitored. It also assumes that staff time booked to projects does not include non-project activities (e.g. support, general administration, domestic phone calls). This should be tolerably accurate, objective, consistent, unambiguous, under-standable and easy to produce (if we 'take as read' the above assumptions). It is certainly important but it is not readily benchmarkable and is certainly susceptible to manipulation through the fudging of the time and costs *actually* recorded to project codes.

With *all* the 'supply-side' metrics it is critically important to ask *very* carefully and with *extreme* cynicism, 'What staff behaviours is the setting of this measure going to engender? Is it actually going to *increase* the value of IT to the business?' In other words, be careful what you ask for because you might just get it! This is rooted in the inter-relationships, and often adversarial relation-ships, between the cost-efficiency and effectiveness metric areas.

For example, in the late 1970s Tesco Stores had an IT function of around 40 staff, generally working in a relatively ad hoc manner. In the early 1980s (as part of the 'renaissance' of the company as a whole) the IT function introduced a plethora of more formal 'professional' practices (I know this because I was a manager in the IT function who played a major role in introducing such practices). There is no question that the 'quality' of processes improved, in terms of deploying 'best practices' (as did the quality of the end product), but by 1984 the IT function had grown to over 500 staff following these processes. The focus on process effectiveness was certainly far from the only reason for this growth in staff numbers but it was certainly an important contributor. The upshot was a dramatic increase in IT costs (reduced cost-efficiency). This led to a substantial redundancy programme to quickly get the costs down. Basically, by 'fixating' on effectiveness (best practice implementation, but not, by the way, best *value* practice implementation) the collective eye had been taken off cost-efficiency.

As another example, throughout the 1980s the IT functions of Rank Xerox were 'fixated' on systems development productivity improvement, and invested heavily in a function point counting regime. Actually, the whole company became fixated with productivity measurement, but that is another story. I well recall attending a conference at which the then corporate IT director for Rank Xerox delivered a presentation, the highlight of which was a (suitably scaled for dramatic effect) graph showing function point productivity trends which 'objectively demonstrated' outstanding improvements in staff efficiency over time. We all duly applauded. Over lunch I engineered myself to sit next to him and asked him directly what his users thought of this achievement. He laughed and replied, 'Now they say the problem is the cost and quality. Oh, and they *still* think we take too long!'

Woody Allen famously said, 'I took a course in speed reading and was able to read *War and Peace* in 20 minutes. It's about Russia.' Speed isn't everything! The much hyped 90 day systems delivery cycles sought in the brave new world of e-business development have indeed placed a much greater emphasis on the speed of systems development. But just as we might question the value of Woody Allen's reading practices, so might we rightly question whether accelerating systems development is simply producing 'even worse code faster'. My point is simply that the measurement and reporting of the speed of IT delivery is not sufficient to indicate IT delivery success. Success is about far more than high productivity (efficiency). It is also about deploying the right (highly effective) processes, at the right (economic) price to produce the right (high value-adding) deliverables of the right (commercially necessary and sufficient) quality.

Basically, if you incentivize people to deliver 'improvements' in one area it may have adverse results in another. That is why I always ask clients to tell me their 'key performance drivers' (that's what consultants call 'what's really important'). In particular, do they primarily want to improve economy, efficiency or effectiveness? No prizes for the universal answer, namely, yes, they would like all of those please. Unfortunately it is, in my experience, virtually impossible, at least in the short (two to three year?) term to optimize all at once. You can't have *all* of your cake and eat it. The important thing is to understand what is *really* important in the foreseeable future and focus on that (but without taking your eyes off the other balls). This is often difficult, but is important if you are going to set yourself realistic objectives.

For example, when I consulted at a large British water utility (that had recently been privatized) I asked them my 'what's really important' question and got the time-honoured reply. This assignment was actually about improving the performance of the whole business and I was only concerned with the IT bit of the equation. So my question was actually put to the board rather than the IT function. But the drivers of the business were also the drivers of IT (unless, for example, a driver of business cost reduction could best be achieved by IT investment – but that is an unnecessary complication for this story!) I explained that 'having it all' was not a realistic option and pushed back. They debated for some days and decided that the key drivers of the business were 'high customer service, low product costs and full regulatory compliance'. They were well pleased with themselves. Unfortunately, this is basically little more than a more specific way of saying that your key driver is to be highly economic and highly efficient and highly effective! I am simplifying now, but basically we asked them whether their customers could, by choice, get water through their taps from a competitor. They, of course, replied that this was an exceedingly stupid question for such highly paid and supposedly intelligent consultants. Of course they couldn't. So why, we asked, do you care about customer service? They're not going anywhere. And what about regulatory compliance? If, say, one of your filtration plant beds overflowed and poisoned a few fish in an adjacent stream, what would actually happen? The answer was basically that there would be bluster from the regulator, a bit of bad press and a temporary dip in the share price. Hardly a catastrophe (except for the fish). And what about if they didn't get their costs down to competitors' levels? Well then they would be quickly bought out by one of the big USA utilities who would probably put most of them out of a job. This helped to focus their minds. The fact was that it was really all about economy. The rest was largely window dressing. In terms of the SAM model they required to be that rather rare thing, an out and out cost centre, at least for a while. My point is simply that you really have to think through *carefully* both your priorities and the implications of the metric targets you set.

5.5 Measuring value-added

Once again, remember our six value-adding CSFs from Chapter 3 and the fact that numbers 1, 2, 3 and 6 all have measurable (demand-side) business outcomes:

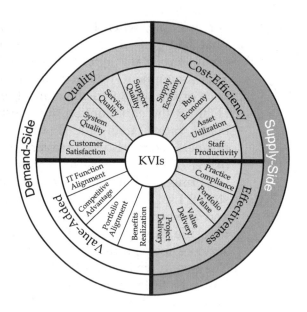

Figure 5.6

1 Optimizing IT function alignment.
2 Optimizing competitive advantage.
3 Optimizing portfolio alignment.
4 Optimizing portfolio value.
5 Optimizing value delivery.
6 Optimizing benefits realization.

First we want to assess the extent to which the IT function and the business have actually ended up 'singing to the same song sheet'. To measure this **IT function alignment** achieved between the business and the IT function we need to measure the extent to which the IT function objectives agreed with the business have been met (achievement of the objectives' KPI targets agreed) and the extent to which they did indeed contribute to the achievement of the high level business objectives. As explained in Chapter 3, I am assuming that the IT function's objectives were suitably 'SMART' and phrased in terms of business outcomes/benefits. In the same way that we selected and shaped the original set of objectives we can simply construct a matrix of the business's objectives against the IT function's objectives and rate each intersection with something like:

−1 = actively hindered the achievement of business objectives

0 = made no direct contribution to achievement of business objectives

1 = made no direct contribution to achievement of business objectives but supported another IT function objective that contributed to the achievement of business objectives

2 = did not directly contribute, but was a prerequisite to another IT function objective that contributed to the achievement of business objectives

3 = did not directly contribute, but was a prerequisite to another IT function objective that directly achieved business objectives

4 = directly contributed to the achievement of business objectives

5 = directly achieved business objectives

The results of each intersection can be 'multiplied up' by the KPI results that show how well the IT function met each of its objectives. These 'business/IT function alignment' metrics will be inherently inaccurate, subjective, inconsistent, fudgeable and unbenchmarkable. However, they will be reasonably unambiguous, relatively easy to obtain, readily understood by non-IT managers and are clearly highly important in helping to assess IT value. Of course, the more knowledgeable business and IT people get involved in the 'scoring' process and the more discipline applied to the process, the more accuracy, consistency and unfudgeability will improve. Ideally the group who originally debated and agreed the IT function's objectives should be reconvened for this assessment.

To measure **competitive advantage** we need metrics for the extent to which IT has enhanced the competitiveness of the business by, for example, using it to create defensive entry barriers, increasing customer or retailer switching costs, changing the ground rules of competition, changing competition from cost-based (i.e. commodity) competition to competition based on sustainable product differentiation or helping build links to (and lock in) suppliers. Measuring innovation levels and contribution to the delivery of competitive advantage is notoriously difficult – it is particularly difficult to see how this could be meaningfully compared across companies (even though this has actually been attempted). In an attempt to 'find something to count' we could just count the *number* of approved work requests that came through into the IT function that (whether identified by the IT function or the business) met to some extent one of our 'competitive advantage' characteristics set out above. This has the attraction of being easy, readily understood by non-IT managers and is certainly a very important measure of IT added value. I don't think, however, it is going to pass our accuracy, objectivity, consistency, fudgeability and benchmarkability tests. It is not entirely unambiguous in that, for example, doubling the number of competitive advantage opportunities that make it past the 'work request' approval stage does not actually tell us anything about how many of them made it all the way through to implementation and actually *realized* the competitive advantage for the business. For that we would have to measure the increased market share, profitability, customer retention (or whatever) that was actually realized and was directly attributable to the system. This is difficult! For example, when Tesco took 3 per cent of Sainsbury's market share within six months of launching their loyalty card, there was a lot more going on out in the business to achieve that 3 per cent than could reasonably be attributed solely to the loyalty card scheme (let alone the *IT* component of the loyalty card scheme). You could, of course, reasonably argue that such a scheme would be unimplementable *without* IT. But that would still leave the issue of how to 'ring-fence' the loyalty card's competitive edge contribution to the 3 per cent. Given that, anyway, it can be argued that this 'extension' is about 'optimizing the net benefits realized' rather than 'optimizing competitive advantage', I am inclined to settle for the simplistic metric (just counting the number of such opportunities). But if you believe you can credibly 'follow the value chain' through to quantifying the actual level of competitive advantage achieved, then wonderful!

Between these two extremes we could assess each implemented solution for its 'competitive advantage realized' using a simple scale such as:

−1 = the solution actively hindered achieving competitive advantage

0 = the solution delivered no competitive advantage

1 = the solution did not directly deliver any competitive advantage but delivered operational efficiencies that delivered a degree of competitive advantage

2 = the solution did not deliver any competitive advantage but supported other solutions that delivered a degree of competitive advantage

3 = the solution did not deliver any competitive advantage but supported other solutions that delivered a high degree of competitive advantage

4 = the solution directly delivered a degree of competitive advantage

5 = the solution directly delivered a high degree of competitive advantage

These metrics will be inaccurate, subjective, inconsistent, fudge-able and unbenchmarkable. However, they will be reasonably unambiguous, relatively easy to obtain, readily understood by non-IT managers and are clearly highly important in helping to assess IT value. Once again, the more knowledgeable business and IT people get involved in the 'scoring' process and the more discipline applied to the process, the more accuracy, consistency and unfudgeability will improve.

Next, we want **portfolio alignment** measures of the extent to which delivered IT solutions effectively supported business processes and are aligned with business unit priorities, i.e. the extent to which delivered IT solutions have actually contributed to the business units achieving their performance targets. This 'portfolio alignment' measure can be achieved quite simply by constructing a matrix of the business units' performance targets against the systems used and rating each intersection with something like:

–1 = actively hindered the achievement of business unit performance targets

0 = made no direct contribution to the achievement of business unit performance targets

1 = the solution did not directly contribute to the achievement of business unit performance targets but delivered operational efficiencies that delivered a degree of support for business unit performance targets

2 = did not directly contribute, but was a prerequisite to another system that contributed to the achievement of business unit performance targets

3 = did not directly contribute, but was a prerequisite to another system that directly achieved business unit performance targets

4 = directly contributed to the achievement of business unit performance targets

5 = directly achieved business unit performance target

It is certainly contentious but I think I could reasonably argue here that these numbers should be 'multiplied up' by the extent to which the business unit actually achieved its performance/ KPI targets, given that we are trying to measure *IT* value here, not just *IT function* value. After all, you do want to create a 'no blame' culture don't you?

These metrics will, again, be inaccurate, subjective, inconsistent, fudgeable and unbenchmarkable. However, they will be reasonably unambiguous, relatively easy to obtain, readily understood by non-IT managers and are clearly highly important in helping to assess IT value. And, once again, the more knowledgeable business and IT people get involved in the 'scoring' process and the more discipline applied to the process, the more accuracy, consistency and unfudgeability will improve.

A similar approach (but focused more on the 'balance' of the portfolio) is to assess the distribution of applications across a spectrum of 'value'. Gartner, for example, use a framework of four categories:

- 'Infrastructure' (the basic technology infrastructure required for business support).
- 'Utility' (basic, essential, non-differentiating functionality delivered at low cost, e.g. payroll).
- 'Enhancement' (new functionality designed to deliver business productivity improvements).
- 'Frontier' (high risk, potentially high reward functionality designed to achieve business transformation).

Unfortunately organizations do not generally (to say the least) categorize their IT solutions in this way and attempts to map the systems portfolio to these categories are inevitably highly subjective and highly dubious from an external benchmarking point of view. Note also that this measure of value is a function of time – today's frontier application is tomorrow's utility application as it becomes copied by competitors and commoditized.

You may be concerned at the question marks over accuracy, objectivity, consistency and fudgeability with the above value-added metrics. Well, in the first place, all of these can be improved upon through discipline and independent assurance. Second, I would argue that even more valuable than the 'scientific accuracy' of the scores themselves is the debate that accompanies the process. An enormous amount can be learnt by both the IT function and the business just from discussing *why* a success was a success and what caused failed expectations to fail (and building those lessons into the future).

Finally, let's look at measuring the value of the post-implementation service. Here we want **benefits realization** metrics which will help tell us the extent to which we have actually realized the tangible benefits that were promised for projects to deliver solutions when those projects were originally authorized. This 'benefits realized' measure might 'simply' be the total value of tangible benefits (increased business revenue, reduced business overhead costs) realized over the year. This will be objective (in as much as it is countable), consistent (if the disciplines adopted make it so), unambiguous (more tangible benefits are always better than less), readily understood by non-IT managers, *relatively* easy to obtain (if you duly prepared your benefits delivery plans and responsibilities) and is, in my view, the single most important metric we need. It is not benchmarkable and it will almost inevitably be fudgeable and inaccurate to some extent, even with your best efforts to attribute benefits to specific IT changes. Such is the importance of this metric I will forgive it its accuracy and fudgeability weaknesses, but suggest that it is worth putting significant effort into assuring (and 'auditing') the validity of the metric results reported.

A simpler metric for tangible benefits realization might be the number of completed projects that realized 80 per cent (say) of the benefits stated in the final approved business case. The fundamental problem with this is that not all projects are created equal. For example, what if one year you deliver 10 low value-adding projects that tolerably deliver their potential benefits and the next year you only deliver one project that actually 'passes the test', but that project delivers value far in excess of last year's 10 combined. On the other hand, such a metric might help incentivize people to break projects down into smaller, more manageable, earlier benefits delivery, subprojects. It is almost axiomatic that, 'ambitious, long, expensive, complex projects with grand goals typically fail – unambitious, short, inexpensive, simple projects with modest goals sometimes succeed'. And I'm not *just* being facetious and I'm not *just* talking about IT.

We have one further key aspect of post-implementation value to measure. This is concerned with measuring our success at applying benefits management 'best value practices' to managing the business case effectively *after* implementation throughout the life of the system and *stop* running functionality that has become non-viable at the earliest possible time, i.e. terminating functionality when it *ceases* to add value. This is effectively measuring the level of 'service delivery wastage' we have prevented. This is the post-implementation corollary of the best value practices to govern projects/subprojects in such a way as to terminate them if they become non-viable during development. Through measures here we want to directly incentivize service delivery managers to say 'stop!' more frequently when systems being run (and, indeed, support services being provided) are no longer credibly delivering more business benefits than they are costing to run/provide. In the case of systems, this is similar to an ASP terminating an application delivery service that has become unprofitable. In the case of services, this is similar to an ESP terminating a service delivery service that has become unprofitable. The difference, of course, with an internal IT provider is that it is concerned with its *customer's* profitability from continuing to run the system/service, not *its* profitability. We have to be careful here. We don't want to incentivize service delivery managers to terminate systems too hastily (e.g. measure: number of production systems/subsystems terminated). That would be an easy metric to maximize. You just switch off all the computers! What we want is to incentivize people to cancel (what have become) *non-viable* systems/subsystems. So our 'system retirements' measure might be the number of *non-viable* systems/subsystems terminated. This should be accurate (you can count them), objective (you either terminated it or you didn't), consistent, unfudgeable, unambiguous (you want, of course, to terminate as *few* systems/subsystems as possible, but you do want to terminate as many *non-viable* systems/subsystems as possible), easy to obtain, readily understood by non-IT managers and important. In fact the one 'test' it fails is, inevitably, external benchmarkability.

This measure is still quite crass because it does not tell you how many systems/subsystems were identified as heading in a non-viable direction and were enhanced to 'reassert' overall viability. That is surely preferable to actually killing the whole system/subsystem. However, I suspect (once more) that this is 'a bridge too far' so far as measurement is concerned!

This measure also does not tell you *how early* you caught the rogue functionality and stopped running it. Clearly, the earlier the better. So you might also want a measure that indicates the extent to which you have minimized the total wasted service delivery cost. This measure might be the *cost* of running systems/subsystems between the time they became 'non-viable' and the time we terminated them. But that implies both that we are able to identify *when* it went 'non-viable' and that we failed to terminate it then. I'm afraid that that is getting too hard! So I suggest we stick with the simpler metric that stands a better chance of success.

Once again, this metric for the measurement of what might be called 'service governance success' might appear tough because systems don't just 'go bad' (turn non-viable) because of factors within our control (e.g. inept service delivery practices). They may well go bad for any number of (often, but not necessarily, completely unpredictable) reasons, such as a business decision to terminate or outsource a business group including all the systems' users, a change in company strategy, a change in government regulations, a change in the economy or straightforward obsolescence. But this is as it should be. Once again, we are trying to assess value, not attribute blame.

5.6 Measuring quality

Many consultants (and I'm probably one of them) argue that the *supreme* KVI is the measurement of **customer satisfaction**, because 'perceptions are reality' and 'evidence' that the IT function is performing highly effectively, cost-efficiently and adding high value will all pale to insignificance if the user community *still* has negative perceptions. Such 'customer satisfaction' metrics are certainly going to be subjective and

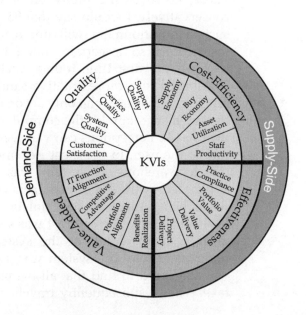

Figure 5.7

unbenchmarkable. However, they will be adequately accurate (if the sample size is large enough), consistent (if you stick to the same questions phrased the same way every time you issue the questionnaire), reasonably unfudgeable (assuming great care is taken not to ask 'leading questions'), unambiguous, easy to obtain, *very* readily understood by non-IT managers and are highly important. They would typically address the customers' perceptions of the IT function and its services, e.g. understanding of business goals, business alignment, commercialism, proactiveness, technical skills, management skills, systems development service, service delivery, systems maintenance and support and training provided.

Our next metric area is the **system quality** of the systems delivered. The user perceived 'systems functional quality' can be measured by user questionnaire, typically addressing such issues as the gap between the delivered functionality and the commercial requirements in data accuracy, data currency, data security, user documentation, ease of use and reporting flexibility. Such metrics will not be objective or benchmarkable. However, they are going to be unambiguous, important, understandable and *relatively* easy to obtain. *Assuming* that the sample size is big enough (and questionnaire fatigue has not set in), *assuming* the 'education' in filling in the questionnaire is adequate and *assuming* there is no 'conspiracy' to mark down a particular system in order to get it enhanced or rewritten, then such metrics will also be accurate, consistent and unfudgeable. Those, however, are pretty big assumptions. Remember that, conservatively, I would say that 95 per cent of the recipients of such a questionnaire will not read even the shortest set of instructions so a certain amount of hand-holding will be required the first time round. Such questionnaires should be distributed to a representative sample of each system's users, ranging from those who only act on the information produced to those who actually hit the computer keyboard (sometimes with their fists!). Perceptions can vary very widely depending on the role of the user. In the most extreme example I encountered of this a warehousing system was more or less universally applauded by the senior managers who saw the results of its use while being more or less universally loathed by the actual keyboard users. The contrast was so dramatic that I asked to be given a quick demo of the system by a user to help me understand why the system was so hated on the shop floor. I was staggered to find that all the user screens were in German text! When I subsequently travelled to the company's German headquarters and asked the head office IT managers about this I found them entirely unrepentant. In fact they claimed that they could not understand the problem. We all learned English, they said (in perfect English), so why don't they learn German? Well, they had a point.

Let's move on to examine the quality of the delivered systems (primarily in terms of availability and reliability, i.e. the *non-functional* quality), services and support and seek measures that satisfy our nine criteria.

Here we want to understand the extent to which our system design processes have produced 'defect-free' code and our service design processes (effectively designing in the 'non-functional' aspects of a system, including resilience) have produced a robust solution. Key metrics here might be the level of 'residual defects' post-implementation, the 'system mean time between failure (MTBF)' and the 'incident volumes' (by severity level) reported post-implementation. Assuming the presence of rigorous call/incident monitoring processes/tools, these metrics should be accurate, objective, consistent, unfudgeable, unambiguous, understandable and easy to produce. The exception to this is arguably the 'residual defects' metric, which would require very careful definition of precisely what constitutes a 'defect'. None of these metrics is realistically benchmarkable. But more importantly, there must be a question mark over the importance of these metrics because they should arguably be subsumed by the following metric, the realization of agreed service level targets. I include them, nevertheless, since truly *credible* systems and support service level agreements/targets are anything but widely deployed.

We want these measures for the extent to which we are optimizing operational service levels because we are certainly not in a position to realize system benefits if the system is not robust, is not available when we need it or is inefficient in use. These come in two main shapes. First, there are *systems* service levels, which characterize the overall **service quality** provided. These can include many factors, such as transaction response times, report turnaround times, the number of system failures, *when* those failures occur, and so on, but principally is typically about system availability. There are also *support* service levels which characterize the **support quality** provided for systems post-implementation. These can include many factors, such as telephone response times, problem resolution times or fault reoccurrence frequency. Actually, the situation is much more complex than this because it is not just 'traditional' production support groups (or ESPs) who provide support services. You might also, for example, have service levels for the responsiveness of a development group in supplying quotes for IT work requests. But for our purposes here we are only concerned with post-implementation service levels. A further potential complexity lies in the fact that SLAs (service level agreements) for both 'systems' and 'support' will often be 'underpinned' by a range of 'operational level agreements' (OLAs) that together 'roll up' into a top level SLA. But for simplicity all we will concern ourselves with here are the top level SLAs.

Our key measure here might be the extent to which agreed service level targets for all production systems ('systems SLA realization') and support services ('support SLA realization') are met on, say, a monthly and cumulative basis. Note that this *assumes* the presence of a rigorous 'end-to-end' system service level management approach and the presence of SLAs that specify *necessary and sufficient* service levels (so that succeeding in meeting the service level target meets, but does not exceed, commercial needs). These are *critical* assumptions. These measures would be accurate, objective, consistent and unfudgeable (assuming you implement the appropriate disciplines), unambiguous, readily understood (at least at a high level) by non-IT managers (*assuming* the services are defined and packaged in such a way as to be immediately recognizable to the business) and they are important to the business (from a value perspective). They are not (ho hum) benchmarkable.

In *Reinventing the IT Department* Terry White says, quite simply, 'Service Level Agreements don't work. So why bother?' Well, I agree with him! I have *never* seen what I would describe as a successful SLA (between an IT function and its internal customer). But that is because they are so often very badly implemented. If you are going to implement SLAs then:

- they must be for *end-to-end* services that the business can recognize and relate to in business terms;
- there must be full accountability on IT to deliver against genuinely stretching, but achievable, SLA targets;
- there must be the capability for the business to negotiate the 'cost vs service level' equation;
- there must be transfer charging for services taken and full accountability on the business to pay for the level of service taken 'above the line' at the point of resource consumption; and

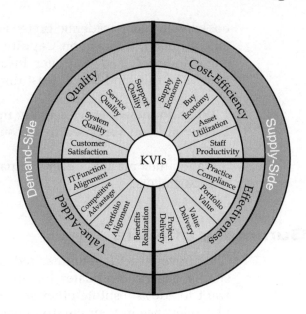

Figure 5.8

• there must be serious sanctions available to 'penalize' the IT function if it fails to meet its SLA targets (and incentives if it exceeds them).

Once these prerequisites are met (and only then) do we have 'real' (ESP-like) SLAs 'with teeth' (see 'The principles of transfer charging' in Chapter 3) that help to optimize value instead of being the typical pointless bits of non-value-adding bureaucracy that Terry White (and I) have so little time for. It is my same message again: either do it *right* or don't bother doing it at all.

Our fully populated 'value compass' of metrics is set out in Figure 5.8.

5.7 Other metrics

Of course there are numerous other metrics that you may wish to consider. For example:

• Staff turnover percentage.
• Number of IT security breaches.
• Average time to fill IT vacancy.
• Average training hours per employee.

I have not included such candidate metrics in my 'sample set' above, however, because they tend to be only very indirect indicators of value and/or they are very ambiguous. Some books with more academic pretensions include such metrics as (and I quote), 'Innovation Capture Indexes', 'Knowledge Leverage Indexes', and 'Supplier Relationship Indexes'. For me, metrics of this kind beg at least three questions, namely:

1 What do these metrics actually mean?
2 How are you supposed to measure them in any meaningful way?
3 Have the authors ever actually set foot in any IT departments?

5.8 Summary of KVIs

The above 30 KVIs (summarized in Figures 5.9 and 5.10) are simply generic candidates for you to consider. You may well want to add/substitute other specific metrics that have particular relevance in your environment. You may also wish to 'roll up' some of them for summary reporting. Certainly there are too many for high level reporting. To that end I have highlighted (in italics) my 'top 16' KVIs, one per metric area (based primarily on selecting KVIs that help to measure business outcomes, rather than the success of practices that should *lead* to better business outcomes).

Be very wary of 'excessive granularity' in your performance measures. On my first exposure to 'balanced scorecards' many years ago I joined a project that had just identified *145* (I am not exaggerating) key performance indicators for the IT function. How can you have *145* indicators that are all *key*? If you asked people the maximum number of things that should rightly be regarded as 'key' I suspect that the average reply would be somewhere around '5'. And I have just suggested 16 to 30, all of which are generic and could well break out into multiple specific metrics. Well I could argue that the 'value compass' model provides just four high level indicators, one for each 'pole' in the compass, cost-efficiency, effectiveness, value-added and quality. These should be more than sufficient for high level (senior management) business reporting. I think that this is a reasonable argument, although not one with which I am entirely comfortable because these four numbers will be an essentially 'abstract' amalgam of underlying specific detail. Were I to ascend to the dizzy heights of the board of a company and be told by my CIO that he had 'improved the IT function's effectiveness by 22 per cent' I'm not sure I would be too impressed! IT is a complex beast and it is hard to measure it

SUPPLY SIDE									
Candidate key value indicators (KVIs)	Accurate?	Objective?	Consistent?	Unfudgeable?	Unambiguous?	Benchmarkable?	Important?	Understandable?	Easy?
COST-EFFICIENCY									
Supply economy									
IT economic metrics (generally)	NO	NO	NO	NO	NO	NO	?	YES	YES
IT financial control metrics (generally)	YES	YES	YES	YES	YES	NO	?	YES	YES
Internal service supply tariffs	YES	YES	YES	YES	YES	NO?	YES	YES	YES
Buy economy									
External service supply tariffs	YES	YES	YES?	YES?	YES	NO?	YES	YES	YES
Physical asset cost	YES	YES	YES	YES	YES	NO	YES?	YES	YES
Staff asset cost	YES	YES	YES	YES	NO	YES	?	YES	YES
Asset utilization									
Physical asset utilization	YES	YES	YES	YES	YES	YES	?	YES	YES
Staff asset utilization	NO?	NO?	NO?	NO?	YES	NO	YES?	YES	YES
Staff productivity									
Systems development and support staff productivity	NO?	NO?	NO?	NO?	?	NO	YES	NO	NO
Service delivery and support staff productivity	YES	YES	YES	YES	YES	NO	?	YES	YES
EFFECTIVENESS									
Practice compliance									
Practice effectiveness	NO	NO	NO	NO	NO	?	YES	YES	YES
Portfolio value									
Planned portfolio value	NO?	NO?	NO?	NO?	YES	NO	YES	YES	YES
Value delivery									
Planned projects value	NO?	NO?	NO?	NO?	YES	NO	YES	YES	YES
Non-viable project terminations	YES	YES	YES	YES	YES	NO	YES	YES	YES
Systems development wastage	YES	YES	YES	YES	YES	NO	YES	YES	YES
Unjustified project work	YES	YES	YES	YES	YES	NO	YES	YES	YES
Delivered projects value	YES?	YES?	YES?	YES?	YES	NO	YES	YES	YES
Project delivery									
Project delivery to budget/schedule	YES	YES	YES	NO	YES	NO	YES	YES	YES

Figure 5.9

DEMAND SIDE									
Candidate key value indicators (KVIs)	Accurate?	Objective?	Consistent?	Unfudgeable?	Unambiguous?	Benchmarkable?	Important?	Understandable?	Easy?
VALUE-ADDED									
IT function alignment									
Business/IT function alignment	NO?	NO	NO?	NO?	YES	NO	YES	YES	YES
Competitive advantage									
Competitive advantage realized	NO?	NO	NO?	NO?	YES	NO	YES	YES	YES
Portfolio alignment									
Portfolio alignment	NO?	NO	NO?	NO?	YES	NO	YES	YES	YES
Benefits realization									
Benefits realized	NO	YES	YES	NO	YES	NO	YES	YES	YES?
System retirements	YES	YES	YES	YES	YES	NO	YES	YES	YES
QUALITY									
Customer satisfaction									
Customer satisfaction	YES	NO	YES	YES	YES	NO	YES	YES	YES
System quality									
Systems functional quality	YES	NO	YES	YES	YES	NO	YES	YES	YES
Residual defects	YES	YES	YES	NO	YES	NO	?	YES	YES
System MTBF	YES	YES	YES	YES	YES	NO	?	YES	YES
Incident volumes	YES	YES	YES	YES	YES	NO	?	YES	YES
Service quality									
Systems SLA realization	YES	YES	YES	YES	YES	NO	YES	YES	YES
Support quality									
Support SLA realization	YES	YES	YES	YES	YES	NO	YES	YES	YES

Figure 5.10

meaningfully without recourse to a certain amount of detail. Therefore you may wish to provide senior management with a few representative ('critical value'?) indicators, probably focused on tariffs, staff productivity, benefits realization, customer satisfaction and service levels.

So what general conclusions might we draw from the proposed 30 generic KVIs?

First, of the 30 candidate generic KVIs set out in the figures, only two tolerably passed the benchmarking 'test'. So external benchmarking is rarely going to be credible (no matter how much time, effort and money you spend).

Second, none of the 30 candidate KVIs fully pass all nine 'metric criteria' tests and one only passes one test (the average is about six tests passed 'unequivocally')! So you will have to accept that any balanced scorecard is going to be a compromise and, at some level, flawed. If you are going to defend all comers from the ramparts of your 'metrics castle' remember that, as the late, great Jimi Hendrix said, it is a castle made of sand, so don't expect to be impregnable at high tide.

Third, if you accept that adding value to the business is the key reason for the existence of the IT function then the measures that have been traditionally applied to IT in the past (typically almost exclusively the supply-side metrics) have been *relatively* unimportant. In fact it is worse than that because the supply-side metrics I have set out are some of the most 'important' I could devise. IT metrics programmes in place in companies today will often include a great many KPIs that are *far* less important than those I suggest.

From this I make seven general recommendations which I would summarize under the heading, 'Don't kid yourself – take a reality check':

1 Accept that it only makes sense to establish a comprehensive '360 degree' metrics programme if you are really serious about it (and all that this implies in terms of cost, time and management attention); but beware of creating a 'metrics industry'!

2 Accept that you may well have to compromise the completeness of your 'balanced scorecard' (because people can't get their mind round all those metrics) and so may have to focus on the metrics which 'add most value' (i.e. they obey the '80/20' rule, of giving you the most important indicators of value at least cost, accepting that these are adequate for

business purposes if inadequate for scientific purposes – but then, I thought we were running a business here, not a lab). Note also that it is almost certainly better to *seriously* implement a handful of key metrics that people actually buy into than half-heartedly implement a shedful that don't really convince. Therefore be clear about *why* you want to implement such a programme. If it is primarily about improving the internal performance of the IT function then you may wish to focus on the supply-side metrics. If it is primarily to 'sell' IT generally, and the IT function in particular, to the business, then you may wish to focus on the demand-side metrics. And if it is (at least initially) mainly about assessing the effect of implementing or improving 'best value practices' then obviously it is the value-added demand-side metrics that you may wish to implement first.

3 Accept that there are no 'perfect' or 'killer' metrics and that any balanced scorecard implemented will be a compromise.

4 Accept that many of the metrics you might want to put in place will only succeed if you have *first* established the corresponding 'best practices', e.g. it is pointless trying to measure the value of business cases if no credible process exists to produce comprehensive business cases. Similarly it is pointless trying to measure success at realizing service level targets if no credible process exits to define business-meaningful, end-to-end, comprehensive, costed SLAs.

5 Accept that attempts to credibly benchmark performance (let alone value) externally are probably doomed. You may be able to con your CEO or CFO (or even yourself) into believing that this can be done credibly but you can't con me. If you really must benchmark externally, think 'laterally' about your preferred peer group. It is not necessarily your immediate competitors. I once asked the CIO of Britain's largest mail order company which company he would most like to benchmark himself against. I expected him to say, perhaps, Sears. Instead he said First Direct, Britain's first telephone banking service. He explained that they were just like him, a nationwide retailer without retail outlets. They just happened to major in selling financial products while he majored in selling ladies' underwear.

6 Accept that the average senior manager has a very limited attention span (somewhere around that of a six month old child) so it is pointless (and counterproductive) presenting him with measures that need hours of explanation.

7 Accept that certain business managers will *never* believe your measures (because they suspect your motives).

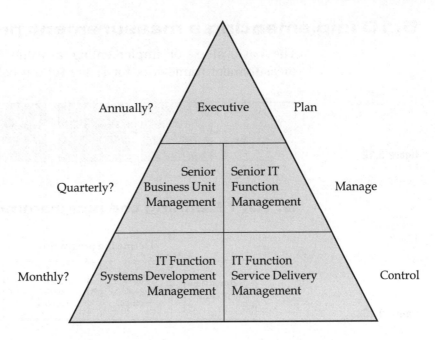

Figure 5.11

5.9 Reporting success

As illustrated in Figure 5.11, different people at different levels in the company will obviously need different reports with different levels of detail and with different frequency. I would suggest, however, that everyone receive a 'top-line' report that focuses on two key things, *target achievement* (i.e. value delivered) and *performance improvement* (i.e. value trends). I would further suggest that it takes the form of a simple set of traffic lights (because everyone who is not visually impaired understands traffic lights!), each of the four quadrants or 16 'spokes' in the 'value compass' being allocated red, amber or green, depending on the granularity of reporting that is appropriate for the audience.

For our 'target achievement' report we might use red for 'targets largely missed', amber for 'targets largely met' and green for 'targets largely exceeded'. For our 'performance improvement' report we might use red for 'worse than last month/period/year', amber for 'much the same' and green for 'we're getting significantly better'. You might want to make it a *little* more pseudo-scientific than that (e.g. what per cent difference constitutes the difference between red, amber and green) but you get my drift. Basically, keep reporting simple.

5.10 Implementing a measurement programme

The basic steps of implementing a value (or performance) measurement framework for IT are set out below.

Figure 5.12

5.10.1 Defining the programme

Define the programme

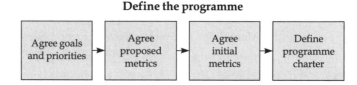

Figure 5.13

- Agree the goals of the value measurement programme (e.g. primarily to illustrate IT value to senior management? primarily to drive internal IT process improvement? Primarily about external comparison? Primarily about internal trend reporting?).
- Agree the immediate priorities for value measurement (e.g. cost-efficiency? effectiveness?).
- On the basis of the goals and priorities, choose (or define) the 'preferred metrics set'.
- Validate the preferred metrics against the 'nine criteria', reviewing them against information already available (or readily available) and so determine the 'proposed metric set'.
- Agree unambiguous definitions for all metrics in the proposed metric set (e.g. what *exactly* do you mean by the term 'IT spend').
- Agree unambiguous baselines for the proposed metric set (e.g. is our baseline for IT spend the budget signed off at last year end? The currently revised budget? The current *actual* spend?).
- Agree the proposed metric set and baselines with key stakeholders in the business.
- Choose a subset of the proposed metric set for an initial implementation – the initial metric set (generally the 'highest value', 'least cost to implement' set that requires least change in existing IT processes and disciplines to be effected).

- Define the programme charter setting out the programme objectives, scope, sponsor, stakeholders, change leaders, deliverables, milestones, dependencies, business case, risks, assumptions, organization, roles and responsibilities, controls and plans.

5.10.2 Developing the programme

Figure 5.14

- Agree appropriate SMART targets for the initial metric set (e.g. 'Development staff productivity >300 function points per FTE per year for applications developed in 4GLs', '>90 per cent of applications meeting or exceeding SLAs').
- Identify any changes in practices or disciplines that will be required (prerequisites) in order to achieve satisfactory accuracy, objectivity, consistency and unfudgeability in the initial metrics set to be implemented; develop an implementation plan to effect these changes.
- Specify, design and develop necessary prerequisite changes in practices and disciplines.
- Specify and design the data collection approach/processes for the initial metrics.
- Specify and design the reporting approach/processes for the initial metrics.
- Specify, select/design/develop automation tools for data collection and reporting.
- Define training needs and develop training materials.
- Define communications needs (internally to the IT function and externally to the business).
- Define and allocate roles and responsibilities for running the metrics programme.

Implement the programme

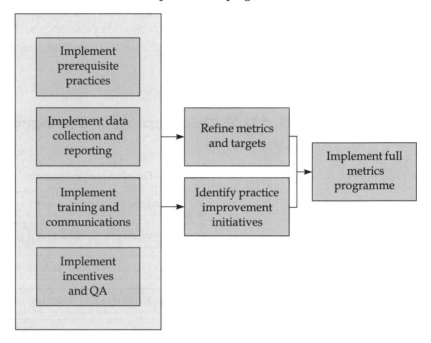

5.10.3 Implementing the programme

- Implement necessary prerequisite changes in practices and disciplines.
- Implement the data collection and reporting systems.
- Conduct training and communication.
- Determine and implement incentives for staff to support the programme and act on its outcomes (and penalties for non-compliance); minimally, incorporate the agreed initial metrics and targets into individual staff performance goals.
- Assess and refine the initial metrics and targets, applying lessons learnt.
- Use the strengths and weaknesses revealed by the achievement, or non-achievement, of targets to develop and implement targeted IT continuous performance improvement initiatives.
- Implement the full (proposed) metrics programme.

5.11 CFFs and CSFs for measurement programmes

That is what it takes to do it 'properly'. What are the key things that most often go wrong in developing metrics programmes? In other words, what are the critical failure factors (CFFs)? In no particular order:

- Lack of clear ownership for the metrics programme. ('Making a success of this is somebody else's problem.')
- Lack of stakeholder buy-in. ('Why should I, an extremely important senior manager, care about your fancy metrics? Give me results, not measures!')
- Implementation of relatively unimportant metrics. ('We've failed to hit our metric targets – well, so what?')
- Lack of mapping from metrics chosen to IT staff *individual* performance measures, i.e. lack of IT staff buy-in. ('The guys upstairs have imposed this damned metrics programme on us – well, so what?')
- IT staff perception that the metrics programme is designed to highlight their failings. ('Gotcha!')
- Metrics not used as key agents of process and behavioural change. ('So we failed to hit our targets – well we must do better next year. What's next on the agenda?')
- Information overload – too many metrics. ('Hey, come join the Metrics Factory!')
- Building on sand – attempting to measure aspects of IT delivery before the processes and disciplines are in place to yield acceptably accurate, objective, consistent and unfudge-able results. ('Over 90 per cent of our projects come in on budget, not that we actually track project budgets accurately.')
- Playing the numbers game. ('By doing this I'll sure *look* better in the metrics reports.')

Looked at a little more positively, crucial to the successful implementation of a measurement programme are the following CSFs, summarized in Figure 5.16:

1 *Do* make sure that your programme objectives are absolutely clear – don't treat it as a 'gotcha' programme; make sure that the focus is not on 'finding the guilty' but on facilitating performance improvement and that this is effectively communicated.
2 *Do* get *genuine* sponsorship from senior IT *and* business executives (and note that 'genuine' sponsorship does not just mean sending out an 'I am personally committed to this' email).
3 *Do* ensure that the ownership of the programme (and accountability for its success) is clear.

13 CSFs for implementing a metrics programme	
1	Make sure that your programme objectives are absolutely clear
2	Get *genuine* sponsorship from senior IT *and* business executives
3	Ensure that the ownership of the programme (and accountability for its success) is clear
4	Ensure that no single metric is taken out of context
5	Be pragmatic about the metrics selected
6	Try to use industry-recognized metrics if you really *must* indulge in external benchmarking
7	Think through the behavioural implications of each metric
8	Ensure that 'tension metrics' are incorporated into the measures for individual groups
9	Ensure that senior business executives *genuinely* 'buy in' to your planned metrics
10	Allow sufficient time to build a credible metrics base
11	Emphasize *trends* in performance
12	Be clear about the different information needs (in terms of scope, depth and frequency) of different recipients of reports
13	Ensure that the metrics programme is periodically reviewed for 'lessons learned' and is allowed to evolve

Figure 5.16

4 *Do* ensure that no single metric is taken out of overall context.

5 *Do* be pragmatic; it is not just pointless, but actually counterproductive to create the 'ideal' set of metrics whose accuracy no one believes. If the metric you seek is going to cost an arm and a leg to obtain and *still* be controversial, don't bother.

6 *Do* try to use industry-recognized metrics if you really *must* indulge in external benchmarking; this will reduce controversy over the validity of metrics chosen. However, in the light of my repeated critiques above of the validity of external benchmarking you might want to take a careful conscience check before selling this to the business.

7 *Do* think through the behavioural implications of each metric (and think it through very cynically). Watch carefully for staff simply 'playing the numbers game' and manipulating metrics in order to 'tell management what they want to hear'. Make sure that all metrics incentivize people to act in the best interests of the company and that the corresponding objectives and measures are built into the staff performance appraisal system.

8 *Do* ensure that 'tension metrics' are incorporated into the measures for individual groups to help incentivize them to

'see the bigger picture' and not act parochially – this is particularly important when groups have, at a parochial level, potentially virtually opposing objectives. For example, application development groups may be primarily driven by objectives (and corresponding measures) to rapidly implement IT solutions into the production environment while operational support groups may be primarily driven by objectives (and corresponding measures) to protect the integrity of the production environment and only accept fully operationally ready applications. By setting tension metrics such as 'percentage of projects delivered to budget/ schedule' for the operational support groups and 'reduction of mean time between failure' for the development groups, a more mature understanding of *common* needs can be engendered.

9 *Do* ensure (*before* you implement the programme) that senior business executives *genuinely* 'buy in' to your planned metrics; if at the end of the day they look at your reports and still say, 'I don't care what your metrics say, I still think you don't deliver what we want and you take too long and cost too much delivering it', then a fundamental part of the rationale is lost.

10 *Do* allow sufficient time to build a credible metrics base (and note that we are talking in terms of years here, not months).

11 *Do* emphasize trends in performance, rather than (as I hope I have demonstrated above) apparent differences from other organizations.

12 *Do* be clear about the different information needs (in terms of scope, depth and frequency) of different recipients of reports; the CEO is obviously going to need a very different report from the data centre manager).

13 *Do* ensure that the metrics programme is periodically reviewed for 'lessons learned' and is allowed to evolve.

Metrics are, in summary, both valuable and dangerous if misinterpreted. Metrics don't just exist to make comparisons. They exist to help you decide how to target your time, energy and investments in improving value. But be very careful about the action determined. Poorly thought through 'knee-jerk' responses to adverse metrics can have ridiculous consequences. For example, several of my clients over the years have, as a result of rising 'IT staff per' metrics (or as a result of business cost reduction drives), set a measure of zero growth in the IT function head count (i.e. a head count freeze). Of course, this didn't stop the demand for systems – so what then happened was that there was an influx of 'temporary' contractors, each costing in the range of 100 per cent to 200 per cent more than equivalent permanent staff. Even when the reins were loosened, the culture of using contractors had become established, since contractors:

- were far faster and easier to 'recruit' (and many, if not most, IT managers are extremely poor at making good recruitment decisions);
- were far faster and easier to get rid of if they were poor quality (in many, if not most, large companies it is both extremely difficult to 'terminate' a member of permanent staff, especially in mainland Europe, and there is a tendency to simply ignore the problem and hope the poorly performing member of staff will just resign rather than sit it out to retirement); and best of all
- they required virtually no man management (all that tedious and difficult motivation, performance appraisal, personal development, technical training, career management etc.) that again, many, if not most, IT managers are very poor at and in which they are often fundamentally uninterested (not, of course, that they would ever actually confess that).

The upshot was that IT costs actually *soared*, and all as a result of an ill-thought through action designed to *reduce* costs. Two of these companies, by the way, are among Britain's biggest retailers (who presumably know a thing or two about commercially astute behaviour), one of which now 'enjoys' over a third of its IT staff being contractors, some of these 'temporary' contractors having spent over 12 years with the company!

5.12 Why bother (reprise)?

So is it worth doing? Well, businesses are increasingly focusing their budget reductions (and outsourcing plans) on departments that cannot *demonstrate* their business value and competitiveness. As the Meta Group put it, 'Measure IT or die.' This (admittedly very defensive) factor alone may justify such a performance measurement programme.

5.13 Summary

Metrics do not *directly* add value to the business but can be very powerful *indirect* value adders by changing people's behaviours to become more commercial. Metrics defined should address not only the 'traditional' supply-side areas but also the 'outcome-driven' demand-side if a truly 'balanced scorecard' of IT is to be established. The relative importance (and weighting) of metrics around the 'value compass' depends largely on the 'SAM positioning' of IT in the organization. Any metric set chosen must be rigorously vetted for its credibility and value. All metric sets will be compromises but should focus on key *value* indicators rather than the more traditional key *performance* indicators that often measure what is relatively *easy* to measure (and/or is primarily of interest to *IT* managers). Reporting should focus on both target achievement and trends and should carefully align with the differing needs of different business and IT groups and levels of management within these groups.

6 Conclusion

> He had been 8 years upon a project for extracting
> sunbeams from cucumbers, which were to be put
> into phials hermetically sealed and let out to warm
> the air in raw inclement summers.
>
> Jonathan Swift – *Gulliver's Travels*

I particularly like the quote above because it summarizes beautifully the pursuit of a valiant, not to say quixotic, quest founded on hopelessly flawed assumptions. That, I'm afraid is the way many grandiose IT transformation programmes are conducted. This is why I am strongly advocating that you focus 'simply' on transforming those practices that will add optimum value, rather than 'try to solve world poverty'.

In this final chapter I want to set out the 'charter' for creating a value-driven IT function. But before I do that I feel I have to address a key question that I am repeatedly asked, namely, is it not just the case that your value-driven IT function simply has to act like an ESP?

6.1 IT function as ESP

I have spent some time in this book comparing (generally pejoratively) internal IT functions with external service providers (ESPs), driving home the need to 'commercialize' (and 'de-corporatize') the former. Indeed, the whole thrust of this book has been to establish practices that will help engender dynamic, entrepreneurial behaviours into organizations that are often beset by internal politics, conservatism and risk avoidance. So, should our value-driven IT function just 'look like' an IT ESP? This is (generally) the currently accepted wisdom (but certainly not mine, as I hope to justify).

First and foremost, I would argue that of the six value-adding CSFs I set out in Chapter 3, *none* will be exemplified in an ESP.

This is simply because even if you were to outsource your 'entire' IT function, you will almost certainly *still* have to do all these value-adding things in-house (in addition to developing strategy, designing architectures, managing the ESP etc.)! ESPs are essentially not interested in adding value to your business. They are, however, very interested in adding value to *their* business! They do this by increasing their revenue and/or profits. Their revenue is your business cost. To optimize their business revenue they obviously want to increase your business cost. And their revenue is basically *their* costs plus their margins. So on the cost-efficiency front they have a strong incentive to reduce their internal costs (in order to increase their margins). Therefore a value-driven IT function should perhaps 'look like' an ESP from the cost-efficiency point of view but will probably learn nothing from a value-adding point of view (the deployment of best value practices in the effectiveness quadrant). And even on the cost-efficiency front, remember what I said in Chapter 4 about the fact that there is little evidence to suggest that internal IT functions cannot be run as cost-efficiently as ESPs. In fact, it is worse than this, because in the case of a number of areas (e.g. service and support quality – optimizing the cost vs service level equation, systems terminations – terminating non-value-adding systems functionality) the ESP has a strong commercial incentive to optimize these in *their* favour, not yours. Optimizing service levels for an ESP means getting you to take as much service as possible. Optimizing the production systems portfolio for an ESP means getting you to continue paying for non-value-adding functionality for as long as possible. So you are not likely to learn much from them here.

Remember, ESPs may indeed be more 'commercial' than the typical internal IT function – but whose commercial interests do they serve? Are they run to maximize *your* profits and shareholder value or *their* profits and shareholder value? ESPs are not just looking to recover the costs of their services, or even just working on a cost-plus basis. Instead they are examining IRR, cashflow, risk, contract growth potential, potential to sell-on other services, length of contract, market penetration etc. with a view to their long-term revenue stream. *And* they will routinely cross-subsidize services and work to low (or even negative) margins at the start of deals in order to 'get a foot in the door'. So we should be very careful about adopting them as our 'role models'. As I explain in a case study below, running an IT function 'as though' it were an ESP can quite easily result in a *lower* value IT service.

275

An ESP wants to maximize its revenue, minimize its cost base and maximize its margins. So, presumably, if we are to manage our IT function 'like an ESP' then it too should be managed to maximize its margins, right? But for an internal IT function the margin should be zero (assuming forward investment is built into the prices) since they are simply recovering their costs. So if we don't want our internal IT function to 'make a profit' at the expense of the business it serves what is its equivalent of 'margin'? I would say that the answer is 'value-added'. The internal IT function should be primarily concerned with adding value to the business it serves, not *its* 'business'. The key difference between an ESP and an internal IT function is that the ESP is geared towards *taking* its margin from your business while an internal IT function should be geared towards *adding* its 'margin' (value-added) to your business. Therefore a value-driven IT function should be managed to maximize value-added, not managed to maximize 'margin' or 'profit' or 'contribution'. Like any 'business' it must also try to optimize its cost base but (assuming this is not a cost centre, in terms of the SAM model) the 'name of the game' is managing the IT function to maximize the value it adds to the business it serves. You may well think that I am labouring the obvious here – but I am increasingly seeing internal IT functions being 'converted' to profit centres and being set profit/contribution targets by the business they serve 'because that's how commercially competitive businesses are set up, right?' Right, and monumentally wrong.

However, note Gartner's recent Strategic Planning Assumption, that 'IT functions that fail to adopt competitive, service-based business management principles will be increasingly marginalized – if not eliminated – in favour of competitive IT services offered by external service providers (ESPs). By 2006, IT functions that fail to adopt these principles will forcibly lose at least 50 percent of their core functions to ESPs (0.7 probability).' From a behavioural change management point of view, this typically will be the 'burning platform' that creates the imperative to move rapidly towards being value-driven. But note that adopting the culture, behaviour and 'operating principles' of an ESP is *not* the same as copying their working practices or running as a 'profit centre'.

So don't just 'go through the motions' of becoming an ESP 'look-alike' – note one more Gartner Strategic Planning Assumption: 'Of the IT functions that are structured as [ESP-like] business units, only 40 percent will do so for the "right" reason (0.85

probability) and 70 percent will fail to bring a business approach within three years (0.7 probability).' A final message to CIOs from Gartner: 'By 2005, 60 percent of IT functions that fail to develop or find executives who can run IT as a business will see their IT service franchise shrink by 20 percent annually (0.7 probability).'

Basically, when senior management do not *really* believe that their IT function is actually able to 'change its spots' or simply that it would take unacceptably long to do so, the obvious 'solution' is to 'give' the IT function to an ESP and let them get on with it. Even then, while the board may happily think that they are 'making the problem go away', the fact of the matter is that they *still* have to aspire to 'value-driven' stature in many areas (in particular all the value-adding areas).

In other words, the majority of the IT practices that are most critical practices in optimizing value from your IT investment will *still* have to be addressed (if only to ensure that your ESPs don't 'take you to the cleaners'). You would have to be studiously blind to the headlines in the computer press each week not to notice the number of ESP deals that go sour, often as a result of a deadly combination of the naive optimism of the customer coupled with the cynical opportunism of the ESP when the deal is being struck. ESPs may not always be 'princes of darkness' (I've met a few princesses too), but the people they send in to make the sale and broker the contract often bear a strong whiff of sulphur.

6.2 Case study – IT function as ESP

I have already given you an 'IT function as ESP' example by citing the difficulty in just one area (namely, 'transfer charging', as set out in Chapter 3). But to examine this more broadly I give you one final example of a recent client of mine, a huge organization in the public sector. They had gone to great lengths not only to implement 'world class IT' best practices, but had also made huge changes to try to adopt a commercial approach, basically running the IT function as though it was a business (even though it was simply an internal division of the 'company' it served). For example, they had implemented an IT 'product portfolio', priced the products in the portfolio based on external price benchmarks, developed product SLAs, implemented internal tariffing and cross-charging for products and recruited hoards of customer management and service level management staff. The business also gave them 'contribution' (effectively 'profit') targets to achieve. However, despite all this (and all this was costing a large fortune as they took on board – and then some – major ESP overheads that internal IT functions traditionally manage to avoid), interviews with senior business management showed consistently that the IT function was still not perceived to *behave* commercially and was still widely regarded as an expensive overhead (indeed, now an even *more* expensive overhead) rather than a value-adding business partner. The IT function was 'going through the motions' of being a commercial supplier of IT services but they were fooling no one, because they had addressed the 'easy' bit, changing the organization and processes, but not remotely adequately addressed the 'hard' bit, the need to address the people issues and the behavioural change (cultural) issues. And, of course, the organization and process changes were designed to make the IT function into a 'pseudo-ESP' profit centre, not a value-driven 'value centre'. Note too that much of the problem lay *outside* the IT function with uncommercial (highly unionized) behaviours permeating the whole organization.

For example, despite the rigorous scope control processes that had been initiated, the only *real* question that was asked by the business as a project progressed was the one that they had always asked, namely, 'Can we still afford this project?' not, 'Is this project actually going to deliver the benefits?' Implementing pseudo-commercial processes into IT will have little or no commercial impact if the business does not actually buy into it (and is itself not behaving in a commercially pragmatic manner). An absolutely key point raised repeatedly by project managers in the IT function was that they were commonly 'obliged' to accept work that they *knew* was somewhere between a waste of money and 'doomed'. Why? Because the business was prepared to pay for it and as far as the IT senior management team was concerned, it was all revenue that helped bump up their 'contribution'. After all, this was how a real ESP would behave, wasn't it? But is that really 'best practice' (never mind best *value* practice)?

And then there was the matter of the 'commercial objectives' of the IT function, the number one of which, as set by the business, was to increase the 'contribution' made (basically the revenue minus the cost). Of course it could achieve this (and win the IT directors their bonuses) by simply increasing the margins on its services. And how exactly would this benefit the business it serves? Alternatively, assuming the margins remain fixed, it will almost always be easier for an organization to increase its contribution, not by reducing its cost base, but by increasing the amount of work it does (its revenue) and so *increasing* its total costs. So it could very reasonably be argued that by asking the IT function to 'behave' like an ESP, senior business management were not only *increasing* the cost of IT to the business, they were actually *incentivizing* the IT function to increase their cost to the business and decrease the potential value added. This is a sad piece of irony that I cite to drive home the care that is required if we are to find and implement 'best practices' that actually do more commercial good than harm while hiding behind a façade of saintliness. Just to drive home the point, this IT function was the one I mentioned earlier that killed an internal initiative that would have increased the value added to the business served because the investment required to implement the initiative would have increased the IT function's costs and so depress the IT function's 'contribution' to the business it served – and their imperative, clearly set by the business, was to maximize their contribution.

The bottom line is that implementing 'world class IT' best practices (and even, dare I say it, best value practices) may actually be commercially *counter*productive if you do not ensure that the business and IT staff who follow them are committed heart and mind and are doing so following the commercial spirit of the practices rather than just 'playing at being commercial', going through the outer motions of a real business, i.e. you have got to have the right people and the right behaviours, and, dare I say it, behave with that most uncommon of things in the world, 'common sense'.

6.3 The characteristics of a value-driven IT function

I have explained how my value-driven IT function would be far more than a conventional 'world class IT' IT function deploying best practices and would also be very different from an ESP. So, on a more positive note, what does our apotheotic value-driven IT function look like – how would we recognize it? There can be no definitive answer to this question because it depends, of course, on the role of IT in support of the business. If, in terms of the SAM model, the IT function is (and only is) a 'cost centre' then it could certainly be argued that the key characteristic of such an IT function is simply that it is cheap (i.e. it has optimized cost-efficiency, even at the expense of effectiveness). I have only consulted in one organization where this was

	6 criteria for identifying a business served by a value-driven IT function
1	It deploys the six key value-adding practices set out in Chapter 3: 1 Optimizing business/IT function alignment 2 Optimizing competitive advantage 3 Optimizing portfolio alignment 4 Optimizing portfolio value 5 Optimizing value delivery 6 Optimizing benefits realization
2	The IT function transfer charges the business for all IT products and services supplied
3	It makes IT users directly accountable for the costs of IT services consumed
4	It makes IT users directly accountable for realizing the benefits of IT services supplied
5	It sets IT value targets and makes IT staff directly accountable for delivering against those targets
6	It measures and reports IT value, focusing IT performance improvement initiatives on value improvement

Figure 6.1

remotely true, however, so as a generalization (and certainly for organizations whose IT functions function predominantly as profit or investment centres, in SAM terms) I would say that there are six key criteria for 'entry into the club', set out below and summarized in Figure 6.1.

1 Deploying (and adhering to the spirit of) the six value-adding practices set out in Chapter 3 (obviously!).
2 Transfer charging for all IT products and services using a tariffed, TCO-based pricing model for standard, packaged, end-to-end IT services, each IT service being accompanied by 'price vs service level' user negotiated SLAs.
3 Making users directly *accountable* (above the line, at the point of consumption) for the costs of IT services and service levels taken.
4 Making users directly *accountable* (above the line, at the point of benefits delivery) for benefits realized; user budgets being adjusted to reflect the tangible benefits proposed in the final agreed business case.
5 Making IT staff directly *accountable* for delivering value by setting IT function value targets (*not* profit/contribution targets) with a *significant* proportion (40 per cent plus?) of the remuneration of each member of the IT function's management and staff being related primarily to the *individual* achievement of *individual* value targets. A base salary would be paid to reflect the skills and experience of the staff member and the commitment and hard work *expected* of them. A bonus

would then be allocated according to the level of individual success at product/service delivery. But the major bonus would be allocated according to the level of *value* delivery.

6 Measuring and reporting the 'business performance' (in particular, the value delivered) of the IT function (e.g. the 'value compass') and continually focusing performance improvement initiatives on raising value delivery.

More important than all these criteria, however, is the calibre of the IT function's management and staff. Your number one goal should be to employ highly competent, highly confident, highly resilient, widely experienced, mature, dedicated, *commercially astute* IT management and staff who trust, respect and value one another (and are trusted, respected and valued by the business). And the greatest and scarcest of these competencies is commercial acumen. Do the management teams in IT functions recognize this? Well, a recent survey by the Computing Recruitment Foundation of 463 IT managers asked them to rate the importance of 10 key skills when recruiting IT staff. The top rating (at 57 per cent) went to 'technical skills' and the bottom (with just 8.7 per cent) went to, you guessed it, 'commercial acumen'. Ever since I began my career in the IT industry [*sic*] I have been reading of the need to develop 'hybrid managers' who are as comfortable in the boardroom as they are in front of a laptop. Well, I haven't met any of these fabled hybrid managers yet. In fact I would not need all the fingers on one hand to count the number of IT managers I've met who looked truly commercially credible in the boardroom. Place many IT managers in a *real* business situation with senior business (or supplier) management and they give off a scent of fear (often combined, interestingly, with arrogance), a scent that is picked up on (and looked down on) immediately by those who operate at this level in business. We need hard-nosed, self-confident (but self-aware) businessmen running IT functions, people to whom the epithet 'leader' automatically attaches itself. It certainly wouldn't hurt if they had come up through the IT ranks, recognized that Java was not just a holiday destination and that a pixel was not actually a small fairy from the South West of England. But so long as the individual's inner identification and allegiance is inward looking to the IT industry rather than outward looking to commerce generally, and the business served, specifically, he or she is never going to treated (and trusted) as an equal by senior business management.

Note that the word (or spirit of) *accountable* runs through my six criteria above. Maximizing the business value of IT is *not* someone else's problem – it is *everyone's* problem, irrespective of whether they are a CEO, CIO, systems analyst or systems programmer. Everyone should be thinking and behaving as though self-employed in a small business. Note also that it is not remotely within the remit of any IT function to meet the six key criteria in isolation. It will be required to bring the business with it and quite probably radically revise long-standing business and HR policies. These policies are often rooted in a lack of clear thinking ('We'll ask IT to run as a profit centre because that'll make it run like a business, and that's good isn't it'), lack of courage ('Yes, they are wastes of space but we can't get rid of these people because they have been here forever'), lack of imagination ('Our policy here is not to transfer charge internally because it doesn't work'), conservatism ('It may not work for you, sonny, but that's the way we have always done it around here'), envy ('I don't care how good he is, no way are we paying him that much') and fear ('If I'm truly accountable for delivering value I'll be revealed as a fraud'). Furthermore, these policies are often combined with (CFO-driven) fiscal policies designed to contain and control IT spend rather than stimulate and maximize IT value delivery, even in organizations for whom IT exploitation may be key to corporate success. Maybe these policies made sense once for blue collar staff and armies of clerical office drones working in business admin (actually I don't even believe that) but they sure as hell are likely to be wholly out of alignment with the need to manage, motivate and extract the best from highly skilled, value-adding, entrepreneurial, individualistic knowledge workers. Why does this sound revolutionary? It's just common sense.

Note also that in my six criteria I have not included sourcing characteristics but generally I would expect a value-driven IT function to be acting as a broker of IT products and services to the business, insourcing those that are core (by which I choose to mean high value-adding services in which they have high competence) and outsourcing non-core products and services that can be provided more cost-efficiently elsewhere. I have also not included characteristics of organization structure because in my 'value hierarchy' this sits right at the bottom. Should you be centralized, decentralized, hybrid, role based, or whatever else is currently vogue? Look at the literature and you will be overwhelmed by opinions on this. I'm sorry (well, all right, I'm not really) but I cannot get up much enthusiasm for these issues, at least, not relative to the 'big ticket' value issues. In the grand scheme of the problem, management surely should have better things to do (like implementing best value practices). However, what I *would* say, briefly, is that the value-driven IT function's organization would be largely project-driven rather than a conventional hierarchy (I'm obviously thinking principally, but not exclusively, here of the systems development function). Conventional, centralized hierarchies were designed to organize armies and make it absolutely clear who obeyed whom without question and, most importantly, who got shot first (the guys at the bottom of the pyramid). It is not an intelligent (commercially astute) way to organize any business I've seen. I refer you back to my 'A hierarchy of value' section 2.3 in Chapter 2, for how management consultancy firms do it, and do it very successfully, dynamically creating and disbanding multi-disciplinary teams to meet specific skill needs at particular times. I have tried on several occasions to 'sell' a more project-driven organization structure to large IT functions and I have always received the same response, namely, 'I can see the value in organizing that way but our people simply couldn't adapt to it.' Really? Have you ever actually tried? And if they *really* could not adapt to even this then you *really* have a problem becoming more commercially oriented.

There is one further key 'people characteristic' that I would associate with my value-driven IT function and that lies in the nature of the 'employment contract' between the value-driven worker and the value-driven employer. This is important so I will spend a little time on it here.

As national and global booms and recessions appear to follow one another in increasing rapidity and as restructuring, rationalization, 'rightsizing', mergers, acquisitions and divestments increasingly figure in business activity, so the need for much greater flexibility in the cost base (and staffing) will grow. I need only look as far as my own 'profession', management consultancy, to see this. If you create a graph plotting the business revenues of management consultancies against indicators of the national economy in which the firms operate you will find an astonishing correlation. This is principally because consultancy is, of course, a 'discretionary' business expenditure, so when the going gets tough the consultants get turfed. This meant that over the 16 years I spent with Big 6/5/4 consultancy firms, I watched British economy-tracking cycles of frantic consultant recruitment programmes followed shortly thereafter by frantic redundancy programmes followed shortly thereafter by frantic recruitment programmes, and so on. There seemed to be a permanent problem of either too few or too many consultants, or, worse, too few in the parts of the business that were growing and too many in the parts that were shrinking. And because it was becoming increasingly difficult to predict which parts were destined for growth or shrinkage I repeatedly saw people and groups being made redundant one month only for their skills and resources to jump back into demand the next. Management consultancy firms cannot go on like that. It is not commercially intelligent and they are extremely commercially intelligent people. Therefore I believe that they will increasingly rely on the use of independent consultants (who will temporarily consult under the firm's brand name) contracted in when the going is good and quickly terminated when the going gets tough. 'Outsourcing', in this personal sense of people having multiple jobs (in serial or parallel) and leading 'portfolio lives', may be in 'all' our futures, because these problems of the increasing dynamism and flexibility required in businesses is not going to go away and is not remotely unique to management consultancy firms.

A corollary to this, by the way, is that the concept of 'company loyalty' is going to become increasingly laughable. You will be very hard-pressed to find a management consultant who (if he or she is being honest) has the remotest loyalty to the current firm worked for – they *understand* that the deal is that they are dispensable (and so they expect to be rewarded appropriately for this risk). Indeed I believe the very concept of 'having a career' will become increasingly remote for many. In short, for many (read 'most') of us insecurity and uncertainty are the future whether we care for it or not. So, as strongly suggested by this book, why not learn to embrace them (and enjoy them) now, and under your own control, rather than wait for them to be forced on you?

In his book *Jobshift – How to Prosper in a Workplace Without Jobs*, William Bridges summarizes the new 'rules of the employment contract' as follows:

- ongoing employment will depend on the success of the employer (and the linkages will be obvious and direct)
- workers must continuously demonstrate value to their employer
- workers must see themselves as outsource suppliers for their allocated assignments
- employers will offer few, if any, 'benefits' like sick-leave, pensions, health care, training etc.

- workers will have to develop their own careers and provide for themselves in sickness and retirement
- the nature of work will switch from jobs and roles to assignment teams. Therefore workers must be able to quickly switch their focus
- workers will also switch from organization to organization more readily. Long-term employment is a thing of the past
- workers will manage their own attitudes and behaviours. Employers will only measure results.

This is an insecure, challenging world, far removed from hierarchic, paternalistic, smothering corporations, stifled by an office culture of 'presenteeism', deference and risk aversion, drowning in internal meetings and beset by puerile internal politics and the pursuit of petty status props; it is a world where people will have to display far greater self-reliance and resilience and earn respect based on the value they are demonstrably adding (day after day) to the business, not their position or seniority. But it is also a much more dynamic, exciting, fulfilling and 'immediate' world with far greater freedom of action, far greater tolerance of non-conformity and far greater reward for excellence. You are no longer a corporate clone 'human resource' – you are a unique (and demanding) person. You are going to have to believe in yourself because you aren't going to get any 'management stroking' in this world – but then did you ever? People who rise to management positions in IT functions rarely have strong staff management skills let alone charismatic leadership skills. Instead they tend to be 'results-oriented' people (OK, I'm being a little generous here). They may well conscientiously go through the motions of being caring managers in accordance with their 'Staff Management for Beginners' course but does anyone really believe it?

This brave new world, dominated by the 'value ethic' (where you are rewarded for hard outcomes rather than just hard work), is, after all, simply the way small, successful organizations (and all the self-employed of this world, like your humble author) have always worked. There is actually nothing new here. It is just corporations (who presumably *started* life as small, successful organizations) reawakening to commercial reality. My value-driven IT function would embody this reality and would 'contract' with its employees appropriately. Look, at the end of day, which role would you rather have in your own private Western – a bit part as one of the Indians massacred in reel 1 or Clint Eastwood moseying into the sunset after cleaning up the town?

6.4 Assessing current practices

The effective deployment of best value practices is obviously key to my list of value-driven IT function characteristics. However, attempting to define and implement all the best value practices set out in Chapter 3 at once is almost certainly going to be overly ambitious. That is why I have added a simple set of 'diagnostic profiles' in the Appendix to help you understand your relative existing strengths and weaknesses in the six value-added CSF practice areas. They require a subjective assessment of existing best value practices and a view on where in the spectrum IT should be placed after a suitable change period (say, 18 months). The best (highest value) way to complete these is in workshops including all the relevant IT managers associated with the practices. It can also be very advantageous to have a 'reality check' by conducting an identical exercise with more junior IT staff (who will know far better how things are *really* done). If at all possible these workshops should also include key users, because their buy-in to the value transformation process will be key (and the earlier they are involved the better) and I can almost guarantee that they will almost invariably rate the existing practices lower than IT managers and rate the desired practices higher, i.e. their 'gap' will typically be wider.

As a general rule you would be advised to focus your value transformation initiatives on the areas with the widest gaps and/or the lowest overall ratings. The value of completing these diagnostic profiles in workshops (rather than, for example, by individually completing them and then averaging the results) is rooted in the General MacArthur saying, 'The plan is nothing. Planning is everything'. Basically, it is the thought processes and internal debate that is important rather than the numbers that come off at the end of the process. Completing the forms together helps to ensure that there is a common understanding of terms and helps to 'bring to heel' people with particular axes to grind. It also helps to avoid the results being skewed by respondents who have either inadequately understood the process or simply completed the forms with half their minds.

The key word in conducting such workshops is 'honesty'. What is important is what *actually* happens, not what the 'procedure manual' says or what you would like to believe happens. This is another advantage of completing the forms in workshops: if one individual has an incurable propensity to 'spout the company line' and answer the questions in a 'politically correct' way (rather than honestly), his colleagues (it is always a 'he') will usually pick him up on it quickly (if only with a mild, 'Oh come on, Jim, you know it doesn't *really* work like that).

Once the scope and priorities of the practice improvement work have been decided in this way, this is followed by the design and implementation of the change programme.

6.5 The triggers for IT value transformation

Recently there does appear to have been an increased focus on the issue of the value of IT to the business. So why have I, for once in my life, been astonishingly prescient, and, more seriously, why is the pressure increasing now on IT functions to optimize, in my terms, cost-efficiency, effectiveness, value-added and quality?

I suspect that optimizing the economy side of IT cost-efficiency has become increasingly critical of late as organizations struggle with global recessions and look critically at their overhead budgets, noting often spiralling IT costs on the back of spiralling demand for systems and bandwidth. Optimizing the staff efficiency side of cost-efficiency has probably become increasingly critical of late as a result of the worldwide IT staffing shortage and the 'e-business evolution' (with its need for 60 to 90 day systems delivery cycles from multiple/parallel development teams). Optimizing effectiveness and quality has probably become increasingly critical of late as a result of the growth of global ERP sites and, again, e-business, and their need for far more predictable systems and service delivery, with heightened expectations of systems availability, reliability, scalability and flexibility. Optimizing the effectiveness of companies' management of their ESPs has become particularly critical as the overstretched IT function has moved progressively into the role of a 'broker' of IT services to the business (and offshore programming has exploded). And optimizing the value-added of IT solutions has become particularly critical of late because of the increased potential of IT to differentiate business services (and create business services), principally as a result of e-business growth.

In summary, I believe that the key circumstances that are tending to create the pressing need today for initiating a programme to transform IT value are:

- Senior management 'backlash' against the IT function (usually on the basis of their perceptions of unacceptable, or

287

unacceptably growing, costs, unacceptable system delivery times, unacceptable quality of systems delivered, unacceptable quality of service or, most critically, unacceptable failure to realize promised benefits).

- A step change in IT service provision (typically as a result of mergers, acquisitions or divestments and, increasingly, business process outsourcing – these factors, which are becoming increasingly key components of business strategy, can result in sudden changes in IT demand levels that centralized IT functions with high fixed cost bases are poorly able to address).
- A step change in the strategic value of IT (e.g. e-business).
- A step change in the business competitive landscape (e.g. e-business).
- A step change in the criticality and visibility of IT services to the end customer (e.g. e-business).
- A step change in the need for higher development productivity (e.g. e-business).

As we can see, e-business has a lot to answer for. It has brought IT service provision much more into the business foreground, which of course is excellent if you are running an optimally cost-efficient and effective IT function that is consistently delivering high quality, value-adding products and services. But it is not so excellent if you are not! And the impact of e-business on IT visibility and importance can only grow if Gartner's prediction is correct that 'by 2008, 25% of consumer spending and 70% of business-to-business commerce (in developed economies) will be web-involved'. The collapse in .com share prices has been famously described as the '.con' revolution. But it was not a con. It was simply an overhyped, 'collective illusion' that obviously had to come down to commercial earth. Obviously companies that are virtually without tangible assets and which make negligible or no profits are not worth billions of dollars. In particular, they are not worth more than the total market value of the 'bricks and mortar' companies that often owned them! But it is now, as the market settles, that the e-business 'evolution' will build, initially in information-based companies (e.g. publishing, travel, financial services) and later to more traditional 'bricks and mortar' companies.

6.6 The objectives of IT value transformation

So what are the typical objectives of implementing an IT value transformation programme? In summary, typical objectives range from the strategic to the tactical:

- To help ensure that the IT function and the business are strategically aligned, so helping to optimize the value that the IT function adds to the business.
- To facilitate the establishment of a more commercially focused demand and supply relationship between the IT function and the business.
- To help ensure that the limited resources of the IT function are deployed to deliver the optimum value to the business through effective work demand management, ongoing value management and management of the delivery of predicted benefits.
- To help ensure that commercially *necessary and sufficient* service levels are provided for business users of the internal IT function (or outsourced ESP) provided services, so facilitating a more commercial partnership between the IT function and its customers.
- To help ensure that all IT services to the business are sourced from the most cost-effective supplier, whether that be internal or external.
- To help improve the reliability of the delivery of individual projects to budget, schedule and quality needs.
- To help increase the likelihood of the realization of programme and project benefits.
- To help minimize the business risks from failing or under-achieving projects.
- To help reduce the total systems life-cycle costs and improve the quality, responsiveness and flexibility of the systems delivery service within the IT function.
- To help improve the integrity of the production environment and help ensure that production service level targets are actually achieved.

6.7 The benefits of IT value transformation

Key benefits of success for the IT function are:

- Increased respect from the business as a result of:
  - the repositioning of the IT function as a value-adding business partner;
  - the increased commercial credibility of the IT function;
  - the increased 'proactiveness' of the IT function.
- Improved ability of the IT function to *demonstrate* its value-adding role to the business (and, potentially, justify *non*-outsourcing of IT services).

- The creation of a far more stimulating work environment which will lead to improved staff career prospects and staff retention.

I want to emphasize this last point. Do you remember my 'value hierarchy' with 'people' at the top? Attracting and retaining the best IT staff is *the* key value improving action you can take. A value-driven IT function will have clearly articulated objectives, cascaded to all staff, clearly aligned with business priorities (giving staff a clear sense of direction), clear recognition and reward for achieving objectives and the satisfaction of feeling you are working in a truly commercial enterprise, a world of 'commercial truth and consequences'. People do not generally leave an organization primarily because of the poor pay. Instead the primary reasons are lack of recognition, lack of purpose and lack of challenge (all typically coupled with a lack of respect for the management team). In a value-driven IT function staff will see their successes (and failures) clearly recognized and rewarded (one way or the other), they will have a very clear sense of *why* they are doing what they do and they will certainly find that working in a genuinely commercial atmosphere is highly challenging and rewarding. If you are familiar with Maslow's 'hierarchy of human needs' you will see immediately how a value-driven IT function caters to the higher needs.

Key benefits of success for the business are:

- Improved IT investment decisions resulting in the demonstrably highest value-adding projects taking precedence, leading to improved profitability.
- Improved probability of delivering programmes and projects that add optimum value to the business as early as possible.
- Improved probability of delivering IT services that add optimum value to the business.
- Minimization of performing work that has low (or no) commercial justification; this, in turn, freeing time to focus on work which demonstrably has, and sustains, a high commercial justification.
- Early warning of programme/project value delivery problems and reduced instances of project failures.
- Minimization of continuing to run systems that have ceased to have commercial justification; this, in turn, freeing time and money to focus on running and supporting systems that demonstrably have, and sustain, a high commercial justification.

- IT cost containment/reduction over time (if required).
- Increased customer satisfaction.

6.8 The risks of IT value transformation

By 'risks' here I mean the key risks of a value transformation programme failing to realize *its* benefits (i.e. truly transforming IT value to the business).

These key risks are:

- The failure (or inability) of the business to 'engage' with their IT function as a value-adding business partner.
- The failure (or inability) of the IT function to 'engage' with the business as a value-adding business partner.
- The failure (or inability) of the business to appreciate that the IT value transformation programme cannot succeed without changes in *their* behaviours and working practices; it is not just about the IT function and how it behaves and works.
- The failure (or inability) of IT function management and staff to 'engage' with the new working practices (i.e. they go into 'denial' until it is too late).

The key ways to manage down these risks are not so much rooted in programme management as in behavioural change management. In particular:

- Identifying and communicating the 'burning platform' for change (i.e. everyone must believe that there is a *compelling* need to change).
- Clearly defined and communicated goals.
- Strong leadership and clearly demonstrable senior management commitment.
- Significant incentives to adopt the changes proposed and significant sanctions for overt or covert resistance.
- Managing stakeholders (inside the IT function and across the business) and their expectations effectively.
- Identifying and publicizing 'quick wins' and success stories.
- Monitoring and reporting increased value delivered (the 'balanced scorecard').
- Implementing changes incrementally, proving them and learning from them *before* implementing them across the business.

Basically, if all parties simply pay 'lip service' to the value transformation programme and its outcomes, not only will it not succeed, it may well actually *reduce* the value of IT to the business as a result of pointless bureaucracy and increased staff cynicism. So only pursue such a programme if you are truly *serious* about it.

6.9 Attaining nirvana

In the Preface I set out some (tongue firmly in cheek) parallels between the Four Noble Truths of Buddhism and IT delivery. I pointed out that the essential fascination of Buddhism for me, as an arch rationalist, lay in its rational, systematic approach to attaining enlightenment. What I didn't mention was that Buddhist teaching also says that *nirvana* is only ultimately attainable by those who have *transcended* the 'Eightfold Path' of Buddhist 'best practice'. So it is, I'm afraid, with IT 'best value practices'. Total compliance with the practices set out in this book is not only not a guarantee of successful attainment of our coveted 'value-driven IT' accolade, I can guarantee it will *not* be enough. For that the 'commercial spirit' of the practices must have so imbued themselves in management and staff that the procedures themselves become an irrelevance. Unfortunately getting to *that* stage is not going to happen overnight. But it is worth the effort.

If you implement, adopt and *adhere to the commercial spirit* of the 'best value practices' (and even if you choose to ignore the cost-efficiency value improvement opportunities) I have no doubt that, for once, the word 'transformation' will be rather more than just marketing hype. However, if you think that adopting my proposed 'best value practices' (and their attendant pre-requisites for success) will be easy then you have not been paying attention. Please don't even try if you are not 100 per cent serious about it. *And* remember that it is largely a 'package deal'. Cherry-picking the bits of the package with which you are comfortable and omitting the 'difficult bits' (like transfer pricing IT services and establishing true IT cost and benefits account-ability in the business) will almost certainly greatly reduce the probability of success, if not be actively *counter*productive (through the creation of additional, non-value-adding bureau-cracy and making it that much more difficult to overcome scepticism when you try to 'do it properly' on the next attempt). But *do* try – and let me know about your experiences by emailing me via *iambic@tiscali.co.uk.* I will then incorporate learning and 'war stories' in subsequent editions (attributed, or, if you want to protect the guilty, anonymous!).

6.10 Heroes and villains

Back at the start of this book I made the bold (reckless?) assertion that (within the limitations of the laws of libel) I would tell the truth. If you work in the IT industry (and, in particular, if you work in a large, corporate IT function) then you will be the best judge of the extent to which this book 'rings true'.

I appreciate that you may think that I have painted a rather depressing picture of the behaviour of many of the protagonists in the case studies and examples; but it is not so much that I am 'down' on these people as that I am down on the uncommercial behaviours that the typical corporate culture tends to engender. It is not that I am prejudiced against corporate culture. It is that I am *post*judiced. It is because I have seen the damage done. But there is hope!

I also appreciate that you may think that the 'heroes' of this book appear to be cynical opportunists – you might want them to run your company but you would not necessarily want them over for dinner. But they are not cynical opportunists – they are commercially pragmatic realists. They simply recognize how the commercial world *actually* works and adopt behaviours that exploit that reality (having a great deal of fun in the process!). The most successful business people I have worked with were, in their 'business persona', consummate actors! Trust me, they won't steal the silver and make off with your daughter if you invite them round to your house! Besides which, the perceived 'cynical opportunism' comes directly from the profit motive. That is why I have been at such pains to emphasize that our value-driven IT function should *not* be run as a profit centre and should *not* make a 'financial contribution' to the business. It should instead be run as a *value centre*. The name of my game is to incentivize people with the *value motive*, to act (behave) in the best commercial interests of the business they serve. This may not make them saints but it certainly won't make them sinners!

Actually, I suspect that most organizations, whether they be in the private, public, or public–private partnership sectors would be run far more advantageously for society as a whole if they were run as value centres (using the term 'value' in its widest sense of 'goodness'), optimizing the value-added to the communities they serve, whether those communities are widget purchasers or hospital patients. This is *my* 'middle way' between the privatization that so enamours the Right and the nationalization that so enamours the Left. However, that is a separate book!

I have simply written what I regard today to be largely self-evident. I don't doubt that many reading this book will disagree! Good. Let's open up the debate. If you don't believe it is true, let's hear from you (my email address is above). Note, however, that in 1830 Arthur Schopenhauer wrote, 'All truth passes through three stages: First, it is ridiculed; Second, it is violently opposed; Third, it is accepted as being self-evident.' Well, we'll see!

6.11 The end

At which point I will follow Lewis Carroll's advice on how to write a book: 'Begin at the beginning and go on until you come to the end; then stop.'

6.12 Summary

While successful ESPs may (arguably) exemplify value-driven IT in terms of cost-efficiency, they certainly will not from a value-adding perspective and so do not epitomize the desired working practices of a value-driven IT function. Running an internal IT function 'as though' it were an ESP can easily, in fact, result in a *lower* value IT service. The equivalent of an ESP's 'margin' for an internal IT function is 'value-added' and an internal IT function should typically be run to maximize value-added to the business just as an ESP is typically run to maximize *its* margins (and profits).

Many factors have contributed to the current urgency in optimizing the value of IT to the business. However, the growth of e-business has been key.

Establishing a value-driven IT function will bring many benefits to both the IT function and the business while creating a much more fulfilling and stimulating working environment for IT function staff. Key to the success of IT value transformation will be the business and the IT function truly embracing, and engaging in, the value transformation process.

Appendix

Diagnostic profiles

This Appendix includes diagnostic profiles to help assess the extent to which existing IT practices comply with 'best value practices' addressing the six value-adding CSFs set out in Chapter 3.

Note that your organization may choose *not* to fully adopt the 'best value practices' for a variety of reasons; for example, existing policy reasons (we have a business policy of *not* performing internal transfer charging between business units), external constraints (e.g. we are not 'allowed' to financially incentivize our staff) or simply because it is seen as too much change in too short a period.

Completion instructions

Please place a ✓ at the appropriate point between the two extremes on the left that in your view best represents how your organization's IT practices comply *currently* with 'best value practices' and another ✓ at the point between the two extremes on the right indicating how you believe your practices *should* comply.

Please note that there are no 'right answers'. Note that the word 'formally' below should be taken to mean that there is an established discipline with which 'everyone' complies (even if it is not a documented, quality assured procedure), i.e. we are primarily concerned with whether or not a practice is *actually* performed.

Current compliance				Best value practice	Desired compliance			
Very weak	Weak	Strong	Very strong		Very weak	Weak	Strong	Very strong
				Optimizing IT function alignment				
				Periodically, senior management in the business and the IT function formally agree *specific* IT project delivery objectives for the IT function based on the business's objectives				
				Periodically, senior management in the business and the IT function formally agree *specific* IT value delivery objectives for the IT function based on the business's objectives (typically in terms of helping the business reduce its business overhead costs, increasing revenues or increasing margins or market share)				
				IT objectives agreed between the business and the IT function are formally validated as being SMART (i.e. Specific, Measurable, Achievable, Relevant and Timebound)				
				The business maintains a strategy that may include several strategy types, such as its investment strategy, its marketing strategy, its operating strategy and its resource strategy				
				The business maintains a set of high level performance objectives and measures (KPIs) based on its strategy (typically relating to such things as profitability, share price, market share, earnings ratios, acquisitions, divestments etc.).				
				IT objectives are selected on a rigorous (formal) basis that helps to determine which *specific* objectives will contribute most to the achievement of the high level business key performance objectives and measures (KPIs).				
				IT objectives agreed between the business and the IT function are weighted to reflect the strategic importance of IT to the business and the relative priorities of cost-efficiency of product and service supply vs the value added by those products and services				
				Agreed IT objectives are formally cascaded down through the IT management structure to set specific performance objectives for all IT management and staff that support the high level objectives				
				Measures (KPIs) to assess the extent to which the IT objectives are being achieved are set at all levels in the IT function and formally reviewed periodically				
				IT objectives, CSFs and KPIs are kept current with changes in business objectives and priorities throughout the year				
				All objectives agreed at all levels are formally assessed to ensure that they are tolerably SMART				
				All KPIs agreed at all levels are formally assessed to ensure that they are tolerably accurate, objective, consistent, 'unfudgeable', and unambiguous				

Current compliance				Best value practice	Desired compliance			
Very weak	Weak	Strong	Very strong		Very weak	Weak	Strong	Very strong
				The performance of every individual in the IT function is periodically formally assessed against their agreed objectives and KPIs				
				Non-achievement of agreed objectives and KPI targets has serious consequences (sanctions) for each individual (in terms of negative financial reward)				
				Achievement of agreed objectives and KPI targets has serious consequences (incentives) for each individual (in terms of positive financial reward)				
				Optimizing competitive advantage				
				Senior business management and IT management meet periodically to develop an understanding of the business and its immediate plans, the current and future role of technology within the business, position the business against the external environment, competitive threats, market trends and political/regulatory constraints and identify potential business opportunities where technology can be used to enhance that position				
				The IT function is active in identifying opportunities for IT to create defensive entry barriers (i.e. make it more difficult for competitors to arise)				
				The IT function is active in identifying opportunities for IT to increase customer switching costs (i.e. make it more difficult for customers to switch suppliers)				
				The IT function is active in identifying opportunities for IT to increase retailer switching costs (i.e. make it more difficult for retailers of your products to switch suppliers)				
				The IT function is active in identifying opportunities for IT to change the ground rules of competition				
				The IT function is active in identifying opportunities for IT to change business competition from being cost based (i.e. commodity) to one based on sustainable product differentiation				
				The IT function is active in identifying opportunities for IT to help build links (and lock in) suppliers				
				The IT function is active in identifying opportunities for IT to help generate new products and services				
				The IT function is active in identifying opportunities for IT to help establish new product distribution channels				
				The IT function is active in identifying opportunities for IT to help facilitate or establish joint ventures				

Current compliance				Best value practice	Desired compliance			
Very weak	Weak	Strong	Very strong		Very weak	Weak	Strong	Very strong
				The IT function is active in identifying opportunities for IT to help improve the image of the business				
				Potential IT opportunities are formally assessed to ascertain the extent to which they might contribute to increased business competitiveness				
				**Optimizing portfolio alignment**				
				Every business unit maintains a set of detailed performance measures (KPIs) and targets				
				The projects in the IT function's project portfolio are partially selected on a rigorous (formal) basis that helps to determine which *specific* projects will contribute most to the achievement of the business units' performance targets				
				Optimizing portfolio value				
				The projects in the IT function's project portfolio are partially selected on a rigorous (formal) basis that helps to determine which *specific* projects will contribute most to the achievement of return on investment (ROI) or whatever indicators are in use (e.g. NPV, EVS, EVA, RONA)				
				The projects in the IT function's project portfolio are partially selected on a rigorous (formal) basis that helps to determine which *specific* projects will contribute most to improving management decision making				
				The projects in the IT function's project portfolio are partially selected on a rigorous (formal) basis that helps to determine which *specific* projects will most reduce business risk				
				The projects in the IT function's project portfolio are partially selected on a rigorous (formal) basis that helps to determine which *specific* projects are best aligned with the technology strategy				
				The projects in the IT function's project portfolio are partially selected on a rigorous (formal) basis that helps to determine which *specific* projects carry least technical risk				
				The projects in the IT function's project portfolio are partially selected on a rigorous (formal) basis that helps to determine which *specific* projects carry least project delivery risk				
				The projects in the IT function's project portfolio are partially selected on a rigorous (formal) basis that helps to determine which *specific* projects carry least benefits delivery risk				
				The projects in the IT function's project portfolio include a balance of projects that have been formally assessed to address needs from the strategic to the tactical, from the transformational to the operational and of varying cost, benefit and risk				

Current compliance				Best value practice	Desired compliance			
Very weak	Weak	Strong	Very strong		Very weak	Weak	Strong	Very strong
				IT function management and business management meet periodically to debate the planned project portfolio in the context of all proposed corporate investments and accept, reject, defer and prioritize projects based on 'objective' criteria				
				What is, and is not, a 'project' is clearly defined				
				Proposed projects are broken down into the smallest practicable 'work packets'				
				Each work packet is formally assessed on a cost/benefit/risk basis to determine those with the highest priority business case				
				The phasing of work packet development is planned to reflect the commercial priorities and deliver the highest net benefits first				
				Project business cases are fully costed, including development, operations and support staff actual total costs of employment throughout the development and full anticipated life of the solution. They also include total technology and physical infrastructure costs associated with the project (whether new or utilizing a proportion of existing technology/infrastructure) throughout the development and full anticipated life of the solution. They also include any outside costs (e.g. package, consultancy) and user costs (e.g. training, testing)				
				Estimates of project costs are derived by a formal process that draws on the estimating skills of colleagues and those to whom the work will be allocated				
				There is genuine project sponsor (and user) accountability for project costs (in terms of budget adjustment) *at their level* in the budget hierarchy				
				There is a formal process by which all tangible and intangible project benefits are defined				
				Tangible financial benefits analysed include reductions in existing IT systems costs, reductions in other business costs, savings from reduced business investment, additional business revenues, business revenue reductions avoided and business cost increases avoided				
				Tangible non-financial benefits are quantified and performance measures set				
				All intangible benefits are defined and documented and every reasonable attempt is made to derive indirect tangible benefits from the intangible				

Current compliance				Best value practice	Desired compliance			
Very weak	Weak	Strong	Very strong		Very weak	Weak	Strong	Very strong
				The baselines from which project benefits will be measured are defined and agreed				
				The actions and responsibilities necessary to achieve project benefits are defined as are the assumptions on which these are based				
				The specific project deliverables expected to deliver specific benefits are defined				
				Project benefits delivery plans are prepared specifying when benefits should be realized (and what *level* of benefit)				
				There is genuine project sponsor (and user) accountability for project benefits realization (in terms of budget adjustment) *at their level* in the budget hierarchy				
				Benefits realization is built into the personal performance objectives of the individuals identified as being responsible for delivering those benefits; achievement is materially rewarded; failure is materially sanctioned				
				Project work *cannot* commence without the allocation of an authorized project code; such a code cannot be allocated without project authorization from the appropriate 'project governance' committee				
				'Project governance' committees are established to assess the business cases for projects and project priorities across the entire business (i.e. not just priorities within a 'business silo')				
				Projects are only authorized by 'project governance' committees if they are compulsory (e.g. required for legal or regulatory reasons) or, for discretionary projects: • have clearly defined ownership, scope, costs, benefits, plans, resources, risks and issues; • meet a clearly articulated business need; • are clearly aligned with business strategy; • are clearly aligned with IT technology strategy; • are technically feasible; • are affordable; • are in the IT function operating plan or, if not, are sufficiently convincing to take funds from the discretionary budget or substitute for a lower valued project in the plan; • do not carry unacceptable project risk; • are likely to realize their promised benefits; • can be scheduled into the work load (or outsourced); • have a convincing (and quality assured) business case; • exceeds the information economics (or equivalent) valuation hurdle set				
				Project staff complete timesheets recording the productive time to be allocated to project accounting codes				

Current compliance				Best value practice	Desired compliance			
Very weak	Weak	Strong	Very strong		Very weak	Weak	Strong	Very strong
				Project financial budgets are maintained and a (predicted) overspend on budget requires user authorization and a corresponding increase in the amount deducted from user budgets				
				Project budget overruns are not 'stolen' from other project or support budgets				
				Projects are formally assessed for their inherent risk				
				Projects are formally assessed for the risks of failing to realize the promised benefits				
				The formally assessed risk of a project is used by the IT function to decide on how to quote for the project (e.g. fixed price, time-and-materials, decline)				
				Optimizing value delivery				
				The business case for projects is reviewed and reassessed at all key project milestones and a decision taken by the appropriate 'project governance' committee on continuing or rescoping or terminating the project				
				The business case for projects is reviewed and reassessed on all significant changes in circumstances and a decision taken by the appropriate 'project governance' committee on continuing or rescoping or terminating the project				
				Projects are only authorized to continue by 'project governance' committees if they are compulsory or continue to: • have clearly defined ownership, scope, costs, benefits, plans, resources, risks and issues; • meet a clearly articulated business need; • be clearly aligned with business strategy; • be clearly aligned with IT technology strategy; • be technically feasible; • be affordable; • carry acceptable project risk; • be likely to realize their promised benefits; • have a convincing (and quality assured) business case				
				Projects are risk categorized and higher risk projects are subjected to closer scrutiny (and permitted lower change in budget, schedule or benefits predicted before being subject to business case reappraisal)				
				Optimizing benefits realization				
				Benefits delivery plans are maintained for all projects				
				Project benefits actually realized post-implementation are monitored and reported on an ongoing basis (against the benefits delivery plan)				

Current compliance				Best value practice	Desired compliance			
Very weak	Weak	Strong	Very strong		Very weak	Weak	Strong	Very strong
				The review of benefits realized includes identifying actions that need to be taken to improve the level of benefits realization, any changes needed to benefits targets, delivery times and performance measures and any lessons that can be learned to improve benefits realization on future projects				
				The results of benefits realization are fed to an IT function 'balanced scorecard' of performance				
				'Business change management' specialists are established (as a job or role) with responsibility for driving out project benefits				
				SLAs are maintained for all significant production systems				
				SLAs are maintained for all significant IT function services				
				SLAs are negotiated between the supplier and the customer to provide *necessary and sufficient* service levels for a specified cost.				
				SLA customers are directly charged for service costs (i.e. they directly hit their budgets at their level in the budget hierarchy)				
				Transfer charging is in place between the IT function and its customers				
				The transfer charging process is based on a 'pricing model'				
				All IT services/products are tariffed				
				Internal tariffs do not cross-subsidize any external tariffs (i.e. IT services sold outside the company)				
				Tariffs for IT services/products are based on end-to-end services				
				The IT function maintains and publishes a comprehensive service/product catalogue				
				IT services/products are designed/bundled in such a way as to be immediately comprehensible to users				
				Production systems are monitored to identify the point when they are approaching being non-viable (i.e. the running and support costs exceed the benefits still being extracted) and appropriate action is taken to phase out (or replace) non-viable functionality				

Index